HANNA

OTHER BOOKS BY
THOMAS BEER

THE FAIR REWARDS
1922

STEPHEN CRANE
1923

SANDOVAL
1924

THE MAUVE DECADE
1926

THE ROAD TO HEAVEN
1928

Hanna

by

THOMAS BEER

Alfred · A · Knopf · New York

MCMXXIX

CONTENTS

A Note To Lewis Mumford

In the summer of 1910 a friend invited me to his father's house at Watch Hill and there I became the awkward cavalier of his sister, a young matron whose beauty was so extraordinary and musical that it persisted as a sounding nimbus about her even when she was shaking sand from the diapers of her small son upon the enchanted beach or pretending gallantly to enjoy a waltz with me. The book which I am dedicating to you was unconsciously begun, one night, while I defended her, on a gentle signal of her fan, in the veranda beyond a ballroom, between lanterns and moonlight. For the yacht of a certain Mr. Dives rode at anchor in the bay, and Dives himself, a pinnacle of creamy English flannels splashed with a tie in the colors of some Harvard club, sulked at the lady's feet, yearning to dance with her. He was dull; he was fifty years old; he attempted a flirtation in tones of a badly maintained boyishness, and the fan informed me that I must be useful, here. So we talked, and it happened that Mark Hanna was mentioned and Mr. Dives kicked alive a curiosity about the great adventurer in government.

He had found Mr. Hanna puzzling. Once they were lunching with some common friend in a hotel when the richest of Americans passed the table and nodded to the Senator from Ohio. Mr. Dives was thrilled. He was the sort of rich man to whom richer men are sacred and he had wanted to meet the grander Dives at once. But Mr. Hanna said that the gaunt financier was not worth meeting. " Why," Mr. Dives cried, " he's worth two hundred millions!" Mark Hanna grunted, " Yes, and what the hell else is he worth? "

Mr. Dives did not understand that question. He recited it to us carefully, the moonlight soaking his white coat and his stupid face. I am glad to report that the beautiful lady did not have to dance with this oaf. The music stopped in the ballroom, and, next morning, his yacht twinkled past the beach in a glory of brass and canvas, bearing Mr. Dives off to Newport. Maybe someone else patiently told him, somewhere, what Mark Hanna meant, but I doubt that he really comprehended it, and he must have died in the satisfaction of feeling that a profound loss to the world was occurring in the separation of himself from his millions of hereditary dollars. He had made me think of Mark Hanna, though, in a new way and the discussions of Mr. Herbert Croly's book on Hanna in 1912 commenced my education in the legend of this man's singular force. I don't mean the public discussions; the capital biography was exposed on the lacteal quagmire of American criticism and sank therein through a scum of tepid reviews. But it was my luck to hear the work tried by a jury of experts, men whose names figured in its chapters, and, listening to them, this familiar image of Marcus Hanna changed for me and was enriched.

He was familiar to me and an awful nuisance of my childhood, although I saw him just twice, once on a train bound to Washington and once as he came stiffly walking down a driveway with little Quentin Roosevelt sticking to his cane, a white moth of starched clothes chanting out a tale about a pet rat's foul misconduct. But Mr. Hanna annoyed me endlessly. He was a substance in Washington or Cleveland which my father had to see, a sort of joss or rune. I conceived him as silent in a shrine, and my father as a messenger hunting oracles. A voice would command over the telephone or a telegram would come, and then the cab was at the door and Mr. Beer was gone to catch the last express for Washington. An upbringing in the political seraglio is like any other; one's father's business is an awful bother; much of my father's business from 1896 to 1904 was Mr. Marcus Alonzo Hanna, and in proof of that I tender to your interest the footnotes and appendix of this book.

This prefactory note was made necessary by the quaint conduct of a veteran publicist and a younger author of fiction in April of this year. The first of five articles compressed from the full text of my study was available to the public on April 11th in an issue of *The Saturday Evening Post*. The veteran publi-

cist, on April 12th, wrote to a friend in Chicago asserting that "Beer has begun to whitewash Mark
Hanna in the *Post*. Ruth Hanna (McCormick) paid
him fifty thousand dollars for his stuff and gave him
the material. . . ." On April 18th the author of fiction had a much higher figure for Mrs. McCormick's
generosity toward me and, in the latest quotations, her
fee has reached terms quite imperial. So I am forced
to deny, on behalf of Marcus Hanna's daughter, that
she has ever seen me, written to me, paid me one
penny, or caused any information as to her father's
life to reach me. About the whitewashing of Mark
Hanna, let someone do that who is willing at the
same time to whitewash the American people as it
existed in the latter nineteenth century — No, he must
do more. He must clean from his account of mankind
that unconquered essential of our being which makes
us bid for a place beyond our fellows; he must prove
that we act and fail driven by some sweeter impulse
than the search for power. I prefer Hanna to another
subject as I might negligibly prefer Grunewald to
Botticelli, any Egyptian stonemason to Donatello,
Hawthorne to Poe, or Faraday to Henry Ford.

But this is not a biography. You know very well
that the biography of an artist is at least a plausible
adventure; if he has the strength to speak his mind
at all, he tells you much about himself. A politician's
art is a long wrestling with the most dangerous of
materials, ourselves. He lives as a demonstration of

the one great modern saying: " It is life, not the individual, that is conscienceless." He puts out his will, not as he would but as he can, and his art is one of concessions, of oblique gestures and perpetual ironics. Search for his conscience and you must pluck it from a hundred battered shards of distorting mirror. He eludes you, and your justice to him is a demand, finally, that his skill and his force be applauded. Try to paint him out and he fades from your perception. You sketch — you strive — you almost reach conclusions, and then you sit at last humiliated by a shadow.

Thomas Beer

Siasconset, July 4th, 1929

HANNA

CHAPTER I

THE YEAR 1865

I

A dark man who smelled of brandy came up through a bright theater in Washington and shot Abraham Lincoln from behind. He then threw himself nine feet down to the stage and for a moment was a clear apparition to the people seated above the President as he shifted a dagger to his right hand, brandished it, and vanished. His pistol's small explosion was not heard at all by many in the galleries. When Mrs. Lincoln's shrieks began they thought at first that Mr. Lincoln had been stabbed, and an old preacher named Hugh Jones stood, shouting in Welsh, "He that took up the sword has perished by the sword!" He was half mad since the death of a third son in battle, and now he mumbled revengeful verses from Ezekiel and the song of Deborah while his scared daughter pulled him down the stairs through a commencing panic. In the cool street he lurched against her, silent. He lived six months, but did not speak again.

Even as men were thrusting Charles Taft in his blue surgeon's dress over the torn flag and gilded rail into the President's box it was shouted in the theater that this disappearing shape had been John Wilkes Booth. His last appearance in melodrama impressed the random young actor heartily; he paused to slash a musician who met him behind the scenes and then stunned the simple lad holding his horse for him in an alley with a blow of his dagger's handle. On the morning of April 15th, 1865, the mob's hot logic answered his performance in like kind. Mr. Lincoln was scarcely dead when a crowd of hundreds swelled into the white lobby of the Burnet House at Cincinnati, hunting Junius Brutus Booth, and the innocent tragedian lay hidden in a friend's room for days until he could be smuggled out of town. Toward noon a pretty girl on Broadway in New York was mistaken for Roberta Norwood by a gang of street boys who penned her against the rails of Trinity churchyard bawling, " Actress! Actress! " Policemen and a naval officer, a Mr. Dewey, rescued her after a real fight. All afternoon a committee of the pious rode through Pittsburgh trying to get signatures on a petition which demanded the closing of every theater in the state of Pennsylvania. That night the mayor of Boston posted guards before the playhouses of his city, and in Cleveland a negro boy who polished brass at the Academy of Music was set on by warm patriots and cruelly hammered.

Mr. John Ellsler, lessee of the Academy, had taken his famous company down to Columbus for a season. He was a reticent, rather stately actor, deft in comedy of the dry kind and competent in everything. He had lifted the whole condition of the theater in the middle West, refusing employment to celebrated drunken stars who entertained audiences by clinging to scenery as they mouthed their lines, often mistaking footlights for an exit. Mr. Ellsler's stock company was a model of drilled conduct; no scandal emerged from it and none entered it. Gentlemen lounged in, between the acts, to chat with the clever manager and to be presented to whatever notable player was being supported by Mr. Ellsler's troupe, to Edwin Booth, to Miss Western or Mr. Couldock. Ralph Waldo Emerson stood in the wings, one night of 1859, watching the Mephistopheles of a farcical ballet shot upward through a trap in a puff of red fire, and the actresses, led by Ellsler's wife, came forward to curtsy in modest reverence before the smiling philosopher.

But now Mr. Ellsler saw a display of ferocious diabolics. His players got the news of Booth's identification at noon of April 15th. They simply did not believe it. Why, this could never be Wilkie Booth! Just awhile ago the mailbox of the Academy was jammed with notes on the most scented paper, addressed to J. Wilkes Booth, Esquire, by ladies fascinated as he stalked in pale robes close to the boxes in *The Marble Heart,* since Mr. Booth repaired his lack of height by displaying his authentic beauty to the populace at close range. It could not be Wilkie Booth. He was too gay and kind and gentle. Mrs. Ellsler wept

5

and little Clara Morris, the hungry child who played everything from Romeo's page to Hamlet's mother, was still weeping on Sunday afternoon when one of Mr. Ellsler's civilian friends found the miserable company keeping its nerves together by a lame rehearsal.

They were a city besieged. When Mr. Thomas Beer walked into the gray place, Ellsler darted at him, begging for news. Was Booth taken? What was being said in the streets? Was the profession to be suppressed? All these people packed around the burly young lawyer from the town of Bucyrus and heaved questions on him. It was a real peril, long forgotten. At the great mass meeting before the capitol in Columbus some man wise enough to be reckless asked the mob's compassion for the shamed players yonder in the theater. A growl stirred, deepening, and the crowd swayed until someone started a thin cheer and the dangerous moment passed. " And verily," says Clara Morris in her memoirs, " we were grateful! " But on Sunday Ellsler had nothing to be grateful for. He handed his friend a telegram from the mayor of Cleveland warning him that it might not be safe to bring back the company to the Academy of Music next week. His restraint broke. He raved, pitching Shaksperian sentences at empty maroon chairs of the orchestra.

This was the end of the profession in America! They would be vagabonds once more, preyed on by moral pamphleteers and sour pastors, shut from society and given the worst rooms in poor hotels! But he would not give up, by heaven! He would take his people back to Cleveland and open the Academy on Tuesday, as he had advertised! Come wind, come wrack! Let the Clevelanders whom he had served all these years lynch him in the streets!

Mr. Beer saw nothing comic in this state of mind, and reported it to a grandson grimly as something hideous he had seen in the year 1865. A terrific emotional machinery had been licensed in America since 1859 and the cool lawyer once had been its victim when he objected to some words of a vindictive orator who was damning Abraham Lincoln for offering to buy the slaves in Kentucky. He had been snubbed and cut on the streets. He had learned, in bewilderment, that all logic and all kindness were lost in this rhythmic billowing of organized hates. The windows of the tiny rural newspaper's office where his dry and sane editorials were sometimes published had been stoned by night, and a benevolent soldier had warned him that the partisans were talking rope. He had experienced the profound æsthetic of a wild drive in a heeling buggy through night and storm, which made him sensitive to the music of *The Erl King*, afterwards, and, in the year 1865, he faced, as gravely as possible, his ruin at the law, because he was a Democrat, and social blizzards because a drunken actor had killed the President. So, having lived for

7

years among people ready to go mad on order, he
saw no reason to laugh at John Ellsler's fears.

But, as it happened, the mob's mood did not last.
For some days actors were insulted in restaurants
and on the street. When Ellsler's company opened
the Academy on Tuesday night, the journals of
Cleveland reported a full house and warm welcome
home for "The Favorites." A very old gentleman
recalls mild hisses in the gallery as the curtain rose,
but the potency of the emotional machine was now
aimed elsewhere: the body of Abraham Lincoln was
parading the United States. On Wednesday carpen-
ters began to lay the floor of a funeral pavilion in the
Square, close to the Perry monument, and Juliet
Araminta Smith probably saw a final demonstration
against actors that same night.

The Smiths have left no trace on the history of
Cleveland unless some venerable gentlewomen recol-
lect a meek, pretty little Mrs. Smith who made
children's clothes in the spring of 1865. She brought
Juliet Araminta and Orion James to Cleveland in
January, on account of economic conditions in central
Illinois. Her father frankly told her he couldn't keep
Nate Smith's offspring in food and copper-toed shoes,
even if it was nobody's fault that Nate had been
drafted into the Army. It was too bad, of course, but
Orion Holt's farm would not support Mrs. Smith and
her children, as well as her nine younger brothers and
sisters.

8

So Mrs. Smith wrote to Cousin Jennie, who sewed in Cleveland, and Cousin Jennie promised plenty of work. Cleveland was growing rich; steamboats and foundries increased; ladies could afford the amplest mourning. The Smiths came eastward and resided, obscurely but agreeably, in one room of a boarding-house. And after young Orion Smith, who was almost eleven, got his job at two dollars a week in the warehouse of Robert Hanna and Company, they lived luxuriously and often had oysters for supper.

The oysters established Mr. Marcus Alonzo Hanna in the mind of Juliet Araminta, who was nine, as a benevolent djinn. She became addicted to oysters and always went with Orion to the fishmonger's shop to revere the salesman who counted oysters into the tin pail. As Mr. Mark Hanna had given Orion his job, because Orion was a soldier's son, her warm and confiding nature caused Juliet Araminta to think that this grandee should be thanked. His munificence rained oysters on her. She accordingly penetrated the warehouse in River Street and presented herself to Mr. Mark. He made the kindly mistake of tendering Juliet a heart-shaped lump of maple sugar out of the tin box on his desk. After that he was seldom without Juliet.

She helped him to escort customers and callers through his firm's premises. She dirtied her pantalettes on the docks of Hanna and Company. She ran

9

diligently with notes addressed to " Angostura &
Bitters, Gin Avenue " or to " Doe & Roe, Mud Street "
and came tearfully back to tell Mr. Mark that policemen assured her there were no such firms and no
such streets in Cleveland. Mr. Mark, refreshed by an
hour of Juliet's absence, fed her more maple sugar
and pulled her hair.

But it was certain that he loved her. He called her
Sawdust and told her that the government should
mint her yellow curls to redeem Mr. Lincoln's greenbacks when the war was over. He slew a monstrous
rat which threatened her on the docks with one blow
of his walking-stick. He — this was glory perpetual
along her street — he even once drove her home behind his black horse Howard, with Orion clinging
awed on the back of the buggy. And it was no good
for Orion to keep saying that a Mrs. Marcus Alonzo
Hanna already existed. Juliet Araminta knew better.
She was Mr. Mark's beloved and he was hers and
when the nasty war stopped they would be married,
and they would eat oysters and maple sugar every
day. So, walking down to the station on the night of
April 25th between Orion and her timid mother, she
wished that Mr. Mark could see her in the full dignity
of her new best dress, as she was sure that she looked
perfection.

Be sure that she did, for she was very pretty at
the age of nine and her mother had composed a costume for her from a plate in the French fashion maga-

zine. This costume survives — a tunic of stiff red silk
nobly embroidered in vast roses of hard white cord.
Under this were four starched petticoats, a shirt of
some kind, a pair of cambric pantaloons edged with
pink lace, and a girdle of canvas. Under all that was
the rosy substance of Juliet Araminta in a condition
of rapture. Somebody sensible had killed the odious
Mr. Lincoln who drafted papa into the Army, and
that had ended the war, and she was going to the
railway station to meet papa. Her views of the war
and the Army and Mr. Lincoln were harsh; it was
all an uncomfortable boiling of tears and belated letters and mamma walking the floor at nights. Juliet
Araminta glanced at the funeral pavilion in the
Square and dared Orion to go and spit on it. But
there was a policeman watching and they had to
hurry, else the train would come in and Private
Nathan Smith would arrive from the wars un-
welcomed.

Private Nathan Smith was discharged from hospital at Georgetown on April 22nd, 1865, after two
and a half years of service, with three fingers gone
from his left hand and no prospects whatever. But
he was still only twenty-eight years old — boys married young in the fifties — and he landed cheerfully in
the smoke of the raw station, seeming taller than ever
to Juliet Araminta, as he was thin and pallid. The
family made a group commonplace in the month of
April 1865: a tired woman crying on a tired man's

11

breast, and two children hopping about in their best clothes.

He must be fed directly; he had been fifteen hours on this train without even a sandwich. The family wandered into what must have been rather a low eating-place near the station, as she recalls that it was lighted by oil lamps and that her mother told her not to look at some ladies in bright dresses who were keeping late hours in one corner. There was sawdust on the floor, near a bar, and when the trouble began, this sawdust flew everywhere. Juliet's father thrust her behind him, against the wall, and she put her hands tightly on her eyes. It was going to be worse than the riots at home in Illinois when the marshals rode through a crowd protesting the draft, and men had their scalps slashed open by blows of the rawhide whips. There was the same dull and thick sound of voices from the jostle at the bar and — clearly remembered, this! — the wail of an old fellow who kept saying, "I am not an actor! I am an elocutionist, gentlemen!" He said it over and over as they pulled him down on the floor. A waiter ran yelling into the street. Women shrieked, of course, and Private Smith roared uselessly, his left hand still in bandages. But when other voices came into her hearing Juliet Araminta knew that everything was all right and took her hands from her eyes. He had come in time! Warned by love's echoes, sounding out her terror, he had flown through the night to aid her. It was not that the waiter had brought in anybody he could find on the street. It was love.

He was standing inside the door, bawling orders at the crowd, just as if the angry men were stevedores on the docks of Hanna and Company. Juliet Araminta peeped around her father's legs and admired him. His silk hat was probably tilted back and sideways on his round head. His whiskers swept in auburn beauty from ear to ear under his pink, shaved chin with its wide dimple. His large brown eyes sparkled yellow as he shouted. In one fragile, long hand he kept a cigar alight by little twitches of his delicate fingers. Behind him a naval officer, perhaps his brother Howard, and some civilians were mere and meaningless shadows to Juliet Araminta. Here was her Mr. Mark! She recalls nothing of the process by which Mr. Marcus Alonzo Hanna quieted the men who had been willing to mob an old stray because he talked like an actor. It is not unlikely that some people in the bar were afraid of Robert Hanna's nephew, the husband of a daughter of the towering Daniel Rhodes. An eminent citizen, in those days, had certain habits of command, and at young Hanna's back was the prestige of a great wholesale grocery and shipping business; the steamboats of his firm ranged the Lakes; every roustabout on the docks knew Mark Hanna by sight and knew that he was not afraid to toss a tipsy stevedore off the deck of the *Northern Light* into the river. The men shied from

him. Someone dusted the victim of applied emotional-
ism and got him through the doors into the safe darkness. Mr. Mark tossed a dollar on the bar, being
already a sound diplomat, and was turning to leave
the place when Mrs. Nathan Smith did all that a lady
in an interesting condition was obliged to do after
a public excitement in those days, and swooned on
the floor.

Juliet Araminta's evening culminated in a pure
bliss of sensations as she sat on Mr. Mark's knees in
a real cab and his whiskers caressed her neck. He
talked pleasantly to the simple family and ordered
the cab to halt at some club or hotel when he found
that Private Smith was still supperless. Waiters came
running with sandwiches and coffee; Orion James
and Juliet Araminta were fed ice cream. It was eleven
o'clock when Mr. Mark lifted her up the steps of
the boarding-house and twelve o'clock struck before
she was in bed. She had never known there was such
an hour as that.

Two hours later Jack and Will Garrett roused from
a nervous nap in a shed on their father's farm near
Port Royal, Virginia. They had not really slept; they
were watching out the night beside the farm's precious horses, one of these a "present from General
Grant," brought home after the surrender at Appo-
matox. All afternoon the handsome, curious stranger
who called himself Boyd and his silly young friend
had been trying to buy the horses for a trip to the

14

South. The Garrett boys mistrusted him and they had locked the door of the frail tobacco house when he and his companion went in there to sleep, for they could not risk losing the horses. Now they nudged each other. A familiar, increasing rhythm had brought them wide awake: a column of horse was pelting through the moist night. . . . It was a detail of Yankee cavalry coming closer down the lane from town. They must have known precisely each echoing detail of the business — the thud of boots dismounting, the chatter of carbines cocked briskly and the separating noise of heels in the dooryard, before Lieutenant Baker hammered on the kitchen door and the boys heard their scared old father answering him. Then it was too much for Jack. He dragged on his gray jacket and loped up the new grass, breaking through the ring of bluecoats on the porch. . . .

A little later and any negro crossing those flat fields heard the crack of Boston Corbett's pistol and saw flames spin up from the burning tobacco house. Soon a shifting audience collected along the roadway — negroes and white folks who had come running to help put out the fire. But the troopers would not let them inside the yard. They could stare across the fence at the boy in manacles who sat against a tree, whistling to keep from tears. That was young Herold. Mr. Booth was a shape under a blanket on the porch, voiceless. Now and then the handsome schoolmistress who boarded with the Garretts bent down and wetted

his face with her handkerchief. He achieved, here, a
fine drama of silence and complete futility. The sun
rose. He died.

Juliet Araminta was not enough impressed by the
morning's news to recollect it. Something local and
pressing had her full attention. A telegram came before breakfast. Orion sped forth and told all his ac-
quaintances that he was going to California on a
ship and danced disgracefully. Mrs. Smith wept,
of course, and Private Smith rubbed his chin while
his daughter plangently wanted to know what had
happened. She was not told, and things became a
muddle until presently she was allowed to guide her
father down to River Street to call on Mr. Mark.

There was a lot of talk. A clerk went out with a
green slip of paper and returned with many bills. Private Smith painfully wrote his name on a note for five
hundred dollars, without interest, payable in five
years after date, and then wiped his eyes. Mr. Mark
stood Juliet Araminta on his desk and drew a pencil
around the coast of the United States on his map,
from New York down past Florida, on below Cuba
— it was south of Cuba that this child saw her still-
born sister buried in the warmer seas — and so
straight on to the Isthmus of Panama.

"If there was a canal through here, Sawdust, you
could sail right up to San Francisco."

The Smiths spoke of this sentence often, after 1880,
but it made Nathan Smith chuckle in the year 1856,

and he told his daughter as they walked homeward
that Mr. Hanna was just joking. There had been
some crazy stuff in the newspapers about cutting a
canal through Nicaragua or Panama. But it stood
to reason that you couldn't cut a canal through mountains. And she was now to be extra good and help
mamma pack. They were all going down on a German steamer with Cousin Jim Holt from New York
to Nicaragua and across to the Pacific slope. Cousin
Jim had made the trip three times and knew the ropes.
Nothing to be scared about (he was trembling with
the thrill of it, himself) — and they would live on
Cousin Jim's land near a town named Santa Clara.

Juliet Araminta had no notions of distance or
geography and was much pleased until it was dusk
next day in the thunderous railroad's station and a
distress came to her in the noise of Cousin Jennie's
snivelling. But here was Mr. Mark. The slim female
with him wore black splendors in token of mourning
for Mr. Lincoln and glittered everywhere with jet so
that she seemed a cloudy wonder from some journal
of fashion. She smiled, though, and Juliet Araminta
had no time to be jealous of Mrs. Marcus Alonzo
Hanna. There was a basket filled with fruit and sandwiches and a smaller basket filled with garments cut,
it mysteriously seemed, for a mere baby. Mrs. Smith
wept gratefully. Orion James began to snuffle as Mr.
Mark handed him up the steps of the tall coach. . . .
She knew, now, that she was being taken from him,

forever, and Juliet Araminta wailed for hours and fell
asleep with her nose pressed to a pane of the lumbering car.

They woke her and told her to look out. It was
dead night where the train was stilled on a siding
among wet fields. But there was no darkness to hide
the rain and the women huddled under wide shawls
or umbrellas. Huge bonfires tinged the world; men
and boys were feeding fence-rails into the flames.
Then an engine neared, with bayonets of guards flashing from the tender and streamers of wet crape swinging curiously. And then all the women began singing
Rock of Ages as the train came by. She saw a lighted
coach brilliant with flowers, and some officer's white
gloves, and she started to cry again, without knowing
why. So Lincoln passed her.

II

Among the important towns of eastern Ohio in
Andrew Jackson's time was New Lisbon, not a big
place, but a thrifty center of farms and trade, dominated by a Quaker named Benjamin Hanna. He and
his sons owned good land, the largest store in the
county, shares in a flour mill, and much else. Their
prestige was enormous in the region; sometimes Benjamin Hanna was called " Squire " in bills and documents. The pioneer societies had not yet come to
value themselves for homeliness, and in New Lisbon
as elsewhere, they tried to reproduce the civil formu-

las and habits of their kinsmen in Pennsylvania, Connecticut, and Vermont. Wandering painters and primitive masters of the daguerreotype report the Hanna tribe in its best clothes for us. The hard Quaker's wife wrote invitations for a son's wedding in a grand, sweeping hand, and, since Benjamin Hanna traded eastward to Pittsburgh or acted as forwarding agent of mills and shops in Philadelphia, his establishment had its mild elegances in the way of handsome silver, miniatures, and pretty trash.

The cleverest and most sensitive of Benjamin Hanna's sons was Leonard, a long young man whose frail hands got him the nickname " Miss " when he was a boy. He had been elaborately educated for medicine and came back to New Lisbon to practice after refining years in Philadelphia. But a fall from his horse damaged his spine. He lapsed into the mass of the family and did as his father and brothers did, although he was always called Dr. Hanna. He dabbled a bit in politics, speaking in debates on primitive abolition and prohibition, trying to rouse sentiment against the Mexican war and forcing his tribe to back small ventures in civic improvement. For the family, when it acted as a body, had great force. It was much admired. The Hannas were tall, imposing men with large eyes, gray or brown, and resounding voices. It was said that you could hear them having an argument or singing a hymn for the space of two miles.

They helped New Lisbon to ruin itself, with the best intentions. A canal was planned which would join the community by water to Pittsburgh and the Lakes. Rather distrustful of the oncoming railroads, the Hannas threw their weight behind the project of the canal, and threw two hundred thousand dollars into its construction. It failed, after a long struggle; the section west of New Lisbon blocked from bad engineering; banks caved in; a tunnel through a swale of rock cost immensely. Marcus Alonzo Hanna, Dr. Leonard's eldest son, must have lived as a baby in the sound of the word " canal." Meanwhile the new railroads were built at a distance from the worried town, and this was the end of New Lisbon's importance. People drifted away; the little cultivated layer of lawyers and clerks went hunting jobs in towns along the railways. One Hanna retreated to Pittsburgh. In 1852 Leonard and Robert Hanna took what money they had left, made an alliance with a shrewd trader named Hiram Garretson, and moved to Cleveland.

In this partnership the nervous, handsome doctor supplied the imagination. Supposedly the firm of Hanna, Garretson and Company was a wholesale grocery. It had that character for a few months, anyhow. But in 1853 Dr. Hanna went off, to rest his nerves, on a sailing vessel up the Lakes and watched something inspiring to a clever man. Hundreds of settlements sent out canoes or dories to the leisurely sloop asking if there was molasses for sale, or a spare

20

steel blade, or a bottle of calomel, or an awl. Dr. Hanna saw a commercial light. He returned to Cleveland and there commenced a period of discussions between the Hanna brothers, often within earshot of young Marcus Alonzo. Robert Hanna was the natural conservative; Leonard was adventurous. In the end the ailing doctor won and soon the firm of Hanna, Garretson and Company had steamboats on the Lakes, dealing out supplies of all kinds, shedding passengers at the developing ports. The ships ran up to wild Minnesota and came back again with pig-iron, salted fish, timber, and skins. When the Hannas of Cleveland backed Abraham Lincoln in the election of 1860, they were eminent men, known everywhere throughout the basin of the Lakes.

But this basin of the Lakes, at the beginning of the Civil War, was an unasserted territory, and long after the war was finished the trade of the Lakes meant little in the everlasting brag of American commerce. Certain families and combinations on the Lakes advanced with a sort of stealth into the literary or journalistic perception of the United States. Indeed, the literary were long in judging what battle had done to commerce. The war deflected all routes of American trade; New York was to become definitely a metropolis; the Confederate cruisers interrupted with decision the advance of American interest in the Caribbean; the appalling importance of the Mississippi was discovered just when the traffic of the

Mississippi was suspended for three years. Robert and Leonard Hanna had no place in the catalogues of wealthy Americans drawn up by the hacks of the seaboard cities in the years before Lincoln's election, and their support of Mr. Lincoln's campaign is not mentioned in the many hundred sheets of raw propaganda which record that fierce episode in emotional politics.

Marcus Alonzo cast his first vote for Mr. Lincoln in 1860. He was born at New Lisbon in September of 1837 and left the failing town unwillingly in 1852 because he was already engaged to marry a pretty girl there. His parents allowed him to consider himself engaged, at any rate, and tactfully permitted the affair to drag itself into staleness for three years, since the eldest son was stubborn as the freckles on his flat face. Among several shaky legends of Mark Hanna's boyhood one is certainly true: he had an astonishing stubbornness. When he was suspended from the Western Reserve University in the spring of 1857 for faking the programs of a solemn Junior Exhibition and successfully distributing his burlesque imitation among parents and professors, his father ordered Marcus to apologize to his mother and Marcus would not do so. But the lady was rather pleased and boasted of her son's refusal in her old age. She was from Vermont, and she despised men who " gave in."

Mrs. Leonard Hanna probably affected her son's whole life. Her own name was Samantha Converse.

Generations of Huguenot and English ancestors supplied her traditions. Her parents came in their own
carriage from Vermont to Ohio with some family
silver and a deal of stiff pride. She was a cultivated
person, but not sentimentally so, for she regarded
the sweet ballads of the fifties and sixties as non-
sensical and terrified people in the theaters of Cleveland by genteel but audible snorts of contempt when
passion gushed too heavily on the other side of the
footlights. She did not regard poverty as an unfor-
tunate condition, but as a disgrace. She gave royally
to charities, but she did it, says a lady who knew her
well, with an air of simple scorn for people who
needed charity. " Any reasonable man," she would
say, " can make a living. . . ." Her eldest son adored
this lady and often did just what she told him to
do, in any unimportant matter of business or society.

In 1861 she confronted him on an important point
and beat down his will. He had voted for Mr. Lincoln
and his natural place, he thought, was in Mr. Lincoln's armies. But Samantha Hanna knew that her
husband was dying, whether his sons understood it
or not. Only Mark comprehended the spreading and
complicated affairs of Hanna, Garretson and Company. After he was suspended from college he went
to work for his father. He wore and was slightly proud
of his jumper and overalls when he handled boxes at
the warehouse. He saw customers, mastered double
entry book-keeping, acted as purser on trips of the

Hanna steamboats, and ranged as primordial travel-
ing salesman through Indiana and Illinois. His uncle
Robert did not see Mark as the model of a business man. "You shake your head," said the dying
Mark Hanna to William Osler, "just like my uncle
Rob. . . ." Uncle Robert's head shook frequently, it
seems. Mark was too much interested in picnics at
Rocky River or in the affairs of the Ydrad Boat Club.
Money spun through those slim fingers inherited
from his father. He had no respect for office hours.
He danced until the bands stopped. His parents did
not worry. Mark never drank and when he slept he
slept in Prospect Street, at home. He might not be
the model of a wholesale grocer, but he was a good
son.

It was onerous to be a good son in the spring of
1861, when the solid society of Cleveland was laid
open by Mr. Lincoln's call for volunteers. A fair half
of the city's grandees were Democrats. Mr. Lincoln,
to them, was an amiable freak who had been rushed
into office by the mob. The Hanna family was Republican, loudly, and Dr. Hanna had even made a
few speeches in the campaign. He fainted on election
day, from excitement, and was insensible for hours.
Marcus now faced his mother, one might say, over
his father's body. There was no private fortune;
Leonard Hanna's income was his share of the firm's
business. Someone must watch the family's interest
and keep unimaginative Robert Hanna wide awake.

So there were long discussions, weary scenes. The argument lasted for two months. Then Howard, the second son, went off to the war and Marcus Alonzo stayed at home.

He then became pathetically conspicuous as his friends got back to Cleveland on leave or furlough. He made himself a committee of one for their entertainment; his mother's carriage was abroad at all hours supporting healthy young officers hither and thither. He gave dinners or swept together parties of twenty or thirty for the play. He was to have given a supper on the night of his father's death, in 1862. Among poor folk it was known that Mr. Mark Hanna, down at the warehouse, would go a length to find a job for a soldier's son. If there was no job with Hanna and Company, there would be a note of recommendation to another firm and a couple of dollars for the boy.

His pride had been hurt, but circumstances arranged a compensation. He met the compensation at a bazaar in the spring of 1862, when she had just returned as a finished product from a school in New York to her parents in Franklin Avenue. Her name was Charlotte Augusta Rhodes and she was very handsome, slim and straight. Marcus Alonzo's consideration of her qualities made him forgive her for being a Democrat's daughter, but her father, Mr. Daniel Rhodes, did not intend his favorite child to compensate any damned black Republican puppy for not being a soldier in the idiotic war, or words to that effect, and his position in the matter was put as strongly as possible.

A romance in the Victorian form now progressed. Mr. Rhodes was unspeakably rich, for the times, entrenched in the coal and iron business and fortified by a natural iconoclasm of temper. One of his legendary remarks is that he respected nobody for being wealthy or respectable. But it is also legendary that he barked without often biting; socially the leader of Cleveland's Democratic faction, he was popular among Republicans and his charities were numerous. Ladies invaded his office timidly, hunting gifts for the Sanitary Commission, and got big checks with a lecture on the asininity of freeing the no-account niggers. He adored his daughter, and as it grew plain that Charlotte Augusta had fallen in love with Marcus Alonzo it grew plain that Mr. Rhodes had not. He had every excuse. He was a cousin of Stephen Douglas, who had been defeated by Mr. Lincoln, and was not Marcus Alonzo one of Mr. Lincoln's condemned screechers for freedom? . . . Charlotte Augusta languished and shed tears. In one of her father's more violent states of mind she dispatched notes to her Marcus by a gardener's red-headed brat named Asa Barnes, and Marcus Alonzo set the boy up as a junior capitalist by paying him a dollar a note for a month of 1863. When Mr. Rhodes cooled down, the wretched child was living far beyond his means, and the withdrawal of revenue ruined him at the candy shop.

The society surrounding this battle was polite. A very strong transfusion of Connecticut took place in the early history of Cleveland. Men of business, in the sixties, wore tall hats made in Connecticut and many had diplomas from Yale College framed on walls of their offices. They took in culture from the same round of lecturers which served their kin at Hartford and New Haven. When Henry Ward Beecher came to lecture on The Beautiful, boring Mark Hanna to slumber, the orator shook hands with people he had known as children in Litchfield and kissed their daughters. Erastus Gaylord's mansion or the house in which Mrs. Leonard Hanna lived on Prospect Street might quite as well have been set on Whitney Avenue in New Haven. A wash of immigrants was sweeping up against this Yankee layer of the city's builders, for Cleveland "boomed" after 1861, but the manners were still those of grave, conditioned Connecticut and the affairs of Charlotte Augusta and Marcus Alonzo were whispered, not unduly aired. Everybody knew what was going on, though, and ladies in skirts of seven layers interested themselves in the sad case of the good-looking Hanna boy. They sighed entreaties upon Daniel Rhodes when he appeared at evening parties where glasses were piled in bright pyramids on tables of real mahogany and eighteen kinds of cake affronted the digestion

besides bowls of punch. It is said that Mr. Rhodes
had no peace. He began to wilt in the spring of 1864.
When Marcus Alonzo went off with his regiment of
militia to defend Washington from Jubal Early's raid
it was admitted that an engagement did exist and,
on September 27th, 1864, Marcus Alonzo and Charlotte Augusta were united at Saint John's Church.
Mr. Rhodes relieved his emotions by boxing the ears
of Asa Barnes when he found the plebeian kid climbing through a window to behold the cakes and bou-
quets of the wedding feast.

III

This sober quality of Cleveland kept the city from
a howling festivity when the funeral train brought
Mr. Lincoln's body to lie in state for a few hours on
April 27th of 1865. The titanic Amasa Stone deprecated an outpouring of women in white gowns to
meet the train, and less tremendous citizens spoke
against display. Crowds slowly filed under the mortu-
ary pavilion in the Square and the legend " *Extinctus
amabitur idem* " on the pennants drooping from a
ceiling sprinkled with hideous rosettes and stars was
admired by those capable of translating it. Elsewhere cities and towns enriched by the war showed
what they could do by way of public grief. Mr. Lincoln had come eastward to his first inaugural through
communities in which a fortune, a factory, or illumi-
nating gas were undreamed. His body now retired

below arches of evergreen twined with silken banners and shimmering at night with colored globes. Ladies clad in fresh white robes posed mournfully near the tracks in choirs of thirty and fifty. Canvas pillars offered such painted consolation as " Go To Thy Rest," or " Ours The Cross, Yours The Crown." A certain new millionaire of Chicago made himself permanently famous among journalists by sending a basket filled with champagne bottles and roses to Mrs. Lincoln — she was not on the train — with his card. In Chicago, too, a photographer named Halstead had for sale at the station a bogus view of Mr. Lincoln rising among clouds into the embrace of Jesus Christ. . . . The train rolled down to Springfield between incessant bonfires and illumined stations. At last he was entombed in a placid valley, close to a soothing brook.

War had favored the cities of the North, although the first historians of the struggle got as far as they could from admitting the nature of the change. They talked mistily of a prosperity caused by the opening of new mines in the West or of free farmlands parceled out under the Homestead Act of 1862. Two or three forthright essayists in religious papers or magazines did say what was true. Something definite and simple had taken place, and yet only a few were ready to admit that the war itself had built factories, enlarged mills, increased railroads and telegraphic services. All trades and crafts had been put to its service, and the labor unions had forced a steady lifting of wages from 1862 to 1865. War tariffs protected industries scarcely existent in 1860 until they bloomed and asserted themselves in unions and associations. A pair of German girls who made roses for milliners in New York before the war sold a business and a trademark in 1866 for a hundred thousand dollars. A whole range of new, eminent families had been created from the rawest materials by the necessities of women's clothing; metal buttons and clasps, corsets, and such unmentionable matters as the cheap lace of drawers thrust up a thousand proprietors and workmen into the beauties of affluence. While millions flooded in official checks from the Treasury on the blanket-weavers and gunsmiths, the civilians paid their hundreds to these protégés of the tariff and the Confederate cruisers. It was a boom, timed to the pulsations of cannon and rifles on the Virginian border.

But the farmers had not enjoyed the fullest benefits of the war. Many rural opera-houses are dated from the sixties, and one who actually chooses to explore rural journalism of Lincoln's presidency will discover that pastors sometimes deplored the spread of fastidious costume among women of the plain people, but there were not enough novelties of the shop and playhouse loosed among the farms to distract mothers from a strict and discomforting attention to the casualty lists. Sons not allured by the recruiting office were often lured away by high wages in the munition plants or by the riot of sudden gain in the oilfields of Pennsylvania. Population of the villages decreased and farms were abandoned in many regions.[1] The prices paid for grain, meat, and hides were high, but the cost of hired men rose incessantly. Women of substance plowed and reaped in the fields alongside their half-grown sons in 1863. And education slowed; a master would enlist or a mistress of some petty schoolhouse marry, and the bothered school-board was likely enough to let the school stay shut until the children were nuisances indoors when snow fell and mothers remembered that book learning was a valuable thing. Many families migrated into the towns near Pittsburgh or into the city itself because their children must be schooled. "The horrors of war," says a veteran, "in my family were not those of the field, but of ordinary household life. My father and my older brothers came home on furlough occasionally, but it was not until I was discharged from service in 1863 as physically unfit that my mother had any one to contribute steady help in her round of tasks and to help her control the lively small children. A mod-

[1] A letter of my great-grandfather to my maternal grandfather, dated August 2nd, 1864, mentions good farmland near Cincinnati sold for sixty dollars an acre "because no help is to be had." Farms were abandoned in western New York, on Long Island, and in the region north of Gettysburg. An acquaintance of my family bought two hundred acres to the north of Springfield, Illinois, in 1864, for one thousand dollars, the price including two years' back taxes. According to Senator Grimes, in 1864, twenty thousand acres had been abandoned in the states of Iowa and Nebraska.

ern woman would have taken to her bed and enjoyed a case of nervous prostration. . . . She was scarcely forty years old in 1865 but she had the appearance of a woman of sixty. . . . She worked all day, and at night, from sheer benevolence, she held a sort of school for the neighboring children old enough to stay up after dark. . . . It is no wonder that she used to say, 'The slaves could have been bought for a billion dollars but nobody will ever know what the Rebellion cost.' . . ."

Nor did these people wholly misunderstand what was happening in the cities and at their capital. The United States was already an uncomfortable topic with foreign essayists; its very peasants who tilled the fields and did what the European peasant had done in illiterate peace for a thousand years could read and write. Cavour pondered that it would be interesting to see the effect of their literacy on their wars and politics. The literate peasants, then, did not enjoy the war too well and knew that it was making money for the cities. The discontents and treasonous grumblings which passed through Ohio, Indiana, and Illinois were protests, not only against the war, but against the city's expanding glitter, and the return of the soldiers in 1865 brought, often, merely the ease of added muscle power. For the boys came home with tales of New York and Washington. They had seen gayeties and luxuries, mixed with urban types in camp, and heard all kinds of unsettling things. It was well that Mr. Lincoln had spoken so kindly of the plain people, for in 1865 the rustics must have learned rather sharply that they were pretty plain.

Yet this rural population derived an intangible benefit from the wretched performance at Ford's Theater on April 14th, 1865. A true folk-hero had been born to them, an obscure man of the plain people who rose to speak equally with kings and to slay monsters. Mr. Lincoln did not rest in his tomb outside Springfield. Very soon his memory was a phantom of rectitude fairly towering while emotional rhetoricians and jobbers ripped his party into quarrelsome bits. His legend was invoked against " the money changers in the temple of Liberty " and " the Pharisees of the Senate " or the divorced woman who dictated patronage from her drawing-room near the Capitol. He was dead; he could do nothing about the soft-handed men of the Eastern cities who had gripped affairs in Washington; he had the profound power, therefore, of King Arthur and Saint Joan. That he might have shown himself shifting and incapable in the problems which hampered his successors became an unthinkable contention. Lincoln would never have done wrong, because he was dead. Since 1900 he has slowly become a man again, but for thirty years he was something else. His figure mingled with that of another gentle bearded dealer in parables, a friend of the humble and outcast, once murdered on Good Friday; the mood of some pastors and journalistic

33

poets in the weeks following his death grew to be an establishment in oratory, sacred and profane: Lincoln was a form of Christ. The cool political humorist and strategist vanished under a softer outline, and his orations with their haunting Biblical music were declaimed on Memorial Day to audiences truly reverent, hushed and tearful.[2]

This cult, like all such reverences, must do its harm. Forty years after Lincoln was murdered Harry Thurston Peck timidly implied in a defense of Chester Arthur that Lincoln's social example acted to the hurt of politicians who didn't happen to be born in log cabins or given to receiving callers with feet in woolen socks spread on a chair. Lincoln's life offered itself to the touchy rural mind in a double capacity: he rose from obscurity to domination and he was as homely as I am. To the cheaper egoist in the bustle of a county campaign this came with soothing emphasis as a form of self-defense: Lincoln was plain

[2] On the appearance of this paragraph, somewhat shortened, in *The Saturday Evening Post*, in April, a gentleman teaching American history in a huge Western university at once wrote to me: "You are like all these other Bolsheviki who are trying to degrade the character of Abraham Lincoln and make him appear an ordinary man. Lincoln was the greatest man born in the world since our Savior, *if it is fair to call him a man at all*. . . ." A dozen other letters in a more temperate tone protested my "irreverence" to Mr. Lincoln. Mr. Rutledge Watson of San Francisco wrote to assure me, on the other side, that as a small boy in Kansas he was taught to mention Mr. Lincoln in his nightly prayers, saying, "Make me as good as President Lincoln." My grandfather once halted a witness before him in a case of manslaughter who swore by "Christ and Abe Lincoln." Mr. Lewis's *Myths After Lincoln*, issued in May of this year, was very grudgingly reviewed. It is plain that the historical interests of Mr. Lincoln are still jeopardized by his emotional values.

34

as I am, so the cultured man — the smart city fellow — is wrong. And this defensive machinery was used by clever men, sometimes wholly dishonest, as leverage in the brawl between the city and the farm from 1865 to 1928. It was really in the year 1928 that the formula reached its highest utility in political blackguardism, when a Republican speaker, a clergyman, addressed a rural audience with the aphorism: "Remember that a country boy is born with the right principles, but a city boy is likely to be bad from the day of his birth. . . ."

In the amusing domain of legislative manipulation, too, the cult worked against the rural population to its infinite damage. Mr. Lincoln had four times signed acts of Congress which, as things fell out, set governmental policies inimical to the plain people in motion and all these policies were later twisted into the fuse of the grand political crash of 1896. Guiltless, so far as is known, of aiding any rogue by premeditation, Lincoln made himself the friend of rogues, the smart men who, more openly than in our times, haunted the economic scene of the United States to the end of the nineteenth century.

The adjective "smart" in earlier New England was not a complete compliment, but was reserved for the inventor of the wooden nutmeg and his imitators. A "smart man" was a horse-trader or a clock-peddler, a licensed trickster excused for his humors in a world where the humor of the eighteenth century was still

HANNA

admired. As the nation expanded, some of this primitive meaning sloughed away from the word, although it was offensive enough to cause an action in libel, in Ohio, in 1858. Lincoln is called " smart " in old newspapers, with a sense of mere shrewdness, before his elevation. And yet, persistently, there was something a little wrong with a smart man; the elder meaning hung around the adjective as the Civil War began.

On Mr. Lincoln's call for volunteers a number of smart men responded to the signal, but without military intentions. A silent " Yo, ho, ho!" rang from mind to mind. They came from everywhere, from apprenticeships in those inns where drovers met, high on the Hudson, or from tours as salesmen of candy or patent medicine in country fairs. Many of them knew the South rather better than did the new President and saw that this would be a war of some dimensions. They were ready, in a fashion, to make it their holy war.

Bull Run was hardly fought when a minor genius named Belknap arrived at the War Department with a large bill for packing sixty-odd dead Yankees in ice and transporting them to their grieved kin. A methodical clerk referred the account to regimental adjutants and found that there were no such soldiers dead. Mr. Belknap vanishes and his petty speculation is followed by the graver adroitness of men who fully knew what they were after. Light history has selected the name of Jim Fisk from this battalion,

36

acting on the wise and always the popular theory of blackening a black sheep to make gray sheep paler. As Mr. Fisk ultimately was killed in a fuss over a courtesan his general reputation does not matter, and he left no acute descendants to specialize in the destruction of testimony against him. But, when one considers the mildness of his wartime exploits, he seems a weak choice. So many smart men were so much smarter and in such widths of roguery. They enjoyed that quality known to Italians of the Renascence as *virtù*, arranging their fortunes without regard to the safety of the Union. Congressional reports, records of Federal courts and the harried Court of Claims, the documents of the Adjutant General, and a hundred military orders exhibit their arrangements.

Twenty officers were disgraced and a pair of Congressmen damaged within eighteen months of the war's beginning, but the smart men continued. Rifles thrown away as unfit for real service by ordnance officers in the East were sold to General Frémont in the West. An expedition was dispatched to the Mississippi in rotten hulls for which the government often paid nine hundred dollars a day. Bayonets of polished pewter, tents of porous shoddy, coffee made of pulse and sorghum, carbines that exploded on the drill ground, blankets so long stored in Boston that water would not soak them to the thickness of a coin, and many other versions of the wooden nutmeg were offered to the Army between 1861 and 1864.

Often nothing could be done. The actual vendor vanished in a cloud of agents and guileless middlemen, or agitated legislators raved usefully when the name of some respected citizen was read out in the meetings of a Congressional committee. Sometimes the cases wound up in a tangle of smart lawyers and angry, inexpert judges. A few smart men were consigned to military prisons or common jails. It was the son of a famous philanthropist who was begged out of a dungeon by Henry Ward Beecher after the bright lad forged a presidential proclamation so as to influence the gambling in the gold room of the Stock Exchange at New York. . . . As one reads the testimony in these affairs Mr. Lincoln's suspension of the Habeas Corpus has an appearance of pure governmental necessity. But nothing could control this adept army of thieves, often so stately in their social placing, as it wrought from the rear. A Fisk is singled out and remembered in the mess; once the names of Wormser, Justice, Vanderbilt, and Simons smelled quite as evilly as did Fisk's sales of mouldy blankets on behalf of two estimable patriots in the city of Boston.

A natural irony followed the apparition of this scattered but most active battalion. When weariness and rural discontent solidified pungently in 1864 and Mr. Lincoln's own family thought he would not be elected a second time, the Republican party discovered in its ranks a number of paying guests, converts to Mr. Lincoln's principles, highly willing to see the war prolong itself. The names of convinced gentlemen interested in the making of sound munitions are to be seen on Republican lists alongside those of men who had been advertised in cases of fraudulent practice on the government. It is entirely true, of course, that successes in the field and the virile efforts of Lincoln's actual friends defeated General McClellan, but it is also true that the costs of the wild campaign were partly borne by men in every degree of shadiness and that Lincoln's party did not disclaim their aid. A political faction invented for the uses of a humane cause thus rapidly became, let us say, both practical and mundane. Smartness entered its being; after 1864 the crazy Western schism was a party of the smart man and of the East.

But the smart men were not all urban or Eastern. In 1863 louts rode through Ohio asking farmers if they had any " crowbait " for the army, and a Federal judge at Cincinnati lost his temper as he tried to explain to some hearty yeomen that they must not doctor up dying horses for sale to the cavalry and artillery. One of General Pleasanton's officers, in that year, presented his commander an affidavit reciting that three mounts just brought to the camp had been sold by himself as useless before John Brown was hanged. In December of 1864 Charles Francis Adams scornfully wrote to his father about the Treasurer's report: " He does not state one principle in sound

finance, but he makes a stately onslaught upon ' specu-
lators in gold.' Why not also on those in flour and
pork? " Waves of cynical talk passed through regiments in which half the soldiers and their officers
came from farms. Tricks of the city's smart men may
not have been fully understood among the tents, but
they did understand about horses and grain and pork,
and a sense of betrayal can be found in the letters of
sailors as well. An obscene variation of *John Brown's
Body* sung in Farragut's fleet mentions wives and
sweethearts lured away by the homekeeping profiteer
" while we go sailing on. . . ." The tedium of war
produced a recoil sometimes fatal to the cordial sentiment necessary to the war itself. " My one interesting
experience with deserters," Colonel John McCook
wrote to a friend in 1900, " was with two fine boys
from Mr. Lincoln's own county. A sergeant caught
them leaving camp in civilian dress and brought them
to me. They told me honestly that their mother and
sisters were practically destitute and were obliged to
' go out ' as hired help by the day. They claimed that
men at home were getting rich by ' sharking ' on provisions for the Army. . . . I got to work through
Anson " — General Anson McCook — " and had the
matter referred straight to Mr. Lincoln. He looked
after them. . . . He has been criticized for his leni-
ency toward deserters. But I believe he knew what lay
behind many of these cases. Mr. [Norman] Hapgood
does not seem to realize the extent of guilt among

dealers in provisions, etc., at that time. The writers seem to neglect this whole phase of the war. . . ." [3]

This phase was not so striking as the battles in which all instruments of civilization were used belligerently for the first time. Potencies of the railroad, the balloon, the iron ship, the machine gun, the telegraph, were declared. Europe had been astonished at us, with much reason. But the war's interior effect on American manners had no immediate students and certain modern writers seem to fancy that a period of corrupt legislation, fantastic morals in public affairs, and ethical sloth commenced only with the end of the war, as if Booth's bullet had released seven devils on the nation. Yet the Gilded Age set in with 1861; no phenomenon appeared after Mr. Lincoln's death that was not plain by the close of 1862, and of many concurrent phenomena during his presidency he, himself, was the innocent producer.

Mr. Lincoln, as is known, was obliged to sign acts of Congress under which an immense quantity of fiat currency was issued. These "greenbacks" were sure to be dangerous. Even the opportunist Thaddeus Stevens fought rather shyly for the passage of the bill

[3] John J. McCook to William C. Beer, June 26th, 1900. It is probably now necessary to inform readers that the "fighting McCooks" were celebrities of the Civil War. The family was distinguished for its piety and physical charm. His men called John McCook "Stunning John" and "Beauty." In 1902 he was standing on Pennsylvania Avenue in Washington when an alcoholized person handed him a dollar bill, saying, "Beauty, here's some money I stole out of your tent in '62, God damn it! I ain't felt easy in my conscience since!"

creating them in 1862. The tempted government issued more and more of the things. In 1864 this fluctuating material had come almost to the sum of four hundred and fifty million dollars. Gold and silver were unseen objects; the public heard of speculation in metal moneys, but the coins had vanished. In 1865 some of his command, wanting to give Major William McKinley a respectful token, pooled their greenbacks and bought a five-dollar gold piece from a jeweler. Ladies wore coins dangling from bracelets, and young children wondered why the pretty gold stamped with eagles was called " money " when it clearly wasn't a paper bill. But from the paper bills arose a superstition in finance; the greenbacks were "Lincoln's greenbacks" as soon as wise men tried to get rid of them and, until 1896, this superstition twisted in and out of the plain people's mind a frozen conviction of the American nation's powers in money-making.

The greenback was not dear to Mr. Lincoln. He may have been no financier, but he is said to have viewed the fiat money with distrust. Yet, in other instances, he played the hand of the smart men cheerfully. It cannot be forgotten that he was naturally an expansionist. He had lived most of his life in the current of the Western migrations; the pioneer and the settler, always tending westward, were commonplaces of his social thought. The United States was a curio among nations in that it could colonize within its own borders. Normans and Bretons were not ad-

vised, in the forties, to leave home in covered wagons
and plant themselves in Provence; Russians removed
to Siberia only under severest compulsion; the cock-
ney went to Wales and Scotland for a holiday and
scuttled home. But to the American expansion was a
vivid factor of existence. It was even a patriotic duty,
and Mr. Lincoln wanted to see the West colonized,
as did everybody else. There is no evidence in any
way denying that he took the swift increase of Western population for a benefit to his country, and he
abetted it by his signature of the Homestead Act of
1862 and by two most dangerous acts creating railroad
corporations with singular rewards and powers.

Nothing seems so harmless as the Homestead Act,
granting settlers Western land if they would cultivate
it for five years. Lincoln and Andrew Johnson thought
westward to a prodigious vacancy in 1862. Through
this arable desert would pass the two railroads — the
Union Pacific and the Central Pacific — forming a
spine for commerce and help to the colonists. Naturally, the railroads must be subsidized and they
might, also, be granted some of this endless public
land. Everything seemed natural while Congressmen
and Senators argued a little as to terms. Four very
smart men of Yankee stock smiled encouragement
from the background of an enterprise which had, too,
a color of military necessity. But the lean and pensive
Senator John Sherman rubbed his beard and wondered, in silence, if trouble might not come of this.

Nobody shouted, "Look out!" although there had been trouble in 1858 and 1859 over a subsidized railroad that was to have made Texas a garden and a pasture. The dignity of the Senate was offended by mad rows over the character of the road's directors and the uses to which they had put the granted lands. Now, John Sherman saw, here came this new bill granting strips of land ten miles deep on each side of the tracks and six thousand dollars in government bonds for each mile finished. Mr. Sherman shivered. But he was a strong Administration man and his shudders did not pass outward in protest. In 1864 he shuddered afresh as the directors needed more help and got it — bonds and more bonds of the United States — although the rails, somehow, were not being laid. And a hazy bill creating the Northern Pacific Railroad, with land grants and privileges, was stuffed through the Senate in a hurry. "These two bills," Sherman wrote in 1895, "prove that it is not wise, during a war, to provide measures for a time of peace. . . ."

Upon these acts a mountain of bright casuistry heaped itself and Mr. Lincoln's name was used, as it grew sacred, to warrant the governmental policies they engendered. What was worse and more pervasive was a certain frame of mind infecting principled men: the government came to be a source of help for private enterprise, of subsidies and candid gifts. It was not Lincoln's fault, but he had armed the smart battalion against his plain people and, in a sort, had made the West a victim of the East. Well, it needed a trained prophet to see beyond what John Sherman feared, and Mr. Lincoln was a prophet only in the popular style.

He was thinking about the West on the last morning of his life. Schuyler Colfax came to discuss the tour he had planned through the mountains to the Pacific coast. The President talked earnestly, deep in his chair. He must get the disbanded regiments and the new immigrants headed to the West, where mines and railroads needed them. Gold and silver would pour eastward, destroying the national debt. The seaboard cities must not be packed with cheap labor, bringing down wages when the mechanics were getting good pay. Colfax was to tell the Westerners that Mr. Lincoln had their interests at heart, and Colfax thrilled. He went away to chat about the President's foresight in Willard's Hotel at a lunch of officers and civilians and came back at night to talk some more.

The gaunt man rocked in his chair and drawled until it was eight o'clock. Mrs. Lincoln walked into the room, with her fan and brilliant shawl, to remind the President that he had promised to see the play at Ford's Theater. Oh, so he had! Well, Mr. Colfax could drop in tomorrow morning. He bowed himself away. . . . The President's carriage was waiting below dim pillars in the pleasant night. Soon the people in Ford's Theater rose and applauded as Mr. Lincoln strolled into his box. . . .

45

CHAPTER II

THE BULLETHEADED GENERALS

I

Mr. Hanna, young or old, was not given to reading books. He went to sleep, even, over the political studies current in his last years which showed him up for a monstrous rogue, and once was found snoring in a hammock, an ear crumpled on a challenge to the Standard Oil Company. But he had a tendency often seen in men of an extraverted intelligence: he sometimes liked to read history. A caller entered his rooms at the Arlington Hotel in 1901 and saw the Senator pondering a great volume of Maspéro, his hands flattened on the pages, lost somewhere in Egypt or Assyria. Perhaps the pictures absorbed him and he was staring at a view of the Pharaoh or the Sār poised in a chariot, casting gold among reverent soldiers. He looked up, after a while, and said suddenly, " Isn't it funny, Jackling, that money and machinery came into the world at the same time? "

His life had been so bound to these two forces that he must have thought them endless partners in the story of man. Everything in Mark Hanna's early time had hung to the new machines. It was because wheels rolled too far from New Lisbon that his father brought him to Cleveland, and his family's success before 1860 had grown as the steamboats paddled money to the offices of Hanna, Garretson and Company. His whole triumph in affairs and politics was conditioned on the wheels and screws delivering purchased commodities, scattering out his agents and his propaganda; he throve by the effects of speed. It might be said that his legend is that of a man who realized the full force of manipulated transportation. He had been born with the railroad's first exhibited potency in American life. He died just as that potency began to be threatened by new machines.

The disaster to America caused by machinery was inscrutable to young Hanna. But the machine clattered under the prelude of the Civil War so certainly that Herman Melville caught the sound and wrote it down in *The Confidence Man*. Obsolescent slavery was defeated by the machine, and it is not badly argued by Oswald Spengler that mere fuel — coal — was the actual victor behind Grant's troops. Latter-day slavery, he says, was " a threshold phase of our machine industry, an organization of ' living ' energy, which began with man-fuel, but presently passed over to coal-fuel; and slavery came to be considered immoral only when coal had established itself. Looked at from this angle, the victory of the North in the American Civil War (1865) meant the economic victory of the concentrated energy of coal over the simple energy of the muscles. . . ."[1]

That is well enough for the speculative historian and the European. For the American, whose history is so short that he can watch its flexures and accidents within spaces of a decade, there is another victory to be mentioned: coal and the railroad and precious metal in the West were three Fates winding out an end of the fine provincial America. Compact social bodies too small to bear defection wilted as "the dream of the plains defeated the dream of the sea"; the romantic motive which perpetually imposes itself upon the economic in this business of migrations shimmered before the men of New England and Pennsylvania, drawing them inland after 1849, not outward on the waters to maintain a liaison of culture with Europe. War accelerated this destruction of the provincial lines. And who saw it? . . . One man at least, it seems.

In March of 1862 legislators, profiteers, and officers smoking at Willard's Hotel in Washington might admire a tall, trim gentleman who strolled past their chairs. He was not old, but his hair seemed almost white, and straight eyebrows showed gray above his dark blue eyes. Some knew the face or remembered that they had seen it engraved in books, and John Hay walked nervously after this magnificent along Pennsylvania Avenue one day, trying to be brave

[1] *The Decline of the West*, Volume II, page 488.

enough to speak to Nathaniel Hawthorne, who had tired of the rumors and the telegrams and had come down from Concord to see what this war was like.

His thoughts were soon printed in *The Atlantic Monthly* as a languid essay, musical with disdain for the mob in Willard's Hotel, where " you are mixed up with office seekers, wire pullers, inventors, artists, poets, prosers, clerks, diplomatists, mail contractors, railway directors, until your own identity is lost among them. . . . You adopt the universal habit of the place and call for a mint julep, a whisky skin, a gin cocktail, a brandy smash or a glass of Pure Old Rye. . . ." The feebleness of modern topers depressed him as he glanced at venerables in frilled shirts swilling Bourbon by the horn. All these mild diluted drinks were tame beside those eight inches of liquid fury! Old times and glories passed in this conglomerate of vulgarities. But he seemed merely to be describing General McClellan's camp, or the prisoners in the roundhouse at Harper's Ferry, a " heap of unwashed human bodies " or the *Monitor* at anchor, a sort of iron rat-trap. Nothing is stressed save his flashing taunt to his friends at Concord who had likened the calamitous John Brown's gallows to the Cross, and his own intellectual satisfaction in seeing Brown hanged for a fool is underscored by an apologetic footnote. But he saw a good deal: the iron rat-trap meant the finish of naval warfare in the adorable grand manner. He pondered for a sentence on future duels of

49

submarines. He saw that something might well come of the poor Southern white when slavery was abolished. And as to the future of the Union, revealed to him in the smoke of Willard's Hotel, why, "one bullet headed general will succeed another in the presidential chair; and veterans will hold the offices, at home and abroad, and sit in Congress and the state legislatures, and fill all the avenues of public life. . . ."

He was really writing a dry little dirge for New England. These railway directors and mail contractors were enemies of that close order which had produced Nathaniel Hawthorne. The nation spread and its several integrities were thinned or slaughtered as troops hurried to the East by rail. Soon the same rails would slide away young men from the decadent villages of his province to the West; it was "the downfall of the Bostonian Empire" that appeared in the smoke at Willard's, and with Boston fell Virginia. . . . But, for Mr. Hawthorne, his own territory had been all America. He was not much interested in this large, raw, collection of states that claimed his devotion only to "an airy mode of law" and had no symbol but a flag. He was not worried about the bullet-headed generals who would rule this hazy space. Something good might come of them. They were Force. "It may substitute something more real and genuine, instead of the many shams on which men heretofore have founded their claims to public regard. . . ."

He had always seen into shams. Boys at college fancied a mystery behind his stare and christened him Oberon as much for this as for his beauty. And now he perfected the strangeness of his life by dying, with his province, as if in protest against the oncoming miscellany. He grew weaker, thinner, smiling at the doctors who could not say what was wrong. Mr. Hawthorne was simply selecting the right conclusion to a grave fantasy about a being who had stared from the shadows of a bewitched wood at man's hypocrisy and man's vain emotions. He vanished. Oberon withdrew, as was most right, while a dog howled below his window among the silent hills, in a cool midnight. . . .

Four years and a day from Mr. Hawthorne's death a Republican convention in Chicago began to fulfill his prophecies. General Ulysses Grant was nominated for the presidency in a roar. There could be no other candidate. And then the delegates behaved unbecomingly toward New England; the expanding nation yawned at the wishes of its intellectual nurse, and Bostonians learned from their newspapers that the West, this region beyond Buffalo, wanted a Western vice president. There is an old lady living who can recollect raucous delegates yelling, " Take yer damn' codfish home! " when the names of Henry Wilson, of Massachusetts, and Hannibal Hamlin, of Maine, were proposed. On a fifth ballot the gay Schuyler Colfax was nominated and the Republican convention of 1868 dispersed, by railway.

It had not been well reported, and facts of the discord between East and West are mostly traditional. But it is true that an unled, formless resentment of New England's postures washed the West during the war. The feeling may be judged by six letters of a Mrs. Dix, an ordinary female of the more cultivated kind who worked in Washington's hospitals in 1863 and 1864. Just one person from Boston way seemed a human being to this lady out of Illinois; she loved Louisa May Alcott. But the wives of the cotton-spinning Congressmen annoyed her, reading tracts to sick men in the wards and " squealing " when some tortured invalid brought out an oath; and so did the Yankee Senators, iced and done up in tight black bindings, patronizing Mrs. Lincoln at evening parties. She could not bear them! " We " — she meant Ben in the cavalry and Geordie in the Navy — " are fighting for Union, and all they want is to see the Rebels humiliated! . . . I hope never to hear the name of Massachusetts again when this ordeal is over. . . ." The Yankees had shoved the nation into hell and now they were sniffing at the Westerners, who did most of the fighting. The rise of Grant and Sherman was a victory of the West. Who won the war? The West! . . . Mrs. Dix died soon after Grant was nominated at Chicago, perhaps in a state of revengeful contentment. Grant would show 'em!

Something of this resentment was working in Marcus Alonzo Hanna on July 3rd, 1868, when he wrote:

"Dear Cap: Lillian just remembered to tell us that you brought those firecrackers for the best baby in Ohio. Dan says to tell you that you are a gentleman. Mr. Rhodes was just putting up a high fence at dinner. He does not want to see Pendleton nominated against Grant. I hope they put up somebody from Mass. or New York, so we can all turn out and lick him. I am awfully sorry about the sheep.

"M. A. Hanna."[2]

The document has its mysteries. Who was Cap, and what happened to the sheep? The second sentence is mendacity. Master Daniel Rhodes Hanna said nothing of the kind, at the age of eighteen months. The rest is simple: Mr. Daniel Rhodes has been bluffing at dinner about affairs of the Democratic Convention, which seemed to be ready to pick George Pendleton, of Ohio, against Ulysses Grant, of Ohio. As a capital financier Mr. Rhodes likes nothing less. "Gentleman George" heads the "soft money" faction of the Democrats and wants to pay the government's debts, foreign and domestic, in greenbacks, the inconvertible paper currency born of necessity in 1862 and now crumbling in all cash-drawers and

[2] This autograph has an odd history. It was found in an old novel in a Washington shop and brought to Mr. Hanna in 1902 to be authenticated. He was just then busy with his negotiations in the coal strike and was giving instructions as to some telegram to his secretary, Mr. Dover. Turning the paper over, he noted on its back, "Wiring Morgan, McCrea, Depew this date," and then apologized for damaging the memento, saying, "I am awfully sorry. . . ." He contended that his use of "awfully" was common in Cleveland in his youth.

pockets. Mr. Hanna, whose son, you see, is "the best baby in Ohio," hopes that the Democrats will nominate some ghastly Easterner, so that the state's loyalties will not be divided between two older native sons.

Mark Hanna had learned things in finance since 1865. A little after his marriage the oil fever took him and he built a refinery for petroleum. That was not enough for a clever fellow, who thought well of himself as a business man, and he built the *Lac La Belle*, the swiftest and smartest of Lake steamers, using his own money for the venture. But the refinery burned and the steamer sank, uninsured, and one morning in 1867 young Mr. Hanna, just convalescent from typhoid, found himself a pauper.

His daughter brought her diminished husband home to Mr. Daniel Rhodes, who viciously teased Marcus Alonzo and planned to make use of him. The teasing would be abominable form in our times, but Mrs. Hanna's brother, James Rhodes, lived to assert that "men joked each other about business losses at that time as if they were country boys having a fight over a stolen ball. . . ." The old Democrat had his joke with Mark Hanna, but, meanwhile, a wonderful perambulator rolled on Franklin Avenue, containing Master Daniel Rhodes Hanna, although his grandfather admitted no concern with the perambulator's contents. He "put up a tall fence" about babies; they didn't interest him, even Charlotte Augusta's brand. But when Charles Nolan came from Washington to get the signature of Mr. Rhodes on a contract, he waited three days in the big man's office and, getting tired of hard furniture at Rhodes, Card and Company's, took himself to the magnate's house. Mr. Rhodes came down from the nursery, snapped his name four times on a paper, and hurried up to resume intensive studies of croup, leaving the caller to be entertained by his son-in-law, an agreeable creature whose name Mr. Nolan did not catch. . . . Yet, in 1888, a burly man whose whiskers now were mere strips of red fur close to his ears stared at Mr. Nolan a time in a hotel at Chicago and then shouted: "Hi, Mr. Nolan!" Mark Hanna's memory worked so; he had remembered a striking person for twenty-one years.

This memory and some other capabilities were put to use in April of 1867, when the renovated firm of Rhodes and Company was announced, with George Warmington, Robert Rhodes, and Marcus Hanna as partners. Daniel Rhodes retired. His son and his son-in-law were to assume his place in the business. Thus, in his thirtieth year, Mark Hanna neatly shifted from dealing in wholesale groceries to dealing in coal and iron, and this was his occupation for the rest of his life in business. He was to be Mr. Hanna, of Rhodes and Company, until the famous firm became M. A. Hanna and Company.

In 1868 his enthusiasm for Grant was natural. Mr. Hanna knew that American paper currency was degraded; Canadians sulkily accepted a dollar at thirty-five cents in the Lake ports, and all dealings of Rhodes and Company in Canada were hampered by the exchange. He must have well understood what General James Garfield, of Ohio, meant, in Congress, on the fifteenth of May. " We are cut off," said the Congressman, " from the money currents of the world. Our currency resembles rather the waters of an artificial lake, which lie in stagnation or rise to full banks at the caprice of the gatekeeper. Gold and silver abhor a depreciated paper money and will not keep company with it. If our currency be more abundant than business demands, not a dollar of it can go abroad; if deficient not a dollar in gold will come in to supply the lack. There is no legislation on earth wise enough to adjust such a currency to the wants of the country. . . ."

That seems clear enough? It made sense to a Mark Hanna in 1868, but it was idiotic gabble to farmers and small editors everywhere in the United States. They could not differentiate business, which is local, from finance, which, after the eighteenth century, had become international. In a nation boasting of its extraordinary financial acuteness there were so few actual financiers that members of banking firms in Wall Street caught up the soft-money heresy and were prepared to back Gentleman George. Sitting near Wall Street was Mr. John Pierpont Morgan, a tall Yankee who had once refused to be a professor of mathematics at Göttingen, keeping the ledgers of his firm in a deliberate double system, one set of books for American money and one set for real money — the sacred token of finance, gold; his cold eyes could examine what his house was supposed to be worth, and turn secretly to what it was worth. To this man General Garfield's words were platitudinous, to a fair portion of interior America they were fantastic. A sentiment had promptly gathered on the greenbacks; they were now " Lincoln's greenbacks." There was a lot of them. They filled the function of money. Of course the government could pay its debts in paper! Anyhow, it was the capitalist and the foreigner who wanted the government to redeem its bonds in gold . . . so to hell with the capitalist and the foreigner! An orator named Chidsey outlined this concept of the nation's case to a crowd in Shobonier, Illinois, in the spring of 1868, saying, " If Europe wants none of our greenbacks, we can blow them on Europe from the cannon's mouth!" That settled it.

Among Mr. Chidsey's hearers was a sickly young lawyer from over in Minnesota who was trying to collect a bill for a client. War had filled Cushman Davis with fevers and made him prematurely bald. Endless lethargies possessed him and he struggled, even in court, with a passion for sleep. But Mr. Chidsey's oration exasperated him and he shouted from the crowd that the United States could not thrash all Europe. The crowd hissed. Mr. Davis went back to

Minnesota, pensive, and, as Senator Davis wrote in 1896: " Here is this Balaam " (Mr. William Jennings Bryan) " telling people just what this jackass was telling them in 1868 and they are believing it. Verily, verily, men are fools when they fall into a superstition about money! " [3]

Ulysses Grant had no such superstition. He had lived through wretched times before the war when the " wildcat " money of banks along the Mississippi fluctuated weekly and might be worthless overnight. He stood boldly in 1868 for the unpopular proposition. " The United States is only one nation among many," he told a small girl, " and its money must be the kind that other nations will accept. You will understand this when you are older." Miss Prudence Watson was proud of the General's communication, but she had to grow up in a country which tried to ignore Grant's little dictum. In 1868 she saw her own brothers out parading for Horatio Seymour, the Democratic candidate, and heard orators bawling that the Republicans were trying to enslave the farmer to the capitalist. Miss Watson's understanding of the word " capitalist " was vague, but she knew that the Corinthian decorations at the top of the veranda's pillars were capitals and worked out her own definition: a capitalist, she reasoned quite correctly, was a man who sat on the top of a narrow post. . . .

From their shaky perches some smart men looked

[3] To James P. Holt, September 2nd, 1896.

down unfavorably on the agreeable George Pendleton when Democracy convened in Tammany Hall at New York on July 4th, 1868. This hall was not so far from their offices; something could be done at short range, in the private name of Democratic bondholders and bankers. Money talked to itself and then addressed the convention's machinery. These forces came together into the life of Mr. Pendleton. After many ballots the delegation of his own state swung against the pleasing man, and Horatio Seymour, aghast, was nominated to head a ticket in which he did not believe. A " hard money " Democrat was nominated on a " soft money " platform. The straddle ended any hope of winning; farmers deserted the Easterner to vote in swarms for the man from Ohio. Next March, as per prophetic schedule, the first of Mr. Hawthorne's bulletheaded generals entered the White House.

II

Pendleton's vogue had been an expression in the most compact terms of the nation's isolation and he had prospered until such time as the smart men saw his implicit dangers. But he had not amused his opponents; intrigue disposed of him, not laughter. The perils of fiat money were explained in America, and broadly, before 1860, but a heavy tithe of the nation's educated men had been taken between Sumter and Appomattox; the cultivated Americans had supported this war, and their mentalities did not survive their

59

bodies. Really, you cannot kill off a medley of poets, engineers, journalists, undergraduates, and sharp young clerks or sterilize them against further ideas by the supreme heat of military experience without damaging the critical life of a nation; and you cannot sever a colony from its several mothers while it is still in the nursing period without damaging its political equilibrium. . . . In the forties and fifties the American had been incessantly stimulated by Europe. His poets, his two real novelists, his lecturers, had expounded Europe to him, if he read books. European heroes and charlatans visited his cities. But after 1860 he moved more and more swiftly into his present condition of "the stripped European." The many and truly informing contacts of simple commerce had been interrupted; in the swirl of his own current emotional adventure he lost all touch with the resolved emotional adventures of foreign arts and political facts. He would face Europe, from this point onward, in the mood of Mark Twain or of Henry James, trying to find it funny and producing just the nervous giggle of a lad thrust into a drawing-room among indifferent older folk, or accepting Europe's own valuations of itself with a fatuous respect. That this miscomprehension affected his understanding of finance began to be plain in 1868. The neurosis had formed; the nation was now in the state of an unconscious invalid who thinks himself wholesome because he eats, walks, and begets. It would need the crash of sensations to assure him that he was shut off by a film of ignorant defenses from the wisdom of mankind, which is not so small. Meanwhile he had money and machinery, and these contented his muscles as playthings. They do so still, some say.

A society of the positively neurotic waited to welcome Ulysses Grant in Washington. Many of these sufferers were soldiers who had served under the taciturn general; others had taken malaria under McClellan in the Virginia swamps. For years their nerves were kept at a certain palpitating pitch, and now they drank and gamed to keep up the tension of nights in camp along the Potomac. They alarmed ladies at dinner by twitchings and bursts of tearfulness over nothing. " Shell shock " had not been invented then, and the ladies did not imagine that a recurrent sense of the inane, war's least comfortable acquirement, was disturbing some giant in broadcloth between the baked shad and the roast duck. One member of Congress always left the House when Gettysburg was mentioned; another could not sleep in a dark room. Nothing seemed amiss with the whiskered men in loose velvet jackets who wore a tea rose in imitation of the Duc de Morny and swallowed champagne before luncheon in Willard's Hotel or drank six of the famous brandy cocktails at the Saint Nicholas in New York on their way to the stock exchange. Their grandsons, after 1919, were just as gay companions, with the whole vocabulary of the neurologist ready to explain their malady. It was the pay-day of a vast military exploit. Only, at the end of the sixties, men were not supposed to have nerves, and there was no talk about neuroses.

Anything for a thrill, though! They turned to ferocious amusements of finance and legislation, and roared in Congress when James Blaine told Roscoe Conkling that he was a dunghill, a singed cat, a whining puppy and some other things. Their taste in oratory had been formed by the sickening, rhythmic vituperations that preceded the war, and their logic had not been increased by fifty months of subjection to mere command. It did not bruise their sense of proportion to hear Abraham Lincoln and the " dead of a thousand fields " summoned up against a bill to deflate the currency, and they did not mind — it was exciting! — if an orator asked God to strike dead the Postmaster General who hadn't given someone's pet orderly an office in Iowa. They must be amused. Our historians primly tell us that " they joined in the mad scramble for worldly success." Perhaps historians may yet discover that success is just a form of amusement, mostly sacred to those who have not brains enough to attain it.

But as for the smart men whose interest in the war had been the costly shipping of soldiers and mail or the sale of munitions, and damn the quality, to the bewildered government, they were now in smoothest function as a medium between the American and his country, ready to explain its possibilities. They had money and machinery at their disposal and useful examples for their argument. The star of Empire, they said, glittered in the West. It was already a traditional saying; expansion was an old catchword. In the fifties there had been little difficulties about grants of land in the territories, but the Homestead Act and the donations to the railroads had countered that precedent. Hotels and boarding-houses in Washington now jammed with people eager to have the government run a railway across their acres, or appropriate ten millions to build a governmental school on their mountain, or widen their river. The popular mind had grown used to the government's benevolences, and smart men would surely not discourage this state of things. The expansionist mania, really, was washing back upon itself; the individual neurosis of the pioneer, his profound belief in future wealth, now mingled with the other neuroses in the East and made the smart man happy.

Huge tracts of Western land passed into the keeping of gentlemen who had rooms and pretty ladies at the disposal of excited Westerners wanting something done at Washington. Everybody was opening the country up. It was a pastime. The pioneers came eastward with charts of their possessions, and the smart battalion at the Saint Nicholas and the Willard entertained them suitably with promises and champagne, a drink popular among Englishmen and Americans

because its gaseous nature recalls the ginger beer or soda water of infantile revelries. Confidence in the government was the note of the smart battalion's discourse to the returning pioneer; all that had been done for the Union Pacific and the Northern Pacific could be done again, and ought to be done. Now, as to expenses. . . . There was a deal of whispering about a man in Washington, who. . . . Soon every Western settlement had its sour loungers, aware of the best bars and hotels in New York and the capital, but bitter forever against the East. They had gone to meet the sunrise and came home shrivelled. They knew all about the damned capitalists of the Saint Nicholas bar, at least. Some of the capitalists locked away deeds to thousands of Western acres and waited for the country's movement to manure this unearned increment. While waiting they roundly applauded the Honorable Roscoe Conkling when he passionately argued, before Federal courts, that the Fourteenth Amendment of the Constitution forbade a mere state to regulate rates of railroads passing through its territories. Mr. Conkling could prove by sheer force of oratory that states should not regulate anything. The less regulation you had, the better. Was not the country being opened up? Even Mr. James Blaine agreed that the country was being opened up. It went on being opened up until the panic of 1873 halted the practice.
. This society, not at all unlike the society surrounding another President from Ohio fifty-two years

later, welcomed Ulysses Grant in 1869. Amusement-hunters, power-seekers, and orators swarmed on the guileless, tired soldier. He was no fool, but his weariness was clear even to the young daughter of William Lloyd Garrison when she saw him at Washington in 1866. That he became the subject of a game is common history, and the game was safe until such time as his stubborn temper roused and his suspicion leaped at his plausible friends. But he was tired and he wanted to be entertained; he had been poor all his days and he had a simple reverence for wealth. Rich people who could dine him in gilded private parlors on steamboats, where colored windows projected sheen on rattling silver and cut-glass goblets, circled the President, with various intentions. Handsome Congressmen who understood a horse, and Ben Butler, who understood the plebeian mind, rose and fell in his favor for eight years. He might buck out of their grooming hands and veto a bill to increase the inconvertible currency; he might sign a bill setting a date for the resumption of payments in real money of the government's debts. He might listen to reformers and establish a commission for the improvement of the Civil Service. He would decide three times to withdraw the soldiers from the racked South and let a conquered people disentangle itself from its miseries by its own will. But, for six days in the week, the smart men had him dazzled. He was tired.

Failure and war had eaten out of this man any

65

essential will; he had been nothing for years, a drudge in a crude community, and then he had been exhausted by an incredible tension of command. "Let us have peace," was not just a political expression, but a personal and immediate prayer. He wanted no more trouble. It was easier to take advice from his friends, and it was soothing to have such pretty things given to him, horses and bonds and jeweled pins. Let the Senators and Congressmen make the appointments to the Civil Service; if the Cabinet made trouble, get another cabinet. Let him have peace!

His presidency will provide gossip for a dozen more biographies. The society about him can be dissected into a hundred layers of scandal. His failures were notorious from the first month of his vacillating reign. But, beyond the orators and the journalists, this general had a special audience, and it saw him not unjustly. He was Grant. He was not the President or the military commander to this legion, but a man. Historians cannot be taught to remember steadily the force of the human aspect on a people. You can pick Grant's effect from any volume of the *Photographic History of the Civil War*. . . . See, here is a circular bench under dusty pines. A group of officers and correspondents gabble in the sunlight. Orderlies and messengers are dimmer upon tall horses beneath the boughs. And here, somehow lonely on the bench, is a hard, lounging body, a plain hat drawn over a bearded face, a cigar, and a pair of dirty boots. This is Grant, familiar to the men watching him as Bill or Ed or Jason waiting outside the smithy at home for a colt to be shod. Everything since dug up by destructive analysts in the case of Grant was a commonplace of his camp. His men knew that he had hauled wood for a living in Missouri, but that did not disturb them. If his staff pumped ideas into him, what of it? A man ought to listen to his friends. He was supposed to drink two quarts of whisky a day. His men were not concerned. He was no figure to be increased by religious lights, and verbal gestures were not expected of him. He was no Liberator. He was their neighbor. He had only to pause beside a cot in the hospital below Vicksburg, saying, " I bet that hurts," to a lad with a smashed arm, in order to have the fealty of a whole county in Iowa. So criticism of the President was immaterial to this grand army. They might curse him for a fool and even vote the Democratic ticket, but he was still Grant.

He gained by an unspoken contrast with his background of noisy creatures on paper stilts. The word " great " flooded the press; great orators, great editors, great railroads, great thieves, and great strumpets were on every page of the newspapers. Mark Twain became a great humorist, as he once said, between two lectures. The rapidity of creation stunned, and the presidential sphinx, who had really done something, seemed larger in this smear of shams. And there was nothing else to look at, now. The giants

vanished or waned as querulous freaks. Thaddeus
Stevens died. Wendell Phillips had gone crazy over
fads, such as female suffrage and prohibition. Sumner was lost in his obsessions, wanting the English
flag washed off the American continent, quarreling
tiresomely with Grant over the annexation of Santo
Domingo or bullyragging the President to get the
fantastic item of two billion dollars for " indirect
damages " inserted among the *Alabama* claims. Ben
Butler wallowed between the parties, grossly impudent and jolly. Roscoe Conkling leaned on a mantel-
shelf of yellow marble, now and then adjusting the
famous curls on his advertised brow, and aspirants
for his favor waited a gesture of Kate Chase's round
fan before approaching the chief of the spoilsmen with
some request or a new slander of James Blaine. This
is the chart of the Gilded Age, a fierce assumption of
greatness in a circumfluent weariness. Everyone was
tired and wanted to be entertained.

Thus the first bulletheaded general becomes an
emblem of his nation in that time. He was himself
a victim in the comedy of the expansionist mania;
his merits, which were solid as the merits of many
men, had been diluted, expanded in all directions;
the force so excellent in the drilling of a raw regiment
exploded vainly. He did small things very well, as
President, and wanted to do large things. But he
strayed among his projects, as the expanding nation
strayed, and his result was a network of incomplete

68

roads towards a proper government, and the demolition of any respect for its rulers that survived in the United States.

Out in Cleveland young Mr. Hanna found that he couldn't interest his friends in politics. "Your newspapers," old Senator Hanna said, in 1900, "used to gas about the great excitement of some election or other. And then we had to hire livery hacks to get the voters to come and vote!" It was his first political lesson. He made himself inconvenient and obstreperous trying to get the Republican voters to attend a caucus or put off a trip to the marshes to shoot ducks on election day. The increase of Cleveland had brought into the city numbers of shabby laborers or immigrants whose votes were already manipulated in 1864, ordered by small bosses or put up for sale. Mr. Hanna profusely objected to the machinery of his party all through Grant's first term. In 1873 he bolted, with other Republicans, and helped to elect a reputable Democrat mayor of Cleveland. He kept fussing about this lackadaisical habit of his friends in regard to the affairs of the city and the state. It took time for cynicism to enter him. He was an Ohio man and a Cleveland man, locally absorbed. He would not see that it was absurd to be interested in a caucus or in the bad lighting of Euclid Avenue; his wife teased him and his friends called him a bore. Let the professionals handle politics and be damned to them. Politics was a dirty game. Nobody dissented at a banquet when

Mark Twain put out his unprinted witticism: "There is a Congressman — I mean a son of a bitch— But why do I repeat myself?"[4] It was not until 1880 that Mr. Hanna shrugged and consented, and perhaps the experience of hearing himself called a rich busybody at a meeting of reformers was the conclusion of his first political mood. He knew, by that time, that machinery ruled in politics and that the machinery was companionably to be oiled by money. This image itself appeared in cartoons, in the time of Grant. All was appropriate. Factories vomited cheap furniture and cheaper machines on the country, and the vital machinery of cities cast up cheap men into place. Behind this apparatus was a point of reality: one might quietly rule in politics without being a politician. One might be an engineer.

III

In 1872 there was a stir and a flutter from Washington. The nation now learned why John Sherman had shuddered in 1864 over the act insuring the Union Pacific Railroad. It came to be said that the mighty construction company known as the Crédit Mobilier had distributed shares of its stock among national legislators. Commissioners were appointed to discover what exactly had happened and the facts twinkled into view. Mr. Oakes Ames, a Congressman from Massachusetts, the son of poor but honest parents,

[4] This was current before 1879. Mr. Clemens dated it about 1876.

was the main witness before the delving commissions. Mr. Ames spoke freely and indignantly and his statements crawled abroad to bite heels. A controlling group of stockholders dominated the Union Pacific and the Crédit Mobilier. As the construction company built the railroad, the railroad paid its friend in cash and stocks. Unpleasant bystanders asserted that the actual cost of building was about one half of what the Crédit charged for its work. It was shown that the Crédit had been paid more than ninety-three million dollars, while the costs could not be run to more than fifty-three millions. Skeptics alleged that the road had truly cost only about twenty-eight millions. Anyhow, stock of the Crédit was a " diamond mine." Mr. Oakes Ames said so himself. He was allowed to know what he was talking about.

The investigation was an affair of two stories. On the lower floor the committee discovered that certain Congressmen and Senators had taken or had bought stock at par from Mr. Ames. In the second story people accustomed to finance had an esoteric sensation. For, mile by mile, the government of the United States kept its contract with the Union Pacific by turning over securities to the road's officers. It was this load of bonds that really paid for the construction of the Union Pacific, on which, said the builders, they had " risked their every penny " and " staked their personal honor." And now the Government must wait until 1895 for the maturity of the railroad's debt.

Engineers, surveyors, and workmen had risked their lives to build the line, but there had been no real risk of anybody's fortune in the deal. The government was the cow and the smart men filled their pails. The fact was there, and very clearly to be inferred in the reports of the Poland and Wilson committees.[5]

Congress meekly voted that a Senator and two Representatives be censured, and casuists defended the legislators minutely through every turn of the business. It is true that no bills affecting the railroad were before Congress when the stock was distributed by Mr. Ames, and Mr. Ames assured the world he was just procuring a friendly influence against the evil-speakers and blackmailers who might threaten his scheme. People laughed over the word "blackmailers," and yet there was a glitter of realism in that statement, for the blackmailing of corporations had begun in the United States as soon as there was talk, in the fifties, of controlling railroads and contractors. However, Mr. Ames settled his case by going

[5] It will surprise anybody reading the journalistic comment of the period to find how seldom this second phase of the matter is mentioned, even in the partisan Democratic sheets. Possibly the method of giving out the reports tended to hide the real issue. Most of the denunciation was wasted on the so-called corruption of Congress. An interesting attitude will be found in *The Last Quarter Century in the United States* by Benjamin Andrews. Andrews was socially in touch with people who could inform him properly, but for a moralist and a reformer he is curiously mild in his recital. Mr. Myers in his study of the great American fortunes seems certainly to be more correct. Mr. Charles C. Nolan, who knew Mr. Poland, told me in 1926 that the investigator put the cost of the construction at about thirty-eight million dollars.

home to Massachusetts and dying. His notebook had done its worst to several careers, as he kept accurate count of the legislators who would pay for the stock presently, but hadn't paid him when the scandal broke. A blow glanced off and ruined Schuyler Colfax, who tried to show that a dividend received from Mr. Ames was a contribution to his campaign in 1868 given by one Nesbitt, chief of the "Paper Ring." Congressmen who returned stock and dividends to Mr. Ames, on second thought, defeated by their example the case of the casuists who kept it. "It was fishy," said one of these former, Allison of Iowa, in 1895, "and you can see what they were after, now. Ames and Huntington wanted to get rid of the debt to the government. They were looking a long way ahead." He spoke as the grandees of the Southern Pacific Railroad were attempting to put off the payment of their huge debts to the public, and the public was resisting the attempt with unusual success. Perhaps Mr. Ames had not looked so far ahead as 1895. He was a very smart man, though, and sprung of the plain people, who, Mr. Herbert Hoover tells us, are the backbone of the country.

This scandal was still piling its gossip in the summer of 1873 when a wide uneasiness troubled the expansionist financiers. Times were bad in Europe, after a panic in April at Vienna. Jay Cooke had to admit that bonds of the Northern Pacific Railroad sold slowly, as Europe would not buy. Europe bought less and less through the late summer, and bright lads in the brokerages now discovered that American finance was not free of Europe at all. Meanwhile sober investors wondered about the government of the Western railroads and a few journals talked, gently, of inflation and unsound prosperity. Then, in seven hours of September 19th, 1873, the whole expansionist bubble descended in water. Nature co-operated handsomely with business; rain fell a dozen times on frantic brokers lurching along Wall Street. Spectators huddled under porticos and umbrellas, staring at the wet show. Jay Cooke had failed, it was known on the eighteenth, but this show of the nineteenth was not wholly due to the collapse of Cooke or of Hatch and Company, although both houses ruined smaller banks and brokers as they fell. The image of the card castle is not accurate. This was real panic, for stocks of excellent value followed the descending railroad shares, thrown away without reason. The almighty American business man became a tremulous sheep in the drenching storm. Everything slumped, racketed, and dropped. Certificates of stock were found lying in the gutter by boys, abandoned — in one case, at least — by men who were solvent. The Exchange closed. People sat on curbs, mumbling to each other. There was nothing left.

And now men who had lived on stimulus since 1861 exacted a last thrill: suicide was constant in the newspapers. Mr. Edward Stokes, who had lately murdered

Jim Fisk, sent word from prison that he was glad to
be in out of the rain. " A horrible levity," Mrs. Henry
Ward Beecher noted, " seems to prevail among the
afflicted. . . ." The more fashionable pastors steered
away from calling their flocks frivolous or supersti-
tious, but mentioned that God's hand seemed to be
on the nation. Mr. Jay Gould quietly swept thousands
of shares into his control at very reasonable prices,
and many sons of stockbrokers left school and went
to work.

At the end of 1873 more than a third of the railroads in the United States were being nursed by receivers. The burden of the panic fell, of course, on
the West, as the ruin of grand banks in New York
brought on the ruin of the rural bankers. Much of the
trouble was simply neurotic.[6] A state of mind succeeded a state of mind; inflation was the mother of
timidity. In the spring of 1874, farms of ninety acres
could not be mortgaged for a hundred dollars, and the
charlatans were wailing to Grant for more money.
Congress, in April, sent an act calling for an increase
of the inconvertible currency to four hundred million
dollars, and the cliques assured Grant that unless he
approved this stupidity the Republican party in the
West was ruined. But the President put his veto on
the folly, and it cannot be decided, now, whether the
new scandals among his odd friends or his veto did

[6] A client of my grandfather, for instance, withdrew all his funds
from solid banks in Ohio, sold his land, and kept more than two hundred
thousand dollars in cash in his house for some years.

most to revive the Democratic party in the elections of 1874.

Business would not revive. The soft coal mines of Ohio and Pennsylvania had been suggesting gold mines until Black Friday. Now scared little concerns combined or drearily summoned creditors to appoint a receiver. Railroads curtailed orders, under stress of economy, and engineers joked about using coals twice over in the yards, as prudent wives used tea or coffee grounds. An association of miners sent its awkward delegates to implore decent wages, but the delegates could report only one friendly listener to the new union. Mr. Hanna, of Rhodes and Company, would hear them out and do what he could for them.

Mr. Hanna, much hooted at by conservatives, had organized an association of operators. Not being talkative he explained his purposes badly to his friends. He had no fancy name for his scheme, but he believed in what is now called collective bargaining. A strike was a nuisance to him, and nothing good, that he could see, had ever come of poor wages and discontent. He listened civilly to the delegates and promised to aid their association if they would promise to use strikes as a last means of getting attention. But he was to be baffled by the weak operators as he tried to keep things smooth in Wayne and Stark counties, called then "the Massillon district." Master Daniel Hanna's first lessons in finance were to be discussions of coal and wages around the dinner-table.

Flushed gentlemen expounded the villainies of the Eastern markets, the horrible terms exacted by cautious managers of railroads, and the general awfulness of everything. Statistics rose in air and battered the boy's head. And then, or later, he learned that his father saw a fraud in all this twaddle of insecurity and bad times. " He held that some corporations and large industrial concerns were deliberately bleeding their workmen as a matter of selfish economy. I have heard the same opinion expressed in regard to the panic of 1873 by other men who were in a position to be acquainted with the facts. . . . But the conditions in the soft coal business at the time were really very bad. It was impossible for Mr. Hanna to keep the rate of pay up. Several of the small operators were on the verge of ruin. . . ." [7]

In these three years of extreme depression Mr. Marcus Hanna began to be apparent to his rivals, for he was a salesman of Rhodes and Company's coal before anything else. He committed seeming miracles. It would be known that a large contract awaited someone in Chicago or Duluth; agents would hustle to the point of demand and meet Mark Hanna coming home with the contract in his pocket. He seemed to smell a chance for a big sale from Cleveland; he shot off to Saint Louis or was met in the streets of Winnipeg. He got there first. And, although it then was thought absurd, he went in for advertising. On his

[7] Daniel Hanna to Henry Adler, November 24th, 1905.

command Rhodes and Company issued leaflets and pamphlets, some written by the literary James Ford Rhodes, which circulated the offices of railroads and factories. It was advertising by indirection. The firm of Rhodes and Company seemed merely to be giving news of the coal-fields to the world.

The private news was saddening enough. Business went on, but prices stayed low and declined in 1875. In the early spring of 1876 the frightened operators reduced wages to sixty-five cents a ton in the Massillon district, over Mr. Hanna's warning, and the union could not keep the men from striking. Only one mine of Rhodes and Company was alive in the middle of April. When Mr. Warmington brought down some new non-union laborers from Cleveland one morning, he was mobbed and would have been killed had not two strikers saved him. A genuine disorder broke out instantly and the sheriff appealed to Governor Rutherford Hayes for troops. The grave veteran at Columbus hesitated and then sent a company of militia to the mines. Twenty-four hours passed. Then strikers set afire two mines of Rhodes and Company, and the militiamen made arrests. A man was shot, of course, and the timid babbled about anarchy in Cleveland. Mr. Hanna limped into his house and threw his hat the length of the hallway, alarming his son by the remark, "God damn militia, anyhow!" This salty sentiment, often repeated by Americans, was Mr. Hanna's first attack of profanity before his son, but excusable. He found himself, as chief of the operators' association, charged with the sickly job of seeing that twenty-three half-starved proletarians were properly punished by the law.

It was not easy to find a lawyer who would defend the miners before an antagonized audience at Canton in June. Some picturesque happenings in Pennsylvania had alarmed readers of newspapers. The "Molly Maguires" terrorized miners around Mauch Chunk, freely assaulting bosses and foremen, sometimes murdering these delegates of authority. There was awful talk of a general conspiracy of labor, perhaps arranged by the Pope or by Russian nihilists. So Major William McKinley's friends begged him to let the case at Canton alone when they heard that he would plead for the miners. He had a great deal to lose. He was being talked up for a seat in Congress and he was popular with the nicest people in his district. But Major McKinley had the unbelievable stubbornness of the mild, pliant man. He elected to defend the miners and take his chance.

His clients at first considered the volunteer a spy sent to entrap them. He was some dapper little devil who would sell them to Rhodes and Company; he was too handsome, too well dressed, too polite. It cost him a box of cigars and large bulks of chewing-tobacco to soothe the prisoners. They talked, at last, won over by his charming voice, a rather monotonous, easy voice with something of the pastor in its tones. People

79

always talked to him, when they liked him, as though he were a professional confessor. "What a priest," said Monsignor Ireland, "he might have made!" His success, in this case, was due to what he had got out of his witnesses beforehand. When he went into court in June, he was fairly sure of getting the men discharged and his legendary appeal against the brutality of capitalism is not even good legend, although it remains a pretty picture, with Mark Hanna shedding tears in the foreground. Major McKinley won his case on the facts.

Mr. Hanna did not enjoy the occasion. He was never vindictive against small people, and the miners were small people in his mind. About this time he let loose his first famous epigram: "Up to his neck a man is only worth the price of a day's labor." This puzzled or offended men who somehow or other tried to believe that one man was as good as another, in some way inexplicable. A man, below his brains, might be just a machine of muscles and worth no more than his neighbor, but it was not a comfortable witticism. In our times it would be called un-American. Mr. Hanna, if he sat in the court at all, was probably relieved to see the soiled machines of skin and muscle let out of their box, but nothing gave him much pleasure in June of 1876; he was suffering abominably with hives on his tender ankles. When he took young Dan to the great Centennial at Philadelphia in July, he was still smeared with sulphur ointment and leaning on a cane. The small boy deplored his father's habit of sitting down on benches in Machinery Hall in contradiction of Daniel's right to hours in the society of an elegant camel attached to the Exposition. It was very hard to get Mr. Hanna away from the machines, anyhow, since he understood what made the wheels go round and the valves open. He talked too busily to clerks and exhibitors, writing down prices and grunting arguments. Once, when Daniel was importunate for camels, the wearied father saw a man in a red fez and said, "Go and ask Abou Ben Adhem if his tribe's increased any." He was then left alone with some humming and clicking interest for a while before Daniel came back to report that Abou Ben Adhem had no tribe. By that time Mr. Hanna was ready to be a good parent and take his son to the camel.

When he was old, in April of 1903, Mr. Hanna leaned on his cane in the midst of political splendors at Saint Louis, where a majestic exposition was to be dedicated. All around him were emblems of power named Theodore Roosevelt, Benjamin Odell, or Senator or General. The machinery of intrigue clicked behind all these shapes. A faction was welding Odell to the President; a faction wanted Mark Hanna for President; a faction wanted Mr. Hanna to cast down Roosevelt and make someone else President. The machines whirred. Experts and reporters watched the show. And then a red-faced, clumsy personage rose on the platform, and the multitude began a lengthening shout which would not die away. They cheered Grover Cleveland, twice President, so hated by half of his party that his name was hissed at banquets of the proper Democrats, who swore by William Bryan. This roar astounded men. It outdid the roaring for Mr. Roosevelt; it was the apology of a people to a courageous man. Mr. Roosevelt stared. The Republican powers and dignitaries whispered lies to him that night, sputtering that Wall Street was backing Cleveland for a third term. But the noise went on, and it was seen that Mr. Hanna was quivering, his mouth tightened in amusement. They wondered if he was laughing at Mr. Roosevelt's humiliation. A friend led him aside when he came limping down from the platform. But he had been remote to the intrigue and the roar for a moment. He was thinking of a quotation that suited Mr. Cleveland's triumph. Lo, he thought, Ben Adhem's name leads all the rest. And that made him think of Dan and the fellow in the red fez, and the days in Philadelphia. Hey, what a grand show the old Centennial had been!

For Mr. Hanna, outside his office, was a simple person. He was not by much different from any well-paid clerk or lawyer who led a son under the Centennial's domes of harsh stained glass. His tastes were plain. He gave his guests champagne and drank water. He doted on stewed corn and rice puddings. He liked a popular play or a good lecture. But he knew each line in whole acts of Shakspere and detested the eloquence of Henry Ward Beecher and Robert Ingersoll. He would play whist a full night without a stake and condescended to euchre if ladies preferred that imbecile pastime. Except that he was a daring pioneer of industrialism and could remember anything that once had interested him, he was the mental cousin of any prosperous midlander who afforded a trip to the Centennial. He resented the patronage of the East, just as they did, and he felt the same way about the massacre of General Custer's troops week before last on the Little Big Horn, and he was still ashamed of Grant for accepting Secretary Belknap's resignation back in March when Congress impeached Belknap for selling privileges at the trading-posts in Indian territory. He may have thought Samuel Tilden would beat General Rutherford Hayes for the presidency in the fall. The Republican party was in awful shape, everywhere. Hayes would never have been nominated if it had been possible to make Blaine and Conkling heal their quarrel at the convention. Mr. Hanna was little wiser, politically, in 1876, than anybody else. He was like the rest of the crowd. His strong cigars were costly, and be sure that his wife had the best rooms in the hotel. If officers of the Pennsylvania Railroad or men from Duluth and Milwaukee saw the heavy man in the press, be sure that they came to shake hands with M. A. Hanna, of Rhodes and

83

Company. But Mr. Hanna was still nobody at Philadelphia in 1876.

IV

War did not make Rutherford Hayes neurotic although his hair and his long, square beard turned gray when he was commander of the Twenty-third Ohio. He didn't understand nerves and he despised excesses. Young officers were politely lectured when they drank too much, but he was indulgent to the enlisted men because they were less educated and had no responsibilities. He liked a soldier to be decorous, if he could, and was delighted with William McKinley's rise. The ironmaster's son was a proper little officer, and aware of his responsibilities.

General Hayes had never been a failure and evaded no responsibility. When he was shot through an arm he lay on the ground before his troops and directed the fire; when an electoral commission assured him that he was President of the United States he took on the job. It worried him the rest of his life to be uncertain if he had been fairly elected in that brazen row when both parties bribed and lied so furiously that the public believed neither side at last, and sat in peace all winter while the case was decided and General Hayes inaugurated. He was then badgered, bullied, insulted by newspapers, legislators and office-seekers throughout his term of office. One gapes at the mass of published but truthless information available on Rutherford Hayes from 1877 to 1881. But the salvation of this Yankee gentleman was that he was a Yankee gentleman, although born in Delaware, Ohio. New England returned to power with Rutherford Hayes, although Yankee journals did not claim him and he was vilified in Boston as he was in California.

He was not one of your fanciful Yankees. He admired Emerson's platitudes, but sometimes could not understand the drifting prose of his pet philosopher; life was a thing of considered rules to the second bulletheaded general; his passion was for conduct, not for speculation. Vagueness didn't please him. He distrusted minds which moved from side to side of a question. James Garfield's cleverness seemed a want of moral principle. But he was not a dull man. As a young lawyer he had undertaken, with a prophetic psychology, to defend a murderess on the grounds that her ugliness and her sense of inferiority had shoved her out of contact with humanity. He talked to people with an alert sympathy until they annoyed him by their perpetual unreason. Then he looked at them as though they were disobedient kids, and gave them up. Mr. Hawthorne would have understood him directly, had they met, for the romancer often talked with such Yankees — stiff, tall, cool — when they brought ships into Salem through a January gale and reported at the customs-house with ice caked in their beards. It was this old strain, scrupulous, hard, and precise in its functioning, that made Hayes loathed by the supple spoilsmen who lived on gifts of office to their followers. He had not been President two weeks when a breach showed between the Executive Mansion and Capitol Hill, nor was it ever filled in with any help from General Hayes. He had a vanity, but it was not wide enough to hold much oil in the shape of flatteries dispensed by Roscoe Conkling: he did like to be called General.

Actually, much of what Hayes did was to carry out the good intentions of Ulysses Grant. Grant had been wanting, at the last, to withdraw troops from Louisiana and South Carolina. Hayes did it and the carpet-bagger governments of both states collapsed at once, freeing the whole South from military controls. A third of the Republican legislators now cursed the President, who had undone the victory of the Union on the glorious fields of etc., etc., etc. Grant steadily disliked the inconvertible paper currency and had favored the Resumption Bill of 1875, which set a date for the redemption of the greenbacks in gold. Hayes and his placid Secretary of the Treasury, John Sherman, accumulated gold in 1878 by an issue of bonds and resumed the payment of gold for currency in January of 1879, while Greenbackers and Democrats howled, literally, in public meetings that this meant ruin, and severe rural patriots upbraided Sherman for letting foreign bankers buy the bonds. But no new panic came; people turned in hoarded gold

86

pieces for bills at the Treasury. Nor was the stiff general afraid to face Roscoe Conkling, the oratorical giant. He made use of his executive powers to clean out a polite gang of Conkling's friends from the New York customs-house. It was not a wholly just performance, but they had been irritating and impudent, certain of Conkling's supreme protection. General Hayes ordered them out of there, as if he were ordering the chevrons off a refractory sergeant's sleeve. The Congress refused to back him, of course, when he wanted to revive the Civil Service Commission, and would not grant him funds.

Washington became a new kind of comic spectacle. The rush of Congressmen leaving the House after the reading of a presidential veto in 1879 was likened by Cushman Davis to the flight of bats from hell. Hayes was incomprehensible to the men hardened by the Gilded Age's acids. He sent poets, scholars, and cultivated lawyers who quaintly spoke several of those foreign languages to Europe as ambassadors and ministers. He made no use of patronage to secure himself a personal machine. One of his Cabinet was a former Rebel, David Key. He appointed unreconciled Confederate ladies postmistresses in Southern towns on the recommendation of Democrats. " He seems," said Murat Halstead, " to have no feeling whatever for the popular thing!" He was, it proved, quite ready to veto a bill shutting out Chinese immigrants from the United States because it dishonored an American treaty with China, and then he patiently observed in his journal that it was the popular thing to burn him in effigy beyond the Rocky Mountains.

It was the nation's luck to have this temperament in office on the night of July 20th, 1877, when Mr. Hawthorne, startled by noises, abandoned a conversation with Pushkin and Miss Jane Austen in the literary heaven to stare down from a golden casement at a web of pink, pulsing irregularly on the map of the United States. The roadways of the machine were ablaze; burning ties and coaches made heaping buds of flame. The great strike had come at last. Black Friday fulfilled itself when the pay of railroad workers was reduced yet again and the men struck " because there was nothing else to do," one of them said. . . . Junctions and roundhouses were seized. The ties burned in six states. Perishable stuff rotted in warehouses and express companies. Cities had no ice and no milk. There was open rioting in Martinsburg, Reading, and Scranton. Militiamen would not shoot into the swaying masses that hooted them. Nineteen were killed in Chicago. Pittsburgh was an insanity of lights and smoke as strikers shoved blazing oil-cars into the huge roundhouse or fired machine-shops. Men lugged stolen mattresses and leaking cans of sirup or frivolous kid slippers from the looted stores up those steep hills to their shacks. It was Wagnerian — a revolt of the dirty dwarfs against the gods at Newport. Sewing-machines were tossed from

halted trucks into the crowd.[8] Champagne puzzled
the finders of a case and they used it to wash their
hot faces, delighted by the fuzzy impact, not knowing
it was wine. . . . At Cleveland it was chattered that
two thousand men armed with revolvers were waiting to plunder Euclid Avenue. In New England it
was observed by Mr. Henry Cabot Lodge that owners
of mills began suddenly to raise wages, finding sharply
that they could afford to do what had been impossible a week before. . . . Ten thousand miners struck
in Pennsylvania. It was a huge and exasperated stirring of the betrayed.

General Hayes wrote three idle proclamations and
sent out regular troops. One of his own kinsmen was
among the militia besieged in the roundhouse at
Philadelphia, but he does not excite himself over that
in his journal. The regulars paraded in cities, took
charge of junctions, and stood guard among smolder-
ing cars in yards. An ordinary revulsion aided the
troops. "We were ashamed of ourselves," says a man
who was sixteen when he helped to loot shops in
Pittsburgh; "we saw that this had not done any good,
but had made people sore at laboring men. . . . we
went back to work as soon as we could. Lots of men
went out west that fall. They bummed along the lines

8 My mother was a witness of the first phase of the strike. She was
taken from Pittsburgh on the last train to leave the city and saw the
sewing-machines in progress up the hills. The detail is mentioned in reports of the strike. One of the surviving strikers is responsible for the tale
of the champagne.

or rode in freight cars. It was said that you could live better out west. I have since met a good many men who have done well for themselves in California who were roundhouse boys with me in 1877. . . ." By the first of August the strike was over. On August 5th the President wrote in his journal: " The strikes have been put down by force; but now for the real remedy. Can't something be done by education of the strikers, by judicious control of the capitalists, by wise general policy to end or diminish the evil? The railroad strikers, as a rule, are good men, sober, intelligent and industrious. . . ." But in the newspapers the strikers were demons waving axes and torches. In New York a great pastor whose salary was known to be twenty thousand dollars a year was persuaded to say, at a meeting of the indignant and comfortable, that a workman could raise a family on five dollars a week, although Henry Ward Beecher was not fool enough to say that workmen ought to enjoy this income. As it was, he had said too much, and there was laughter. People live who joined in the titter. Americans of those days still had humor and they might not have heard a presidential candidate putting forward the existence of the electric ice-box as a proof of his party's integrity, without laughing a little.

The strike was over, but it had sharply shown that something was ruptured in the being of the United States. Mass employment had swelled in time to the increase of all machines. It was only in small brickworks or petty shops that owners now saw their men at all. Mark Hanna strolling out on the dock of Rhodes and Company, a cigar in his teeth, to listen to the firm's foremen stating a grievance as he sat on a barrel, which stained his trousers, was a survival of an elder order, a wholesome singularity left over from a tradition. Laborers, since the war, had grown used to feeling that the boss or the company was remote, unfriendly, an entity designed to keep wages down. There was a conspiracy of wealth against the masses, a dozen brittle parties of reform affirmed. The machine, spreading everywhere, had spread with it the dingy shack, the smoky flats. Mass thinking codified its simplicities and found the point against which its anger with its own weakness must be projected. This was Wall Street's doing. Wall Street was now to be the emblem of oppression.

General Hayes was badly placed to do anything about the judicious control of capitalism. The powerful legislators were openly his enemies. Quiet people and reformers packed his table at the White House and the number at his wineless evening parties grew, but the great figures of Washington did not condescend to the President. Congressman McKinley was a favorite caller, sometimes squiring Mrs. Hayes to lectures on foreign missions, but the journal says nothing of Roscoe Conkling and James Blaine. Congress passed, over the President's veto, the Bland-Allison Act of 1878, forcing the Treasury to issue at least twenty-four million dollars annually in full face of the fact that silver would not rise to par and that its depreciation had begun. Congress did everything it could to make itself loathed by Rutherford Hayes. His last act as President in 1881 was to veto a monstrous thing named the Refunding Bill. He then shook hands with Senators who had insulted him in speeches, with Congressmen who had jeered at his beautiful wife for her modest little addresses on temperance; and so he went home to Fremont, where he was glad to see that his new country-house in its grove of fine trees had a low, plain, old-fashioned look. He had not wanted to be President a second time; it was such a slavish, exacting job. And, he told his friend William Dean Howells, you had to deal with such extraordinary people. They seemed to have no principles at all. They were like unruly cattle.

Mr. Hanna hoped to see John Sherman nominated in June of 1880 at Chicago. The Secretary of the Treasury had two merits at least that made Mark Hanna think well of him: he was from Ohio and he really knew what business was all about. But Mr. Sherman had two vices in the reckoning of the Republican party's leaders: he was not any more a good showman than Rutherford Hayes had been and he was critical of fellow politicians. Had he not called a Senator an ignoramus to his face and publicly, even though he asked the man to dine afterwards? He was still pensive, he was proud, and he annoyed the smart men by his tendencies toward a reformed Civil Service. He jested sourly about New York's financial heroes. He refused to meet Jay Gould at a dinner in 1879. He was not on smooth terms with James Blaine, and Roscoe Conkling despised him for a friend of Hayes.

Roscoe Conkling now reached maximum. The superb showman was truly able. His narcotic oratory was backed by a soothing tact in private relations; he could stun the public by three hours of pointless invective, and get his way with a caucus by bland courtesies. He had the kind of sarcasm which covers a shortage of real wit, and the effrontery of a practiced harlot. All this equipment was mottled and disfigured by the most humorless egoism. He liked power; he had power and he did nothing with his power save to consolidate his hold on the politics of New York and to place Congressmen under obligations. Would he see John Sherman nominated? " This," he said, "would be fatal. . . ." Assertions of the sort were his daily offering in Republican councils. He addressed ten men across a table as though a thousand gazed at his curls and his gestures. He would suspend the reading of trivial notes to a committee while a page brought him water and resume his unimportant suggestions in the case of an Indian reservation after frowning in silence over the delay. It was right, in his mind, to assert that Sherman's nomination would be fatal, as though that meant anything outside the

Republican party. For he had the charlatan's most valued gift in public life: he created excitements out of nothing and made simpletons believe that his causes were real issues. Sherman was unobjectionable to the party, but he was not that which Mr. Conkling liked to see in movement toward the White House. What could be played against him? Of course, there was Grant.

Grant landed at San Francisco from his voyage around the world and came eastward in a glory of applause. He was still Grant. Smart men arranged processions and banquets in the cities, but they needed none of that out in the country, where the special audience of this general gathered by the weathered stations at any hour of night in hope of seeing just his private car pass by. Cowboys raced their ponies alongside the tracks. Miners put burning boughs together, after dark, below the numerals of some old regiment carved white upon a hillside and hoped that Grant would look that way. The cheers were screams, and celebrating shots cracked the ears of children in the crowds swept together by this name. Here came Grant, and the noise of the welcome was soothing to Mr. Conkling after his dose of Hayes. He gathered the smart men behind him and appeared at Chicago with three hundred and eight votes of the Republican Convention pledged to Grant. They were Eastern votes, for the most part. Out on the prairies veterans hated Conkling, not altogether justly, as Grant's evil

THE BULLETHEADED GENERALS

adviser in times past, and farmers knew him to be a pet of the railroads. They would take Blaine or Sherman before they would take Grant with Conkling's hand on his collar. Mr. Conkling did not know this.

His own insolence now spoiled the rhetorician's chances of a nimble victory. In his pounding speech, nominating Grant, he sneered at Sherman and Blaine. He was applauded for twenty-five minutes, or Grant was applauded. But he was answered by General James Garfield, of Ohio, nominating John Sherman, and something happened. This convention's numbers were mixed with a younger variety of politician. Garfield's speech was not wholly new in style — he had to say that God was preparing the outcome of the nominations — but he talked on amiably and courteously, without sneering, and the young men, sick of allusions to Appomattox and to envy's poisoned chalice sat up, listening. Once someone shouted, " We want Garfield! " and cheers disturbed the speaker. Mr. Conkling sank in his chair, staring at this unpleasant symptom of a change in public taste. When he sensed that he was watched he turned his stare to the galleries and kept it aimed there when the roar began as Garfield stopped.

On the thirty-sixth ballot Garfield's sudden following had risen to three hundred ninety-nine votes and he was nominated. Mr. Conkling's faction was handed the nomination for the vice presidency and chose Chester Arthur, of New York. The maudlin

95

convention broke up. Mr. Conkling retired to New York in a state of mind and openly sulked. His language for some weeks is legendary and cannot be proved, but he talked too freely and an edge of the ridiculous entered his situation. He had personally been hit in full sight of the party by an expression of the party's will, after a fierce, maintained contest. It was stiff. Polite messengers and intermediaries could not budge him to meet Garfield. Chester Arthur had to persuade him to make any speeches in the campaign and Mr. Arthur, not caring to be defeated even for the vice presidency, lost patience with his patron at a dinner in Delmonico's. " I hope you understand," he said, " that if the Republican party is defeated, we are defeated with it! " The inner party of smart intrigue must not be allowed to go down. So Roscoe Conkling consented to appear as a loyal Republican. He collected a group of names and loaded them into a private car, summoning other great folk to meet him in Cleveland, whence the whole crowd of dignitaries would be lugged to Warsaw, Ohio, and would exhibit its devotion to General Garfield in the candidate's own state.

Mr. M. A. Hanna of Cleveland had demonstrated to the Republican leaders of Ohio that he was valuable in campaigns. The basis of campaigns was shyly kept in the background, owing to an old conventional sentiment which denied that money had anything to do with Americans around election day. Cabs and

hacks took lazy voters to the polls and someone had
to pay for that, and for bunting, posters, and brass
bands. But there was never much chatter about the
campaign funds except the rude words of the losing
party. Still, someone had to collect for the local committees, and Mr. Hanna, genially persuasive, had
been useful in 1876. He roamed northern Ohio, smoking cigars, and collected. It was a weary job and it
had no dignity. It was like the function of some
trusted priest in the Middle Ages, arranging the loans
of Holy Church to the Jews and Italian bankers. It
was business to be done quietly, by a solid man.
As a reward, in 1880, Mr. Hanna was allowed some
fuss and feathers. He understood transportation, to
be sure, and that would make him useful on the trip
to Warsaw. He went along to see that all these persons
of great name were comfortable.

It was a fine mass-meeting. The crowd yelled for
Grant when he mounted the platform and gaped as
Roscoe Conkling expended five minutes in empty
music of his noble voice. Logan, Cameron, and the
rest were pointed out to children. Mr. Hanna smoked
and admired the great or maybe wondered if they were
worth the price of a day's labor from the neck down,
or up. He was not conspicuous, unless one looked at
his eyes; nobody paid attention to his emotions when
it was whispered among the reporters and understrap-
pers that the party would go straight back to Cleveland, ignoring General Garfield in his pretty house at

Mentor. Mr. Conkling's loyalty to his party had limits. He would not meet the candidate or be reconciled to him. He would leave Ohio without acknowledging Garfield as chief of the Republicans. . . . The great filed down from the platform and were transported to the house of a state senator for luncheon. Mr. Hanna stayed outside with the small fry and listened to the indignant buzz in the dooryard. His friend Charles Foster lost sight of him for five minutes. Mr. Hanna had walked into the dining-room and bowed to Ulysses Grant.

" General, it has been arranged that we return to Cleveland by way of Mentor, and if you propose to stop there and see General Garfield, we shall have to start in a very short time."

Roscoe Conkling scowled. He had brought Grant into Ohio as a condescending favor to the party and now this plump imbecile with the brown eyes was going to drag him to Mentor, to the house of his enemy. It would seem a reconciliation, an admission of fealty to Garfield! But he could not speak; he did not dare to command Grant.

" We will stop at Mentor," said Grant.

Mr. Hanna came beaming out and told Charles Foster what he had done. The crowd at Mentor went mad for Grant, and the great men stood about on the candidate's veranda for the world to see, then vanished from Ohio. Mr. Hanna set dutifully to work collecting Republican funds. He did not know that his small ruse worked the damnation of Roscoe Conkling. He had oiled the heels of the charlatan for a fall.

Conkling's egotism now spun him into a reverse of his position. He boasted of his aid extended to Garfield's campaign in "the West" as well as in New York. He spoke of the new President's obligations to him, and the simple creatures of the metropolis expected to hear of a cabinet picked by Garfield on Mr. Conkling's orders. Had not Garfield invited Mr. Conkling to his home in Ohio and told him that he was in his debt? But there was chuckling in New York itself. John Logan had turned loose a version of the scene in Warsaw; it was known that some friend of Garfield had challenged Grant to ignore the candidate and that Grant, not Conkling, had caused the party to call at Mentor.[9] Even Mr. Conkling's prim, industrious ally Senator Thomas Platt was not so sure that General Garfield would be biddable. Spring came; battle came. General Garfield made James Blaine his Secretary of State. General Garfield appointed a Secretary of the Treasury without Mr. Conkling's consent. Mr. Conkling forced an odious scene in Garfield's apartment at the Riggs House, and cold spread even in his own clique as the news of his language got abroad. Garfield coolly retorted by appointing an enemy of Conkling's machine collector of customs at New York. Mr. Conkling's rhetoric became a continuing thunder. He wagged his curls and vaticinated before a committee of

[9] See Appendix, Notes to Chapter II.

conciliation, imitating sentences from the Bible, threatening to expose a disgraceful letter written by Garfield. He exposed it, and it was nothing but a hint for campaign funds sent to an official. Committees and orators worked between the President and the Senator for days, but Conkling's anger sent his conceit floating upward. He would have the President humiliate all his enemies in New York and nothing less; Garfield must eat dirt. The two men met for a last time in a lady's drawing-room, bowed to each other below a chandelier while watchers gulped, and were blocked from each other's sight by a movement of resolute friends as Conkling seemed about to speak. On May 16th, 1881, Mr. Conkling and the mild Mr. Platt resigned their places in the Senate, as a gesture of outrage, knowing that the Senate would confirm Garfield's collector of the port of New York. The legislature of their state would, surely, elect them back to the Senate. . . . But the legislature wouldn't. Conkling was done for.

So was Grant. He soon gave the use of his name and his money to a smart man who had a scheme for a bank, and the smart man finished off the money. But the name was good. Poets and critics, sunflowers of emotion, turned to Grant again when it was known that he was dying, valiantly writing his memoirs in hope of paying his debts. Sympathy was a fountain. But his special audience had never turned from Grant and did not have to show its sympathy by calling at his house on the mountain. It knew Grant. He was doing the right thing for his folks. The farmers clubbed dollars and sent subscriptions for "the General's book" to Grant's publisher. . . . Clumsy coats and tanned faces appeared in the streets of New York on the day of his funeral. Rutherford Hayes nodded to men of his old regiment as he was driven past them on the curbs. Mr. Hanna lent veterans the money for their fare to New York and back. Soldiers and their grave children came to look at this burying-ground, where Grant was. And, after years, they came to New York once more on the windy day when Grant's white tomb was consecrated, with foreign soldiers parading before William McKinley and the Hudson dark with ships. Some of us who were children then, heard all around us the murmur of a man's name. They were talking of Grant, of this picture in a schoolbook. Because we have seen machineries creating sentiment for Presidents without honor, actors and empty sportsmen, we can grin at sentiment. But we dare not grin backward at this sentiment a man created for himself. He was Grant. The name, as they spoke, had the sound of a drum briefly pulsing, and no other name has sounded so, in this long time. There are illusions of the dead so firm and hard that they cannot be dissevered from their causes. He was Grant, to them, and that meaning was recorded in the mention of his name, the curt admission of their faith in him.

CHAPTER III

THE HUMAN MACHINE

I

Without notice in Eastern newspapers, on April 1st, 1873, Mrs. William McKinley began to alter American history. She gave birth to a second daughter and had a bad time of it. Her mother died while the pretty little lady was still in bed, and it seemed that Major McKinley's wife would never be well again, after the new baby vanished in August. She would sit for hours in a darkened room, holding Katie on her lap, weeping in silence. Katie was not allowed out of her sight, unless the major took the child for a drive, and poor Katie left just one childish saying to sting in the memory of her uncle, Abner McKinley. He found her swinging on the gate and invited her to take a walk with him. " No, I mustn't go out of the yard or God'll punish mamma some more. . . ." Then Katie died in June of 1876. God, revealed to Ida McKinley in the chatter of old women, had punished her some more. Presently the literal children of Canton told each other, across fences, that Mrs. McKinley had fits. A form of epilepsy showed; the handsome young Congressman was pitied at home and in Washington. A cloud of sympathy settled on William McKinley with the beginnings of his public life.

His buoyant manner changed. He became a soft-spoken, watchful nurse in his own house and a worried guest if he was in company without his charge. About 1880 there was something worse. "Please," said the major to a pretty girl, "don't walk into the yard with me. Ida might see you. . . ." For a year or so the fading invalid thought herself neglected. When the major came down from President Garfield's funeral in the autumn of 1881, he mentioned a handsome lady seen at Cleveland, and his brothers were witnesses of a frantic scene, cut by an epileptic attack. The phase ended. She was a gentlewoman, and the wife of a personage. Public business might be interrupted by Mrs. McKinley's messages to the Representative, the Governor of Ohio, or, at last, the President of the United States asking his opinion of a scrap of silk for a new frock or the flowers of a bonnet, but Mrs. McKinley behaved herself as well as she could. She had a certain bright intelligence and was sometimes witty enough to amuse John Hay.

McKinley ascended into the headlines of newspapers with this burden, and it was genuine, wasting his time, hurting his health, and wearying his friends so that they canonized him before he was forty years old. A man who loved tramping in any weather and who broke wild colts for his neighbors was reduced to driving a bit, when Mrs. McKinley wanted some air, or to strolling through Canton with a bowl of blanc-mange sent to an ailing child.

She loved children, although she might cry if a child came to sit on her knees. In 1892 a Mrs. Saxton lectured on the work of Presbyterian missions in a church at Columbus and Mrs. McKinley seized upon her when she was through her talk, asking if they might not be relatives (her own name was Ida Saxton), and then insisting that the missionary come home with her to meet the Governor. She ended by dining with the two and telling them all about India. " It was a curious experience. They seemed positively fascinated by my stories. I have never been a good talker and have always known my deficiencies in conversation. It startled me to have them hanging on my account of my work in the hospitals. . . . Mrs. McKinley said, ' Oh, how wonderful to be like Lady Dufferin and help all those poor children and their mothers! ' I did not know of her losses and did not understand how keenly my talk about the Indian children must have hurt her. . . . She began to cry when I left and begged me to come back some other day. When we met afterwards in Washington, in 1899, she fairly implored me to see what could be done by the Presbyterian board of foreign missions for the children in the Philippines. . . ." Other people had like experiences. The women and children of the Orient lured McKinley's wife. He was murdered. She shivered through winters in Canton, cowering above fires and hot pipes, and wailed to friends that, if she had any strength left, she would go out and teach the babies in the Philippines. And the major had planned to take a trip through the Orient. And now she would never see all that. . . . Out there, perhaps, had been a paradise of colors and warm flowers, with Katie and baby Ida born again, brown and naked for her kisses, waiting to be brought up as Christian ladies. . . .

The major had been thriftily reared, being the son of an ironmaster who had a large family, and he rose through politics on a notion sacred to thrifty provincials. It was the tobacco-growing Connecticut farmer who demanded a tariff on tobacco from Sumatra, and the rural American ironmasters were noisy, primitive agitators for a tariff on iron and steel. Major McKinley was not amused when Winfield Hancock, the Democratic candidate of 1880, called protective tariff a " local issue." He said, " The protective tariff is a great combination of local issues. We can not neglect the force of so many local issues in judging the nation's great need of protection for its industries and produce. . . ." [1] He believed heartily that these amalgamated local issues made a demand on the government and that better wages for the laboring man would result from a high protective tariff. Many of his speeches in Congress are plausible and well made; his voice was charming and the adroitness gained by constantly tending a nervous, fanciful woman helped

[1] Unprinted autograph, addressed to J. C. Parton, December 30th, 1889.

him with irritable opponents; he nursed his subject along and grew famous as the champion of the tariff.

Tariff is a method of deliberated stealing from foreigners — that is, from a class of human beings in which the native has no sentimental interest. It is an old institution among men, but men have always shown their small faith in the lawfulness of tariffs by admiring smugglers, just as Americans of our time show their disregard of the ignoble Prohibition laws by tolerating sellers of alcohol. In the nineteenth century this theft, called a tariff, was sentimentalized by honorable men just as honorable men excuse a mother who steals for her young. Madison's catchy phrase " infant industries " echoed comfortably and, as William McKinley could justly complain in Congress, Europe was given to playing the hog against American necessities on occasion. Chicago burned, and prices of paints and metals rose too suddenly in Europe. A manufactory of cathedral glass in Missouri was destroyed; the value of European glass was suspiciously rising within a week. This game went on, and to oppose such jockeying by legal pillage did not seem wrong. McKinley's attitude was no more narrow than that of Thomas Reed, an educated, traveled, clever man. The protectionists were sincere enough — are sincere enough — but their final vision of a world's economics is small. They limit their concept within the art of successful government.

Successful government, up to the year 1929, is any

kind of domination which assures a particular flattery to the most powerful factions of a state. The collective egoism of a landholding minority or a landless majority or a party of moral reform, backed by rich industrials, is soothed by the enunciation of principles which tend to flatter it. Physical comfort and the humiliation of another faction are practically the alternate offers of the artist in successful government; a full dinner-pail, "the highest standard of living ever known in the world," protection from workmen rendered careless by strong drink on Monday morning, and such benefits unforgettable are tendered and accepted. Anything will go in common times. But an uncommon period, when more than one powerful faction has to be placated, calls for someone able to suggest the grand art of government. And the period extending from the panic of 1873 to the end of the century was uncommon in the United States.

Mr. McKinley's merits in the eyes of an examining tactician were many. He had good looks, a good voice, and good manners, with an amusing trace of the country boy about him to conciliate the plain people. This last was valuable. The real tacticians in politics were now learning their job. They began to transmute Fernando Wood's epigram on pandering to the moral sense of communities, and, as the plain people grew defiantly proud of being plain, they pandered to this pride whenever it was possible from 1880 to 1928. Garfield was not advertised as a finished expert in currency and economics, but as a lad who had led horses barefoot along the tow-paths of canals. Grover Cleveland's rough simplicity and early poverty were duly expounded. It was difficult to exalt Benjamin Harrison as a son of the plain people, but wasn't he the grandson of a pioneer hero? . . . The plain people, curtly, had become a faction so powerful that even dull Eastern observers faintly recognized the point and some of Major McKinley's earliest followers were politicians in Connecticut and Rhode Island. This " shadow of Lincoln " was the thing demanded by the West. " I am unable to see," said Professor William Sumner, drawling to students at Yale College in 1888, " that a boyhood spent in poverty among simple people peculiarly qualifies a man for political preferment, but such seems to be the general argument. . . ."

As for the rest of McKinley, he was fond of red carnations, lilacs, and the music of brass bands. He was a Methodist, but not convinced that a guilty soul suffered eternally for its misdeeds in this world. Might it not be extinguished, sent into oblivion? He was uncertain on the topic of perpetual franchises for street railways. But he approved the classified Civil Service and he spoke up handsomely for arbitration in case of strikes or disputes between common carriers. He had no time for reading, what with politics and nursing, and said wistfully to his Vice President in 1901 : " You make me envious. You've been able to get so much out of books. . . ." His memory was well trained, and this does him credit, for it had once been weak.[2] He liked his town and loved to dawdle around a farm.

He was adored, but this adoration prophesied the downfall of American character in the next generation. To be adored for negatives is not so well. The children of pioneers overvalued the conciliator, the very pleasant neighbor, everybody's friend. McKinley had the strength of certain opinions; he could be stubborn. Beyond him drearily appeared the caricature of the modern American; the jellyfish of satire, amiably afloat in a society of like mediocrities, agreeable to everything, the " good fellow " of the golf-club and the office.

But the adoration of McKinley was genuine. In 1928 a shrewd and *rusé* old gentleman of Cleveland amazed some youngsters by telling them that William McKinley was the only person he had ever known who suggested the possible personality of Jesus Christ; on the day of the President's funeral, in 1901, guests and uncomfortable servants in the alley of the old Manhattan Hotel stood watching a man, accounted brutal in finance and politics, who had just crumbled against a wall, sobbing in a roar of pain as the hush of

[2] My grandfather judged several cases in which McKinley was concerned. One of these the major lost by simply forgetting what a witness had said before him. He notably improved, afterwards. Mr. Abner McKinley said that the concentrated stare which annoyed people was really an effort of attention. Mr. McKinley looked straight at you and steadily, to the point of seeming rude.

the street told him that the service at Canton had begun. The major was adored, early in his career. " My opponents in Congress," said Thomas Reed, " go at me tooth and nail, but they always apologize to William when they are going to call him names. . . ."

At the Republican convention of 1888 an accident displayed Major McKinley favorably to Marcus Hanna. A distinct faction, made up of men from every part of the country, approached him with a suggestion that he let himself be nominated. McKinley refused and bluntly.[3] He had come there pledged to support John Sherman and he would support John Sherman. Much whispering indicated that Joseph Foraker, in charge of the Ohio delegation, was willing to shift grounds and join the Blaine faction. The Eastern leaders were willing to try a trick. If a " stampede " for McKinley could be started, his own state's delegation would be driven to sharing the movement. John Sherman would be removed from the list, and a deadlock arranged in favor of Blaine. But McKinley halted the attempt by declining to hear himself mentioned as a candidate; he interrupted the roll-call of states when his name was shouted from the delegation of Connecticut and succinctly denied that he was in the running. The nomination was thrown to Benjamin Harrison, and Marcus Hanna contented himself by

[3] " I heard Mr. McKinley use violent profanity only once in his life. It was when he refused to be nominated by the Platt crowd at the convention of '88. . . ." Charles Foster to William C. Beer, November 15th, 1901.

reflecting, "Well, Harrison was born in Ohio, anyhow!"

Mr. Hanna's admiration of Major McKinley was profuse. He appreciated men who stuck to a losing bargain, for he kept his contracts even if they were only oral, and delivered coal at the promised figure to customers at a loss. He would accept a back-drop painted for the Euclid Avenue Opera House ten feet too short for the height of the stage because he had given the dimensions to the painter and could not complain. He detested people who did not stick to a bargain, once made. The major's rectitude impressed him at just the right time, for he was quarreling with Joseph Benson Foraker.

Foraker and Mark Hanna were made to quarrel. The rich man from Cleveland accepted political theatricalities as so much chaff. There had to be processions, all these speeches, and " a lot of gas " about precedence. It amused him. He liked a phrase much used in conversation by Rutherford Hayes, "the hurrah boys." Mr. Foraker accepted the chaff as something else. He felt that a bit of parade and circumstance was becoming to him, at this time, as Governor of Ohio and as Joseph Benson Foraker. He was imposingly designed; he spoke with force and certainty; he had regulated the Republican machine of lower Ohio to an extraordinary smoothness of operation. Mr. Hanna's lack of dignity annoyed him. He was sharply disgusted when the millionaire failed to arrange proper rooms for him in the hotel at Chicago, and when Hanna obliged some Negro delegates from the South by taking over their tickets to the gallery of the convention at a price, he was outraged. Mr. Hanna was not behaving as a sound politician should.

On his side, Mr. Hanna was tired of the handsome Governor's attitudes. He had shed a deal of money on Foraker's campaigns and the Governor inconveniently had not done just the right thing about a job promised to one of Mr. Hanna's deserving campaigners. And, on June 8th, 1888, the Governor had let it be known that he disapproved a plan of Grover Cleveland. The President wished to restore the captured Confederate battle flags to the South, but his action brought on a shower of partisan protests. Mr. Hanna admired Grover Cleveland and he liked Southerners. When he met Mr. Foraker at Chicago, he tactlessly told him that his gesture of June 8th was " stale " and might damage John Sherman's candidacy, remarking these things before half a dozen men, one of them a stranger to Mr. Foraker. The quarrel swelled in a flare of suspicion, and the alliance of Hanna and Foraker ended with the last day of the convention of 1888.

Mr. Hanna was nobody in particular in the hotels at Chicago. He did not stand about bars, and few of the delegates met him. Charles Nolan heard him indicated in a crowd as the head of Hanna and Company in Cleveland, the man who owned the Euclid Avenue Opera House. But people were not interested in this stout and quiet person sitting with Benjamin Butterworth or Charles Foster in lobbies and restaurants. Mr. Hanna was now an actual millionaire, the possessor of his own business, the director of street railways developed from some ramshackle properties of his wife's dead father, the president of a bank, concerned in a ship-building company, partner in three rolling-mills, and nurse of the Republican party's finances in Cleveland. But he was not conspicuous; he was technically not in politics at all. He spent money on politicians. There was a difference, in 1888, which has since disappeared. Anyhow, the East dominated this convention. Reporters and sightseers were keen to talk to Mr. Platt of New York and Mr. Quay of Pennsylvania, the unbreakable bosses, who had knocked down John Sherman and got rid of Allison's promising little boom. So Hanna was nobody in particular at Chicago in 1888.[4]

II

Benjamin Montgomery, chief of telegraph service in the White House, had callers in his small office on a night in the autumn of 1902. A great strike in the

[4] Mr. Hanna's remarks on Foraker's criticism of Cleveland are not mentioned in Senator Foraker's memoirs or in Mr. Croly's biography of Mr. Hanna. But the matter is touched on in a letter of Charles Foster, who may have been present; and Mr. Charles Clery Nolan, who was present, is a living witness. A piece of gossip about a quarrel between Mr. Foraker and Mrs. Hanna over the Confederate flags seems plainly to be a mixed version of the alleged scene between the Forakers and Mrs. Grover Cleveland at a reception in Philadelphia.

coal-fields made this dim little chamber the most important point of the United States. Privileged correspondents and an agent of John Pierpont Morgan were talking to Colonel Montgomery as they awaited the end of a dinner-party elsewhere in the banal residence. Montgomery was a gently oozing spring of information on the Civil War, and this night he was reviving the siege of Petersburg when an apparition grew in the smoky door, and all these men in dinner jackets started. It was an old man, who seemed ten feet tall, towering in a wet ulster, and a soft black hat with the device of the Grand Army. He had got into the Executive Mansion, they could not find out how, and he would not leave it without speaking to Mr. Roosevelt, he would not say why. There he was, an immovable substance, an awkward fact. The President was at dinner? All right. He would wait. He stood just outside the door and inimically considered the official and the journalists, patently distrusting the lot of them. He did not take his hat off when Mr. Roosevelt came limping through the hall to write a telegram, but watched the President finish the message and then said, " I seen in the papers where you hurt yer leg, colonel."

Mr. Roosevelt spun and stared. There began the strangest conversation. The old man spoke slowly as a plow moves through rocky ground. He had come on east to thank the President for giving his son a " gover'ment " job. This Jim or Bill had been shot in Cuba and needed something quiet to work at, and this was one of Bill's or Jim's children. A minor apparition, three feet long, edged around the columnar ulster. The President snatched a carnation from Colonel Montgomery's coat and knelt painfully on the floor, talking to the child while he fastened the flower in its clothes. Then he looked up at the specter and asked if it was a Republican.

"I used to be a Republican when it was Lincoln an' Grant an' Hayes an' Garfield. Then I was a Demmucrat some. I was a Populist in '92 and I was for Bryan in 1896. An' now I'm for you, colonel."

The President stood up. One of his hands helplessly felt the silk of his evening coat. His eyes squeezed shut behind his glasses. For once he had no answer to a compliment. He bowed and limped away, the veteran watching him. But when the old man spoke, it was in a level tone of sad censure.

"Lincoln would never have wore them clothes."

"Why, my friend," said Colonel Montgomery, "I can show you a dozen pictures of Mr. Lincoln in evening dress!"

But the Westerner knew better. His Lincoln was now firm in his mind and the mind of his likes out there, a friend of the plain people who scorned the silk-stocking crowd. Without heat he told the gentleman, "You're a damn liar," and then he vanished, with Jim's or Bill's child hanging to his fingers. . . . A bit later one of the reporters showed Mr. Roosevelt

a note of the scene, but the President shook his
head, saying, " No, as a favor to me, Dunn," and
there was no pretty anecdote in next Sunday's paper.

This apparition had told the story of a certain rural
mind. He voted for the heroes of his war while they
lasted and then he had been a Democrat because he
could not vote for smart Jim Blaine, the trafficker
with railroads; then Populism gave him a cause without a hero, and then Mr. Bryan was the hero of his
cause in 1896. This was how he thought about things
in a world without telephones, a world in which news
was the county's newspaper or the babble along the
road from the telegraph station when someone great
died or a river flooded. He was a colonist, within his
own country, unaware that he hurt his country's
finances with manias and heresies, sure he was doing
something fine for the United States out here on the
prairies. He might have understood just the last sentence in William Sumner's arraignment of the colonial idea. " The notion is that colonies are glory. The
truth is that colonies are burdens — unless they are
plundered, and then they are enemies." This last he
would have realized; he had been plundered. He was
the enemy of the East, where all his good money,
taken by the railroads, went to join the interest on his
mortgage. It cannot be judged, now, whether he hated
the railroads with their rates for shipping grain worse
than he hated the mortgage. Let the son of such a man
speak for him. This is Mr. William Dunn McCready,

born in 1874 in southern Nebraska in a house four miles from town, half a mile from the next house, youngest of eight children and five sons. He first saw a metal faucet on a train taking him to Omaha for the funeral of an uncle, in 1884.

"There must have been faucets and similar appliances in our town, but I presume they were in the houses of our banker and the man who had the store. I was never admitted to those glorified precincts. The banker had a telephone put in about 1886. I can remember the profound sensation of the event. . . . I must try to convince you that our district was victimized by a kind of swindling that increased the hard times of 1891 and 1892. The railroad overcharged for everything. You know that it was cheaper to burn corn for fuel in 1888 and 1889 than to try to ship it. We were absolutely at the mercy of the railroads and the express companies. The performance of the Octopus [5] in California is always treated as an individual kind of high piracy in conventional books. What else did the middle Western states get, may one ask?

"Another form of swindling was that used by some storekeepers in such small communities. I know that a lot of sentimentalism has been expended on the dear old whimsical fellow who has a general store by some of our writers of rural hokum. But the storekeeper was frequently a hard-fisted cheat. In 1890, when the McKinley tariff bill passed Congress, this smart

[5] The Southern Pacific Railroad.

Heinie in our town put up all prices 'on aggount of the dariff.' It was then that our banker came to the rescue. He told this robber baron to put the prices down or he would open an opposition store. Of course the storekeeper dropped his prices instanter. But it gave him an awful black eye with the community. He sold out to my uncle in 1891 and left town.[6]

"It was natural that our county went Populist in 1891 and 1892. I want to say for my father that he was about the only person who understood the fall of prices between 1885 and 1890. This was on account of his mania for geography. He comprehended that there were such places as Russia and the Argentine Republic. He would tell neighbors at calamity meetings that if Yurrupeans could get grain from South America and Rooshia for less than we sold it they would naturally buy it. But I swear that he was the only person I knew who did understand that. I am not saying we were a lot of fools. But the world was shut out from us and to a degree you people cannot get, even from the best descriptions in Willa Cather and *The Grandmothers*. My dear old man did know a little about external conditions affecting the price of crops. On the other hand he could not be made to understand that fiat money was not real money, any more than I could until your father banged it into my head at Saint Paul. He had been used to paper currency ever since he was

[6] Other storekeepers did the like in 1890. There are instances in Iowa, Ohio, Illinois, and Massachusetts known to me. Democrats were accused of this trick as propaganda unfavorable to the McKinley tariff.

a boy back in the fifties. If the government said a thing was money, it darned well was money. The Populists perfectly believed that in 1892, at the time of the convention in Omaha. They were so simple about anything financial that it is cruel for historians to laugh at them. Their delusion was this proposition: If the government will issue a lot of greenbacks per capita to the population of the United States, there will be more money in circulation and our crops will sell for more. If you tried to explain that this money was a drug in Europe and could not go abroad to purchase goods, they just did not get it. Europe was too far away. The Free Silver craze was part of the same delusion. I think I might say that they did not understand the depreciating quality of money at all, or so few of them understood it that it came to the same thing.

"May I add that the historians do not seem to realize the extent of the Free Silver advertising? It is funny to me that when this silver propaganda was so widespread and so openly shoved at us by men who were in the employ of the silver-miners nobody remarks the purely mercenary motive underlying the whole game. The silver-miners had a product to sell and they were trying to keep it sold by making up a bogus moral issue out of it. Because the suffering of the farm belt was intense and it really had been browbeaten and smacked behind by the railroad kings, it does not follow that Free Silver was anything but a

119

financial hocus-pocus worked up by interested men.
Bland, Bryan and Company were agents of the silver-
miners, no matter how they stated the case to their
consciences. The way the business is sentimentalized
is what astonishes me. . . ."

In 1890 a remarkable instrument called the Sherman Silver Purchase Act passed under President
Harrison's pen and became law. Four million five
hundred thousand ounces of silver bullion were to be
purchased monthly and the Treasury was to issue
against this gift to the silver-miners notes redeemable
in coin at the discretion of the Secretary of the Treasury. This meant that the nation was to purchase ap-
proximately nine-tenths of the nation's monthly out-
put of silver and that the Treasury could not refuse,
since these notes were legal tender, to redeem them in
gold if it was required to do so. Here was subsidy, in
short. The silver-miners were secured from any loss
by the people of the United States, and the people of
the West were gravely informed by orators that this
astonishing performance in pure capitalism was a
method of giving the farmer a plentiful, assured
currency.

The friends of silver did not discuss one or two
facts. Silver was depreciating everywhere in the world,
as they knew; all important countries of Europe were
now using gold as the standard of value in finance.
They knew this, as they knew that they were getting a
subsidy for the silver mines and causing danger to the

currency. But the act was signed and bankers began hoarding gold. Europe must be paid in gold, of course. . . . A bulk of silver dollars accumulated in the Treasury. Loans for small factories tightened at once. Little industries of the midlands were caught. In April of 1891 young Bill McCready came in from feeding the pigs and found the women petting one of his brothers. Nick had walked all the way down from Omaha when a factory closed, throwing sixty men out of work.

Many sons now came home to all these farms. If they were proud, they had come home on a visit; if they were honest, they had just come home. Democrats said it was the McKinley tariff and the banker said it was the Silver Purchase Act. But neither legislation produced the drought of 1891. That autumn one of the McCready boys took his long legs into the Army, the last resort in those days, and one of them tramped off down south to look for something to do in warm country, and Bill went up to a cousin in Saint Paul, on borrowed money, and found himself a job as an office boy at four dollars a week. This family of kind people split, under the mallet of his sacred majesty, hazard, and was never drawn together again.

Among callers at the office where Bill worked was a big young man of affairs, Mr. William Collins Beer, western agent of the National Surety Company. He would rave against the Silver Purchase Act by the

hour or discuss it logically to any length. Mr. Beer
was such an abominable mathematician that he had
been decently discharged from West Point in 1883
after a battle with calculus. He could never add sums
in his checkbook certainly, but he understood the
movement of money. The office boy gaped, listening
to Mr. Beer's prophecies of a panic. Having been born
after 1873, Bill was not aware of panics. He had a
secret thirst for mad, exciting things. He tired out
older people asking them what had happened in 1873.
One evening in June of 1892 he asked an amiable,
stout man sitting beside him in the gallery of the Republican Convention at Minneapolis if he remembered anything curious in 1873.

The gentleman remembered all about it, and talked
in short, undecorated sentences, saying "by God" a
good deal. He spoke of suicides, ruined banks, and
battered businesses, and the gang of clerks sitting with
Bill listened to his stories instead of attending to the
speeches which flowed down on the floor of the hall.
This assemblage was distinguished and very dull, and
the stout stranger seemed more amusing to these lads
who had come over from Saint Paul to hear marvels. The only entertainment was Governor William
McKinley of Ohio, president of the convention, who
blandly conducted proceedings with a palm-leaf fan.
Bill and his friends admired this personification of a
statesman. The stout gentleman with the brown eyes
admired Mr. McKinley, too, and told them many

anecdotes of the Governor's kindness to all kinds of people. And what did they think of Thomas B. Reed?

They thought nothing of him. The fat, famous Speaker of the House of Representatives was no hero in the West. Out here he paid for his habit of being wittily rude to raw Congressmen. He was a smart man, the boys told the stranger, but. . . . Yes, the stranger argued, but what is it you have against him? Aw, said the nobodies, he's stuck up! They were all chattering their opinions, while the stout gentleman watched them with his brown eyes. People would talk to him torrentially and then wonder why they had talked, or what he had said to them, discovering at last that he had seldom opened his lips except to put a cigar between his teeth.

Mr. Hanna was gathering opinions. He had nominal headquarters of a McKinley movement at a hotel in Minneapolis, and there, on June 10th, 1892, he declined to combine his idol's admirers with those of Mr. Reed, although he was promised the Secretaryship of the Treasury for Mr. McKinley as a fee for helping Reed to the nomination. But he knew — he had been listening to the delegates — that this listless, discouraged convention would nominate Benjamin Harrison once more. He made no fight for his candidate, then, but was interested to idle in the gallery with these boys and to drive back with them to a respectable German beer-hall in Saint Paul. They liked him. He told them he was in the coal business, before he paid for the cabs and the beer and vanished. But, says Mr. McCready, "if anybody had told me what Mr. Hanna's name was . . . it would have meant absolutely nothing to me. I never heard of Mark Hanna from any source until the Hearst papers began cursing him in the spring of 1896. . . ."

Really, he was so located as to be unheard of. The Eastern newspapers discovered Chicago early enough in its history, but Cleveland remained unknown. Its rich folk were not scandalous or showy; its politics had not the violent quality essential to American fame. Easterners knew that a street named Euclid Avenue existed, and actors knew that Cleveland was a good town in their profession. Mr. Henry Adler, for instance, was advancing on Cleveland in 1884 simply because it was a good town for the show business. He was connected with the theater, in those days, only by some pink ribbons and emotions, but he happened to be reading a French technical magazine which contained prints of theatrical machinery, and the stout man who picked up the magazine for him asked to have legends under the plans translated. Mr. Adler was obliging, and discovered with interest that Mr. Hanna owned the Euclid Avenue Opera House. As the young traveler was moving to a seat in Mr. Hanna's theater because of the dazzling lady who would tonight ravish Cleveland, he talked to Mr. Hanna cordially and told him all about the lady. Mr. Hanna must have said to himself, "You poor little fool!" but he went on asking questions about theaters in France. When the train reached Cleveland, he invited Mr. Adler to dine at his house before the play.

In the hall of the big dwelling a small girl was uproariously pretending to be a dog. Mrs. Hanna alarmed the guest by showing signs of tearfulness. There had been another terrible editorial in the *Leader*! Mr. Hanna read whatever his enemy Mr. Cowles had written about him that day, grunted softly, and made the newspaper into a roll which he tossed to his youngest child. Miss Ruth Hanna fell on it and worried it.

"Marcus! You're not going to let her eat that ink!"

"Well, old lady," said Mr. Hanna, "it's the same kind of ink we use on the *Herald*."

Gentlemen now swarmed into the house and a couple more arrived when the crowd was seated. Mrs. Hanna told Mr. Adler, shy at her right, that she never knew how many there would be for any meal; Mr. Hanna loved company. Yet, the new-comer asked, were they all in the theatrical business? Mrs. Hanna explained that her husband was interested in coal and iron, and owned the *Herald* as well as the opera-house, and was managing a street railway.

"But," she said, "you're from New York. I suppose the only man you've ever heard of in Cleveland is Johnny Rockefeller."

Down the table they were talking of actors. A florid, jolly boy announced that he didn't like Henry

Irving. This Irving was a player who established a character with the audience by ten minutes of lucid and graceful performance and then, just when you didn't expect it, allowed his art to change into something richer and so strange. He gargled, hurtled, writhed, and yawped through some passage of simple emotion. He made Shylock a gibbering neurasthenic at one side of the stage and took him off at the other side as a nobly dignified English gentleman; he appeared as King Arthur in armor designed by Burne-Jones and declaimed for ten minutes so intensely that nobody knew what he was saying at all, but applauded him in a daze of apprehension lest they should not do the right thing. He became a fetich of the latter nineteenth century and was supposed to have contributed something to the pooled culture of England and America. Young Daniel Hanna did not like this actor, he said, because he was not like a human being.

"Don't you be a fool, Dan," Mr. Hanna grunted. "Why, you don't want a tragedian to act like a human being, do you? There wouldn't be any fun in that!"

But he judged comedians differently and watched them from his box in the Euclid Avenue Opera House with the attention he gave to a machine's first movement in a rolling-mill or to the conversation of his youngest child. Joseph Jefferson, William Florence, James Lewis, and the younger men as they rose were valued and discussed. His mouth would stiffen in contempt if a salty scene was allowed to drop into foolery; Mr. Hanna became an ugly, disapproving mask suspended above the public, scowling at the stage. When disapprobation was final, he began to rub an ear with a fist, and his emotion might take him out for a cigar in the lobby. If a play went sour, he was precisely the disappointed boy.

Actors loved him, because he complimented their profession by understanding it. He knew the mechanics of their game — how a fast exit was made and how one fell without breaking one's knees or smote down a villain without bruising one's knuckles. There were also big suppers at his club and occasional generous loans. He was not so familiar toward actresses. That night in 1884 he was taken into the dressing-room of Mr. Adler's bright lady, but stood silent, perhaps not sure that he was privileged in beholding her.

He became a habit of Henry Adler, idle, rich, and melancholy, as cultivated Jews so often were in that period of American society. When his lady led the boy to Cleveland he would drop in at the offices of Hanna and Company and sit for an hour beside Mark Hanna's desk while shipping men, naval architects, customers for coal and iron, and little officials of the swelling city filed in and out. He discovered why his broker in New York had never heard of the mighty Mr. Hanna. This was a lord of the Great Lakes. The formula of his father's success served Mr. Hanna. His iron ships rolled up to Milwaukee and Duluth to fetch back ore for the mills at Cleveland in gross quantity. He had allies in all the ports, men held to him by affection without contracts. But a hundred miles from the edge of the Lakes, Mr. Hanna ceased to be. He was blotted out in the mere size of America, and in New York he was unknown. Mr. Adler saw him walk through a crowd of bankers and business men one crowded night at Delmonico's with his youngest brother, Leonard, without getting a nod. That was in 1888.

He had the fascination of a constant surprise for the clever idler. He knew so much; he knew nothing. An English tourist suggested that the United States would still be colonies of England if the Stamp Act had not been passed. Hanna thought and shook his head. No, the colonies and England would have quarreled in the nineteenth century as soon as the question of immigration from European countries commenced to be important. And his memory had picked up the system of Indian government with which to floor this same tourist in the same talk. And then he didn't know what the letters M.F.H. meant, or what the Reichstag was. He did not know the name of any eminent painter then alive, except James Whistler, but he spoke shrewdly and tartly about pictures sometimes, for his mechanical sense made Mr. Hanna keen on lines and curves. " He was certainly," Mr. Adler wrote in 1904, " one of the best and worst informed men I have ever known. . . ."

Just before Christmas in 1889 Mr. Adler's lady

played in Cleveland and her victim walked into the office of Hanna and Company, and into a confusion of clerks around a weeping charwoman at whom Mr. Hanna was fairly roaring. To one side of this mess stood a beautiful little personage in a frock-coat who was trying to soothe Mr. Hanna. The rich man's eyes were yellow in anger and he would not stop shouting even when the Honorable William McKinley said, deeply, " Hanna, I'm ashamed of you! " Yesterday the major had been playing with a gold piece which he kept in his purse because his men gave it to him at the end of the war. He had left it on Hanna's desk when the millionaire took him away to dinner. And now where was it? Mr. Hanna did not care what she had done with it. He wasn't going to put her in jail. But, he shouted, she was to get back that " same, identical God-damn " coin from her husband or the saloon or the grocer, or, by God, he would find out who her priest was and tell him on her! . . . About then the gold piece rattled on Mr. Hanna's desk from the woman's hand. She slumped on her knees, inelegantly, and howled for pardon. Mr. Hanna stepped back from the suppliant and began to rub his ear. " Aw, get out of here! I'm not going to hurt you! "

Presently Mr. Adler was taking supper at The Players in New York with Lawrence Barrett and mentioned that one of the actors in the poor melodrama by Mr. Oscar Wilde in which Mr. Barrett was appearing looked like Marcus Hanna of Cleveland. The cold, superior tragedian positively warmed to an austere beam. He put his elbows on the table and talked about Hanna for an hour, saying that Mr. Hanna knew more of machinery than many engineers. " He's a human machine himself," the player said, " with a heart of gold." And then, on Mr. Adler's next visit to Cleveland, he saw the human machine at its function. Mr. Hanna sat on the floor of his office with Howard and Leonard Hanna perched behind him on his desk, all watching the model of a dynamo as it tried to lift a weight hitched to a tiny crane. There was an engineer to discuss things with the nervous inventor, but Mark Hanna gave judgment. He had nodded to Mr. Adler as if he had seen him yesterday, when his admirer came in. Then he went on studying his toy. . . . Would this thing do, or wouldn't it? . . . It wouldn't. His big head fell back. He looked at the inventor and said, " Not for me! "

He probably rejected Thomas Reed in the same fashion. He liked Mr. Reed, but Mr. Reed was not for him. He brought Mr. Reed out into Ohio to speak in William McKinley's campaign of 1891 and Reed was charmed by an evening party at Mr. Hanna's house. Cleveland gave the celebrity a good time, but rural Ohio did not like his speeches. The people laughed and applauded, and were not won to him.[7] There was

[7] Mr. Hanna had employés listen to the effect of Mr. Reed on the crowds, he told my father. He never took Reed seriously as a possible President, his brothers assured Mr. Adler. I am told that a letter of Mr. Roosevelt to Nicholas Robertson, of San Francisco, makes a contrary asser-

nothing Lincolnian about Reed, obese, dapper, and sarcastic. He wasn't too friendly when they came up to shake hands after meetings. He was an Eastern product.

The swoop of American affairs between 1890 and 1896 made Mr. Hanna believe that no Easterner would do. In 1890 came the Silver Purchase Act. In 1891 business slackened. In 1892 here was the People's party in convention assembled crying out for government ownership of railroads and telegraphs, and for more silver to keep plenty of money floating into rural banks. The " soft money " heresy of 1868 had come alive again in this new form. Silver was the friend of the lowly and agricultural; silver was something clean and radiant, while gold was a red devil friendly to the rich of Wall Street. Gold was England's weapon against the United States. Gold was all wrong and silver was all right. Gold belonged to the capitalistic East, and silver was mined in the free and democratic West. . . . The Populists wanted other things. Explore the pamphlets and the lumbering speeches and you find the popular election of senators, the restriction of immigration, the subsidized farmer, the income tax, the regulation of rates for common carriers. You find everything, if you look, that had been stirring in the minds of reformers since the Civil War. Emotional

---

tion. But the letter dates from 1896, when Mr. Roosevelt was possibly influenced by his affection for Reed. It is well known that he wanted to see Mr. Reed nominated at Saint Louis in 1896.

politicians are seldom original; Mr. William Jennings Bryan, speaking rhythmic pieces at county fairs and religious festivals, heard all this chatter close to the soil, and listened attentively, his wits absorbed in the task of becoming a great orator.

A great malefactor rose in the East to collect upon himself the grievances of the West. President Grover Cleveland caused the repeal of the Silver Purchase Act in 1893, in the midst of the panic which sent young Bill McCready home from Saint Paul because his employer was ruined outright, and cost Henry Adler the favor of his bright lady, who, as Mark Hanna had warned him, wrung him as one wrings a moist rag and chucked him away when his income was suspended. In 1894 Mr. Cleveland sent federal troops into Illinois to aid in restraining the strikers at Chicago after Mr. George Pullman's stupidity brought about a general strike of railroad men, a thing costing more than has yet been computed. And here Mr. Hanna, furious in Cleveland, displayed himself in his odd duplex nature.

First he raged against Mr. Pullman for failing in common sense. The damned idiot ought to arbitrate, arbitrate and arbitrate! What, for God's sake, did the manufacturer think he was doing? He made a scene in the Union Club, surrounded by gentlemen who rather sympathized with Pullman. Mr. Myron Herrick tried to quiet him. Another friend claimed that Pullman had done fine things for his workmen. There was the town of Pullman, the model suburb, with its neat

132

homes for workers and its pretty square and library. "Oh, hell!" said Marcus Hanna. "Model —! [8] Go and live in Pullman and find out how much Pullman gets sellin' city water and gas ten per cent higher to those poor fools!" He knew too much to take Mr. Pullman's claims as a philanthropist on the high plane. He knew too much about workingmen not to see that Pullman's stockholders, Eastern and midland, had forced the commonplace millionaire into a folly against the state. "A man who won't meet his men half-way is a God-damn fool!" His words sped out and came into Chicago; in 1896 there was a difficulty in collecting money for the Republican campaign fund from Mr. Pullman's office.

The odious and Eastern Cleveland went on affronting the West. He demanded of Congress that it help him get rid of the fluctuating currency which was making the Treasury a pool for capitalists who could collect gold on notes until the reserve of coin was low and then sell back to the government at their profitable convenience. He blundered and appealed to Wall Street for help in marketing bonds. Wall Street, in the person of Mr. John Pierpont Morgan, dealt out the bonds and collected handsomely for its services. Mr. Cleveland's second term of office was concluding in a series of crashes; it was Wagnerian music, politically expressed.

A certain madness, an apocalyptic tremor, passed

[8] Primordial American noun, compound, meaning latrine.

about the world in this last phase of the nineteenth century. False scientists wrote novels on the end of the terrestrial globe, and flashy magazines printed them. An Englishman fancied the Martians invading London with poisonous smokes and flashing rays of heat that killed. Had the century failed, after all Macaulay had claimed for industrial machinery and progress, to make the world happier? Cheap men wondered what Christ would think of Chicago, as if the Nazarene would have concerned himself with Chicago any more than he valued things rendered to Cæsar which were Cæsar's anyhow. The disintegrating, halted Christian socialism of the century's middle period recurred in terms of emotion. Western speakers read *Progress and Poverty* again and there was talk in Kansas of the houses of Have and Want. Silly people in banks worried about revolutions. . . .

There was a nervous conversation at lunch in the Union Club at Cleveland. Someone got windy about a revolt. This Altgeld and that man Tillman from the South might start something serious, with the Populists following them. Mr. Samuel Mather laughed, saying that all the country needed was some protection for its industries and solid money. He left the room. Heads shook. Mr. Hanna took his cigar out of his mouth and grunted, "Sam's right. There won't be any revolution. You're just a lot of damn fools."

That autumn all the youngsters who called him Uncle Mark and hunted his advice on details of business had a chill. Uncle Mark had quit! He had handed over his share of Hanna and Company to his brother Leonard. He was through. . . . He had taken a house in the South, at Thomasville in Georgia. It was incredible. But it was true. Mr. Hanna had retired from business. He really had not time to manage Hanna and Company and squabble about franchises of the street railways when he had to make William McKinley President of the United States.

III

The Republican National Convention would convene on June 16th, 1896, at Exposition Hall in Saint Louis, but Mr. William Collins Beer arrived with the haste of all political amateurs on the tenth of June. He arrived perspiring; heat was already in possession of Saint Louis, and his room in the Southern Hotel was a decorated oven. He was full of ideas and advice which he yearned to bestow on the high powers of the party at once. He wanted to have the United States openly join the nations of Europe in declaring for the gold standard in finance. The National Surety Company had transferred him to New York in 1893; he had met Europeans and had dined with bankers and presidents of life-insurance companies. His pockets were full of letters introducing him to Eastern delegates, and he knew many delegates from the states of Iowa, Minnesota, Nebraska, and California. He wanted to meet the grandees. He was told that he must meet Mr. Hanna before he met anybody else.

He recoiled. Since April, Marcus Alonzo Hanna had been revealed in the newspapers owned by William Randolph Hearst as an amalgam of all sins. He was foulness compact. He was the Red Boss of Cleveland's politics. The town council trembled when he sent minions to address it. He had stolen a theater from poor John Ellsler, foreclosing a cruel mortgage and rejecting the man's pleas for time.[9] He ruled Cleveland from his office, terrorizing unions and ruining rival street railways. He sent poor sailors, forced on his ships by bestial labor masters, out to sea on the wintry Lakes, cold and starving, unpaid and mutinous. He had bought the poor old *Herald* and then had wrecked it, which meant that he had sold his newspaper after five years of steady loss, in 1885. He had corrupted William McKinley's government of Ohio. He was a hypocrite as well, affecting to be a strong churchman and drawing down the curtains of his house on the Lake when he had guests to Sunday dinner. Now the Red Boss lay in wait at Saint Louis with a train of purchased Southern Republicans, ready to make McKinley the candidate of his party.

It was too wide an indictment for anybody to swallow whole, but Mr. Beer did not want to meet Marcus Alonzo Hanna. William McKinley was an old friend of his father. He would wait until he recognized some

[9] See Appendix

honest associate of the major. He hung about for two days, boiling his arguments for the gold standard in his head and drinking ice water. Then he gave in, and let Mr. Joseph Kimball lead him to Mr. Hanna's den on the floor below his own room in the Southern Hotel.

Mr. Hanna was a quiet object in a gray, plain suit, deep in a chair beside a bottle of mineral water, and placid as the bottle, in a room packed with vociferous personalities. The only other placid thing in the room was a tall, comely gentleman, excellently clad, who leaned on a wall and fanned himself with a newspaper. Mr. Beer knew Myron Herrick by sight. They had met in the office of John McCall, president of the New York Life Insurance Company. But the other men were strangers, and, somehow, this heart of the great party wasn't imposing. Mr. Beer decided, suddenly, that the grandees were just noisy, worried men. They did not stop talking when he was presented to Mr. Hanna. Under cover of the noise Mr. Hanna's memory now ticked, adjusting itself to the problem standing before him, very hot.

"You from Ohio? . . . Son of Judge Beer?" The young man was startled. "H'm, your dad cost some friends of mine in the oil business a lot of money once." The young man was pleased. "Some Democrat judges," said Mr. Hanna, impersonally, "are a damn sight more honest than lots of Republican judges. . . . Let's see —" the memory caught at something — "Got an uncle down at Ashland, haven't

137

you? " But, the young man thought, this is omnis-
cience! " And now," said the Red Boss, "what's it
you want to tell us about the platform? "
The amateur spoke. There had to be a statement
in the Republican platform promising outright that
the party stood for the gold standard. He had heard
that Mr. Hanna was a bimetallist and he knew that
McKinley had dallied with Free Silver in a cautious
speech. He now attacked Mr. Hanna with statistics
and financial reports. He soared into complexities of
English banking and hopped the width of Europe to
speak of Russia. He quoted from the resolutions of
European conferences and congresses. He recited the
wisdom of Mr. John McCall, although Mr. McCall
was a Democrat. The grandees listened. Mr. Beer discovered in himself a talent for oratory and he talked
and talked. Ferocious voices answered out of the jam.
Two Westerners retorted with arguments from essays
of theoretical professors. Mr. Beer's rapid tenor voice
shut them up. He had begun by talking to Mr. Herrick and Mr. Hanna. He was now personally identified with the forces of sound finance; he was the gold
standard defending itself against Free Silver. He threw
out an emotion while his collar wilted and his clothes
darkened with sweat. His throat was raw when he
stopped talking.
"Very interesting," said Mr. Hanna.
The others were more cordial. Mr. Herrick asked
the young man to dine. Mr. Beer walked, dripping,

down the corridor with Mr. Kimball, sure that he had saved the United States from another panic. When Mr. Kimball cackled and fell against a wall, he could not imagine what was the matter with the gentle little man from Arizona.

"You're about the hundredth person who's made that speech in there. Don't mind me!"

Mr. Beer went off to his bedroom and sternly took a bath. His father had always warned him that Republicans were coldly perfidious. He had been allowed to entertain the Red Boss and the rest of them for half an hour. He would leave Saint Louis directly. He would report to Mr. McCall and the president of the National Surety Company that Mark Hanna was a thug and a churl. He was moping in fresh underclothes on his bed, waiting for a page to bring him up more iced lemonade, when Mr. Hanna trundled in, bearing a cigar and a long sheet of typed names.

"Know any of these men, son?"

The bruised amateur looked down the list. He saw that this was the mass of the Silver faction in the party, delegates, bankers, editors of newspapers. Yes, he said, he had met many of them on his trips for the National Surety. He said so with a deal of injured dignity. Mark Hanna stared at him.

"All these men are in town already. Go and talk to 'em. Feed 'em. If you run out of money, come to me. If you can't catch me, see Herrick. If he ain't around, get hold of Andrew Squire."

139

Mr. Beer had plenty of money for dinners. But just what did the man want? He asked, " Am I to say that you — "

" You're not to say anything about me. You," said Mr. Hanna, " go and talk gold to those men. Tell them everything you told us."

He was not even polite. He trundled out. But the dynamo in the gray suit had energized the bruised young man on the bed. It is emblematic that Mark Hanna was one of the first, if not absolutely the first, of industrialists to attach a dynamo directly to a machine. He had the quality possessed also by Theodore Roosevelt and Tom Johnson in his times. He could energize. Mr. Beer pulled on his clothes and went into operation, armed with many lozenges for his delicate throat, certain that Mr. Hanna was for gold. He commenced a round of the hotels and wallowed in the society of men who wanted something done for Silver.

This Silver faction was partly made up of bimetallists, men who believed, quite correctly, that there was nothing wrong with a double standard of money. There was nothing wrong with bimetallism, except that international finance condemned it. The trouble of these gentlemen was that finance was not international to them, but American. They still did not comprehend what James Garfield had explained to Congress in 1868. Truly, they were victims of their sentiment for the American life. Money-making was the permitted field of the search for power in that

America, and they had grown up in that rhythm. Men worked; work was life. And while that rhythm, now broken, lasted in its strength, this American life satisfied; they were happy men, memorable in their enthusiasms, more charming than their sons who cannot believe in business as they believed.

But the bimetallists who thought that American interest was somehow damaged by submitting to the rules of world-finance were in a minority. The bulk of the Silver faction was made up, candidly, of the politicians to whom silver-mining was a home industry, a local issue. They wanted to see the Silver Purchase Act of 1890 restored and maintained; in other words they wanted the silver mines subsidized at the expense of the United States. They were bitter with fright and selfishness, of course, and among them moved quietly Mr. William Jennings Bryan suggesting that, if the Republican party rejected their patriotic enterprise on behalf of the plain people, they would find friends in the Democratic party.[10]

There were plenty of bitter Republicans entering Saint Louis from the East on every fast train, followers of Thomas Reed, and henchmen of Thomas Platt and Matthew Quay. They came to the convention knowing that this unknown monster of Cleveland had already secured William McKinley's nomination. His allies had caused the Republican conventions of nine

[10] Mr. Bryan was reporting the convention for a newspaper in Omaha. His own memoirs assert that he " conferred " with the Silver delegates.

states to pledge delegates to support Mr. McKinley, and the Southern Republicans of the " rotten boroughs," as Foraker called them, were loyal to the major. Mr. Hanna could thumb his nose at the Eastern bosses and the Eastern aspirants. His hero had refused to promise offices to Platt and Quay in exchange for their favors. All right, Mr. Hanna could do without the Eastern machines. His own machine supervened. The clever men of the party knew what had happened; Mr. Hanna, of Cleveland, Ohio, was the master of this occasion. But that was not enough. Mr. Hanna was doing what he should not; instead of being solemn and dignified, Mr. Hanna was amused. His mouth wiggled into grins as he stood in the lobby of the Southern Hotel with reporters purring and clawing his sleeves; he was openly entertained at his own show.

Meanwhile his human machine worked in the boiling of hot, discomfited men in those hot rooms and restaurants. Five unpaid amateurs were tackling the Silver faction. Mr. Beer spent all one night in useless argument with Richard Pettigrew of South Dakota, and crossed trails with another amateur in the rooms of Senator Teller of Colorado. Mr. Hanna himself was working out a subtle bit of fencing with a less public faction. Experts saw that a committee of the American Protective Association, the half-secret anti-Catholic society, was worming after Mark Hanna as he flitted from hotel to hotel. A messenger shot from

142

Hanna's quarters to a quiet lawyer in Saint Paul on the fastest train and, suddenly, there was a vehement telegram from the great Monsignor Ireland demanding that the Republican party should not disgrace itself by any action against his sect. The telegram was published. There could be no further question of conciliating the A.P.A. Mr. Hanna was much surprised by Monsignor Ireland's telegram.[11] He was about to be described by a sensitive Eastern observer as " coarse, insolent and incapable of tact in the detail of politics. . . ." What is tact?

His machinery moved in triple time. He had three problems. He must conciliate the East, if he could. He must keep the Silver faction in the party, if he could. He must clearly have the convention declare for the gold standard in its published platform. A declaration for sound currency would be insufficient. So he blended two of his problems. Let the Easterners themselves force him to declare for gold, then, by all means. The grandees were heavily telling him that he must get a firm statement for the gold standard written into the platform, and they went on telling him so through Saturday and Sunday. Next autumn several dignitaries muddied the rill of history by declaring

---

[11] Mr. Maury in *Wars of the Godly* correctly points out that Ireland's telegram kept the religious row alive and really strengthened the A.P.A. But the pressure on Mr. Hanna was serious. Many of the delegates from the central states were touched by Protestant bigotry. Senator Allison of Iowa had a violent scene with a man named Murchison who attacked him before my father and John Baldwin on behalf of the A.P.A. Saint Louis was full of religious busybodies, on both sides of the quarrel.

that they, severally, had caused the words "the exist-
ing gold standard must be maintained" to be written
into the platform. Three Eastern politicians made this
assertion and, in sketches of the episode, written by
Easterners of recent times, their assertions still seem
to be believed. But on Friday night Senator Redfield
Proctor of Vermont told Charles Gleed, a Vermont
man transplanted in Topeka, Kansas, that the word-
ing of the sentence had been accepted by Mr. McKinley and Mr. Hanna before dinner. On Saturday morning William Merriam of Minnesota whispered to Mr.
Beer that a gold standard plank was in the platform.
At half past nine the young amateur telegraphed to
the National Surety Company: "It is all right." However, the Easterners continued on Saturday and Sunday to force Mr. Hanna to declare for gold. Mr.
Thomas Platt, Mr. Henry Cabot Lodge, Mr. Edward
Lauterbach, and several others addressed this dunder-
headed millionaire, with the authority of older politicians and cultivated financiers. His reluctance showed
them what a fool he must be. They suffered a great
deal.[12]

[12] "Why does Hanna not come out and tell these prominent burglars
the truth? The gold standard sentence was in the platform by Friday night
or else Proctor and Merriam are a couple of liars. He is pretty deep. . . ."
Charles Gleed to William C. Beer, November 20th, 1896.

"I think Mr. Hanna was right to let it seem that the eastern end of
the party forced his hand in declaring for the gold standard. Herrick and
he had it all arranged when they came to Saint Louis. Lodge never got
there until Sunday. He came on the same train I did. His claim is just one
of his conceited pieces of bragging. I suppose he thinks he had something
to do with it." Bruce Higginson to William C. Beer, August 1st, 1896.

Late on Sunday night the dunder-headed million-aire made a play for Senator Cannon of Utah, the best speaker of the Silver faction. He did not know Senator Cannon, even by sight, and Cannon had pungently refused to meet the Red Boss. But William Beer had soothed and blandished a follower of Mr. Cannon, a jolly parasite named Ira Gillis, and he led this conquest to Mr. Hanna's rooms. Mr. Hanna received his callers informally, in a nightshirt, and demanded at once their opinion on his ankles. Some red blotches had appeared. Were they hives? He would not be assured that this was just prickly heat.

"A fortune teller told me this spring I was going to have a bad summer. I had hives all the summer of the Centennial. I can't stand 'em!"

He tramped the room, directing his attack on Mr. Gillis. Gillis could tell the Senator that Mr. McKinley would send a commission to Europe to find out whether an agreement in favor of international bi-metallism could be reached. No reason why all that silver should be wasted. He and the major both hated to think of it. But you couldn't run the country on depreciated currency. He picked up a bit of cold toast from a tray. If all the nations of the world agreed this toast was money, it was money, and gold would be worthless as silver, and silver would be more worthless than it was now. Couldn't Cannon and Teller and Pettigrew see reason? . . . Mr. Beer saw this stout, worried man in the flapping nightshirt become dignified, leaning on a little table and holding a piece of greasy toast as he talked in harsh, short sentences. . . . Did the Silver Senators want to see another panic? Didn't they know that, back east and as far as Chicago, able workmen were starving and shopgirls going on the streets? He promised that the major would do what he could for Silver. And if Mr. Cannon had been reading the stuff in the newspapers about M. A. Hanna, let him wire any man in Cleveland, even Tom Johnson, by God, and see if M. A. Hanna ever broke a contract! He had promised; he would have a commission sent.

" I've been in the coal and iron business pretty near thirty years. You go and roust out a man that's done business with me and see if I don't fill my contracts! "

Mr. Beer left him talking and did not see Mr. Hanna again until the convention assembled, but he saw Mr. Gillis and even tried his hand on the decorative Senator from Utah. He was sitting in the gallery close to Gillis when the gold plank was read out. Mr. Cannon's friend turned to grin at him. An hour later Teller and Cannon had made their speeches. The Silver delegates washed from the hall, and even Henry Cabot Lodge joined in the yells as the rebels stalked out.

Nominations were now in order. William Allison, of Iowa, was nominated by John Baldwin. Thomas Reed was proposed by Henry Lodge. Levi Morton, of New York, was inaudibly tendered by Chauncey Depew. Senator Joseph Benson Foraker of Ohio then put the

146

name of William McKinley in nomination, never
looking toward Mr. Hanna. The applause lasted
twenty-five minutes. . . . The obedient Governor of
Pennsylvania now nominated Matthew Quay, who
had sense of humor and liked to display it indirectly.
The roll of the states was called. Mr. McKinley had
six hundred sixty-one and one-half votes. His nomination was made unanimous. Delegates bawled for
Hanna, and people stood up in the galleries for a first
glimpse of this new power. Young Bill McCready
jumped, recognizing the plain citizen who had been
so friendly at Saint Paul as the plump figure appeared on the platform. . . . Mark Hanna faced
the crowd and barked out some limping sentences,
his hands behind his back, his face watering his collar,
and then he beamed at the collected party just as
a child smiles when its birthday cake comes to the
table.

People ebbed downward from the gallery. Mr. Beer
saw a group around his wife's cousin, John Baldwin,
who had nominated Senator Allison, and walked over
to join it. He was standing with ladies in the medley
when a tall, dramatic man shoved past him to shake
hands with Mr. Baldwin, rolling out a flattery on
" your beautiful oratorical effort . . . " in a wonderful, clear voice. Men from Omaha and Council Bluffs
grinned at each other. Why couldn't Bill Bryan have
said what he wanted to say without all that bosh
about beautiful oratorical efforts? . . . But the ladies

147

turned their little feathered hats as Mr. Bryan's curly dark head steered away into the press.

IV

" The oddest thing about Hanna," Theodore Roosevelt said, on November 13th, 1916, " was that numbers of intelligent people thought him a fool. . . ." This impression, to be sure, had been riveted by the cartoons in the spring of 1896 producing Mr. Hanna as an obese money-bag or a stupid man lugging a hurdy-gurdy, with McKinley as a dejected monkey hitched to his master's wrist. None of that, though, excuses the subtle bankers and political lawyers in New York who, at a conference before the first of July, decided on McKinley's cabinet for him. Having decided on the cabinet, they went the further length of offering each other places in it, or " sounding out " various men to find that posts would be accepted. Colonel John McCook was airily appointed Attorney General of the United States in this manner, and Mr. Chauncey Depew, it was heard from the neighborhood of his offices, was to be Secretary of the Treasury. As for Mr. Hanna, he was said to be yachting off the coast of Maine, on the second of July, and they did not bother about him. Perhaps he would like to be an ambassador or something. Mr. Hanna was in Cleveland, really, but, for all the New Yorkers cared, he might be at Monte Carlo. Out of sight was out of mind. Soon enough these smokes were blown askew. The voice of Mr. William Jennings Bryan sounded from Chicago, in the swells and pauses of a beautiful oratorical effort, and the East became poignantly aware of a great leader in the West, acclaimed as a new Lincoln, a son of the plain people, nominated by the ecstatic accord of the plain people.

At the time of Mr. Bryan's death, editors refused to print articles on his career in which commentators mentioned that his nomination by the Democrats at Chicago in 1896 wasn't a thunderbolt. But since 1925 Mr. Silas Kent and Mr. Charles Willis Thompson have asserted the truth: Mr. Bryan had a considerable following before he appeared in Chicago, and it had been guessed by several Republican observers that he might win the Democratic candidacy. Senator Allison of Iowa, among others, accounted Bryan a dangerous man in May of 1896. So did Harvey Scott of the *Oregonian*, out in Portland. So did Charles Gleed in Topeka, Kansas. So did Redfield Proctor in Vermont. Their letters on the topic exist. Nevertheless, the melodrama of his appearance and his famous speech are dear possessions of history, and your great-grandsons will probably read in schoolbooks that this handsome fanatic conquered the Democratic convention in 1896 by a single speech and so made himself a political hero. It will be true and untrue. He would not have been nominated except that he seized the nomination with cordial intent, and his speech was a deliberated, reliable method of seizure.

Properly analyzed, this address is an arpeggio of
appeals to popular belief and prejudice, each paragraph calculated to rouse emotion. It contains a fuse
for the conceit of the pioneer, a defiance of England,
a gesture toward the cemetery, and a suggestion of
Christian martyrdom. He made the Republican party
wicked by four strokes of the voice and lifted himself
into the position he kept until death took the American people from him. He became a moral force, as un-
critical persons understand morality, and his more
critical opponents had to resort to calling him wicked
in turn. That Mr. Bryan, enemy of capitalism, was
the half-conscious agent of a faction of capitalists, the
silver-miners, and that he proposed to crucify the
plain people on a cross of depreciated silver are obvious facts. His sincerity is no longer important. " If
you tell a crowd of Americans that you are a good
man," said David Graham Phillips, " they will politely take you at your word. . . ." Mr. Bryan's virtue
was announced. He was nominated for the presidency
of the United States and at once began operations as
an eager artist in success.

One of his most efficient enemies was a wrecked,
fidgeting middle-aged lady in the small town of Canton, Ohio. She was effective in a quiet but condign
manner. By direction of his friends Major McKinley
stayed at home, speaking to deputations and pilgrim-
ages from every quarter of the United States. These
deputations couldn't get off the train at Canton with-

out learning that McKinley was a devoted husband to an epileptic wife. Ladies often came with their own husbands to meet the Republican candidate and were impressed, although Mrs. McKinley was not displayed, and the curiosity of the deputations as to her health annoyed McKinley so acutely that several times he had her driven off to the farm of an old friend when his front lawn would be full of Republican pilgrims. But sympathy for the gentle little man poured out of Canton as the pilgrims retired. While women in crowds everywhere gulped as William Jennings Bryan spoke of God's will, and his curls glowed and his eyes flashed, other women talked of William McKinley's virtues. And everything was grist that came to mill in the summer of 1896.

The general tone of talk at Republican headquarters in Chicago and New York was angry confidence. Of course McKinley would thrash Bryan, and thrash him completely. But there was an undertone. Mr. Hanna's machinery worked with a delightful smoothness. There seemed plenty of money for the pay of speakers, for brass bands, bunting, golden elephants of paper or metal, and posters. Only on July 20th the major was almost fantastically glad to hear that the population of Nantucket Island, off Massachusetts, was solidly Republican, and on July 29th Mr. Hanna acknowledged a load of Republican pledges and some news from Connecticut forwarded to him by way of Canton with a singular warmth. Everything seemed all right in New York. Clergy and bankers and owners of huge department stores denounced Free Silver cordially. Mr. Cornelius Bliss received journalists at the Republican bureau and talked with grave assurance. Good news was always coming in and going out. But on August 5th John Hay wrote to Henry White in London: " I find the feeling a little nervous; unnecessarily so, I think. I talked with Hanna and some of the Executive Committee, and while there is nothing like dread of defeat, there is a clear comprehension that Bryan will get the votes of a good many others of his kind, and that it will require more work than we thought necessary last spring to beat him. . . ."

Mr. Hanna came unostentatiously to New York on August 3rd and conferred with selections of the leaders. The feeling, as Hay wrote, was a little nervous. Americans were then more dignified, if they were men, than they are today and it was not considered form to display fright. It trickled out among the workers of the party that there was a good deal to be done. Mr. Hanna's idea of what was to be done scandalized Colonel John McCook so that he scribbled to William Beer: " I wish that Hanna would not talk so freely about money. But I know that we are going to need more. It is disappointing that a Democrat like [John] McCall has more sense of the real situation than Mr. Depew. Depew's attitude is simply disgusting. It is turning out the stiffest campaign since the war. . . ."

It was, but the Lincolnian figure was not in the Republican party, and Mr. Hanna knew that a lot of money was needed against the shadow of the Liberator. Bryan's weakness, as Hanna knew, was what Harry Thurston Peck rhetoricized in 1905; Mr. Bryan had picked up the wrong weapon. He was making his campaign on Free Silver. " He's talking Silver all the time," said Mr. Hanna, " and that's where we've got him. . . ." He sat in a chair at the Union League Club with another bottle of mineral water at his elbow and faced the New Yorkers, his cane across his knees. The proper Republicans of the metropolis were upset and stood staring at the obtuse coal-merchant from Cleveland who thought they should raise three million more dollars for the campaign fund. Money! Wouldn't he see that revolt was threatening? It was very well to say that Mr. Bryan was not in favor of abolishing the Supreme Court or confiscating railroads and telegraphs. Those were notions of the Populists. But the Populists were backing this bastard Lincoln! Altgeld was a maniac, ready to plunder the cities in Bryan's name. A somber wave thundered from the West. And Mr. Hanna sat talking of speakers and brass bands and educational pamphlets on sound money when the world was turning upside down, as if mere words and music could stop this thing.

Something furious stirred the air around heads of children on sea beaches. Ladies were gasping, with hand on corsets, about rebellion and the horrible things John or Mason had told them about Mr. Bryan. Mr. Bryan was a black tower, like the Iron Man in *The Garden Behind the Moon*, smoking as he strode about in a clangor of bands, inciting revolution. You might be told that Mr. Bryan was a harmless person, normally resident in Lincoln, Nebraska, who thought the country would be better off if silver dollars were coined at a ratio of sixteen to one gold dollar. But even the voice of a father assuring you that he'd often talked to Mr. Bryan in Omaha and Lincoln without being damaged was not conclusive. Bridget could soothe. The matter was simple to her in the kitchen, because Monsignor Ireland himself had spoken against this crazy man from out west, and the saints were with Mr. McKinley, that was good to his wife in her trouble, and so don't you fret, and, for God's sake, be taking that dog out of this place, now! Still it was slightly awful to be a child in the summer of 1896.

The East took fright and high regions of the Republican party were troubled. Mr. Hanna did not seem to be spending enough money on New York. The metropolis heard that Mr. Hanna was trying to carry the midland states for McKinley. But the metropolitans saw no sense in that. John McCook was exasperated and delivered a whole lecture on the importance of the midlands to an audience in the Union League Club one afternoon, and Mr. Theodore Roosevelt followed up his stately exposition of the point with a few words. The metropolitans were not convinced. A young man of large means and advertised name drawled that he had arranged for a *maisonnette* in Versailles. If a man like this Bryan was going to run the country, he would certainly leave it. He then left the room. Mr. Roosevelt said in falsetto, "There might be compensations in seeing Mr. Bryan elected!" But it was a serious little meeting, for Mr. Bryan was soon to accept the Democratic nomination before a mob in Madison Square Garden. People were betting that the new Liberator would carry New York and Connecticut. And this fool of a Hanna was wasting money on the middle West!

Mr. Hanna returned to New York. He was there on August 15th, again, in a gray suit, drinking mineral water. Also there was James J. Hill, the railroad king, who had words to say in certain offices. Mr. William Rockefeller did some rapid telephoning from his house in the Hudson valley. Mr. Cornelius Bliss went personally, in a closed carriage, from place to place around the lower end of the city. Late at night twenty or thirty checks were in Mr. Hanna's wallet, and a new phase commenced in the high regions of the party. The bluff of the Wall Street set had been called, in one day, and a number of men who'd been talking of the sums they had paid to the Republican campaign fund had now actually paid those sums. There was also a new tone in remarks made about the dunder-headed millionaire from Cleveland. "The feeling about

HANNA

Mr. H.," William Beer writes on August 20th, to Mr. Harvey Fleming in Kansas City, " has changed. He has made a lot of these people see that he knows what he is doing. But there is a bad scare here. . . ."

Pastors, politicians, and even some gentlewomen broke out and raved against Mr. Bryan. The scare was bad. Behind the plunging orator in his private car was this wave of queer names and uncomprehended identities, Altgeld, the anarchist, Debs, the socialist, Populists, and Silver Republicans. Bryan was cursed grotesquely, in speeches violent with fear. And under the fear was a little justification. An element of the Populists did a good deal of vicious talking on street corners and in railroad yards. Threats were chalked on coaches of the fast express trains. A spellbinder named Fletcher dropped in a fit as he howled against the Rockefellers in a crowd at Coney Island on the first of September. Cartoons showed Hanna and McKinley discussing policies across a whisky bottle. Slander, to be sure, was so current that it moved into McKinley's own party. Men who knew the candidate were cornered and asked, confidentially now, if McKinley wasn't pretty much of a sot. And wasn't there something funny about his wife? [13]

[13] " I know that Mr. Hanna has refused to answer any of the libels as to himself. His position is sound. But I think this low campaign against Mr. and Mrs. McKinley ought to be dealt with. . . . The offices [of Wells, Fargo and Company] report that scandals are in circulation in Missouri and Kansas. Several men of some intelligence have asked me if it is true that Mrs. McKinley is an English spy. These reports prejudice a certain

The failure of Mr. Bryan's speech of acceptance in New York, introduced at unutterable length by the Governor of Missouri, did not cheer the men at Republican headquarters. On September 8th John Hay wrote to Henry Adams: " He [Mr. Bryan] has succeeded in scaring the Goldbugs out of their five wits; if he had scared them a little they would have come down handsome to Hanna. But he has scared them so blue that they think they had better keep what they have got left in their pockets against the evil day." On the same day he wrote to Mrs. Charlton Paull: " And are you going to join the grand exodus from our wayward native land that is to occur when the Goldbugs are squashed under the heel of Silver's champion? Many of my friends are saving their money for the purchase of suitable residences in Paris. Shall we next meet on the Place de la République? " He might be gay on paper, but he was privately rasped. He broke out, in that week, dashing a newspaper from him, " They dare

kind of second rate citizen intensely. . . ." Dudley Evans to William C. Beer, August 27th, 1896.

" Horrible stories are being told about McKinley's habits by Popocrats out here. He is called a common drunk and a deadbeat. A letter of Tom Johnson is circulated showing him up as a general reprobate who swindled the state of Ohio out of three millions on some deal for new poor houses. . . . You have no idea how the country brethren love free Silver. Tried to explain to one yesterday that 16 to 1 does not mean he will have 16 times the money he has now. He called me a liar. . . ." Nicholas Lemke, in Fresno, California, to William C. Beer, August 30th, 1896.

" We are all of the opinion that it would do harm to answer the slanders on Mrs. McKinley. My brother thinks it would make the matter worse. . . ." Howard Melville Hanna to Cornelius Bliss, September 1, 1896.

to call this mountebank a new Lincoln!" And this hurt, everywhere. It roused old generals of the Civil War; it disgusted a son of Robert Lee; it even made men shrug who had not loved Abraham Lincoln. Yet there it was, the image of the tall man from the West, the new folk-hero.

On the 9th of September William Beer was quietly summoned to the office of Cornelius Bliss in New York and there told that an idea, proposed to Mr. McKinley through Julius Whiting of Canton, had been approved at last by Mr. Hanna. Mr. Beer was to be allowed to conduct a special train containing some famous veterans of the Civil War through the West and middle West, making a demonstration for Major McKinley. Mr. Beer knew that his invention was already accepted by Hanna. Howard Hanna had sent him word from Cleveland that the generals were being collected. But he beamed on Mr. Bliss and said he was proud of the trust conferred on him by the party. He knew all the right things to say, by this time, for he had created an awkwardness at a luncheon by observing that some converted Democrats, speaking in the metropolis for Mr. McKinley on salary, were not worth what it had cost to convert them. This episode taught him that the inner mechanism of political conversion should not be mentioned abruptly. So he beamed at Mr. Bliss and reached for his hat. . . . The grandee twiddled a cigar on a brass tray, glancing at the shut door. As Mr. Beer had to report to Mr. Hanna in Chicago, would he

— er — deliver a list of suggestions made by some —
well — important people to Mr. Hanna. Bliss allowed
his flat mortification to appear. But these people were
handsome contributors to the funds, and. . . . Mr.
Beer copied down a list of sixteen suggestions and told
Mr. Bliss that he expected to be kicked out of Mark
Hanna's office; the important people, vestrymen of
correct churches and what not, were willing to turn
the election into a religious feud. They had listened to
anti-Catholic tattle. They proposed to antagonize
every Irishman in the United States by hinting that
Monsignor Ireland's support of McKinley was insin-
cere, and accusing prominent communicants of the
Catholic Church of secretly aiding Altgeld's " German anarchists." Nevertheless, the list must go to
Marcus Hanna, since these were important people, as
importance was judged in New York. One of them
gave exigent balls and another had been an ambassador, and another saw himself in Mr. McKinley's
cabinet as Secretary of War.

Mr. Hanna was checking over a new pamphlet on
sound money when the bearer of this idiotic document came before him on September 13th. After reading the suggestions he said nothing, but Mr. Beer now
discovered that Mark Hanna's eyes seemed yellow
when he was angry. He threw the paper on his desk
and asked in a chugging, metallic voice, " Who gave
you that God-damn stuff ? " When he was answered,
this unpoetic man leaned back in his chair and spoke

in a figure. He was like a weight in the middle of a seesaw, he said, and both ends of the plank had damned fools on them. As for poor Bliss, he couldn't help himself. As for this lot of God-damn sheep in Wall Street, it would serve them right if Bryan kicked them to hell and gone. What were they made of? All you got out of most of them was a thousand dollars and a lot of condescension. If they had been allowed to nominate Tom Reed, Bryan would have walked over them. They could not even see the sense of his simple pamphlets against Free Silver. They couldn't see anything! Give him a farmer or a laboring man who wasn't a lunatic and he could make the man see the fallacy in Bryan's money scheme. "They'll read this stuff," he said, slapping the pamphlets. "It gets on to the table in the sitting-room and they read it!"

His breath gave out. He stopped. Then he was imperious. Mr. Beer was to tear up the list and not to talk about it. Mr. Hanna would send on some thoughts to New York. His ugly mouth relaxed. He began to laugh. It was a funny world! Here he was, with his name mud in the Democratic papers, trying to keep the country out of a panic! He saw the humor of his own position: the Red Boss was the friend of the plain people in this pass, and their champion was their enemy. An irony made the pragmatist outweigh the idealist and moralist. By God, it was a funny world! . . . He chuckled, and roared for his secretary, dictated a curt order to all the railroads, commanding passage for General Alger and his party, and then rapidly told Mr. Beer how to get along with General Howard and General Sickles.[14]

The young amateur now entered on a crazy period of nights in a circle of cigars — he did not smoke — and heard the Civil War rehearsed in a purely professional way without compliments or sentiments. He dove from the train at all hours into towns still unknown to satire, hunting Bourbon whisky, bottled milk, liver-pills, and mineral waters for his convoy. He had to suppress the grandson of one hero who was learning to use a pea-shooter and tried its range on hats in Kentucky, where gray Confederate coats showed in the crowds alongside the halted train. He lay sleepless while a wooden leg which General Sickles sometimes wore got loose from its place in the darkness and rolled furiously down the line of berths as the train ascended slopes. He descended among the people with Republican pamphlets, or express agents sweated through the mob to meet him with fresh boxes of ammunition, buttons and leaflets and flags. He knew all the words of the speeches that would be made and blessed General Howard for an impromptu,

[14] This conversation is summarized from an extended report rendered by my father to the president of the National Surety Company. The report excludes any description of the questions submitted by the important personages to Mr. Hanna, which were naturally confidential as between Mr. Bliss and Mr. Beer. Mr. Hanna's order to the railroads is interesting, as it is dictated to the general managers of the lines, describing the railroads merely by initials, as "C.B. & Q." It was Mr. Beer's only authority for the transportation of the special train, but no manager questioned it, although the traffic of the roads must have been seriously distracted.

now and then. He fed bandsmen jujubes for their
blasted throats and settled a quarrel between a cornet
and a bugle over a wench in Nebraska. He struggled
with the lunacies of reception committees and county
chairmen. He played checkers with General Stewart,
and ruined his palate for a day while testing a cocktail
made by General Sickles. Outside the train a sentiment shouted, sometimes sobbed, as these old men
spoke; inside it, Mr. Beer wondered why anybody
ever went into politics. And were not unlimited mon-
archies the best governments, after all? And were not
tribes in Africa happy without money, tariffs, and
policies? He hated everybody on cold October morn-
ings when General Sickles whistled an air from
Rigoletto or General Howard spoke with feeling of
the wronged Indians. But he was fighting Free Silver.

So the machine swept against the Democrats in an
explosion of pamphlets, blue and gold emblems, placards, and voices. A dynamo whirred inside Mark
Hanna's head. This man knew how to carry West
Virginia? Send him speakers or money to hire them.
Crowds in California liked a lot of music? Give it to
'em! . . . Two or three times in quiet rooms he let
friends know his contempt for New York. It had
taken Jim Hill and Bliss working like hell to make
those sheep see what they must do for him. . . . But
the top of the scare was passing. Money poured out of
stately offices in New York and Boston. The oiled
machine ran smoothly. On October 28th he thanked

Henry Adler for a check, but returned it, writing: "It is all over. Reports are satisfactory just where we wanted them most." He had broken Mr. Bryan's sorceries in the middle states. There was jubilation already among his workers because now the farmers were scared of a panic, if Silver won. He threw away an affidavit brought to him by Bruce Higginson proving that Democrats had bought promises of votes in Louisville. "What the hell of it? They're licked, anyhow!"

On Saturday before election day a parade of one hundred and fifty thousand men passed up Broadway in New York City. It included even the languid millionaire who'd been thinking of a *maisonnette* in Versailles. The city gaped at this monstrous production of so many well-dressed men, so many gilded elephants, so many buttons, so much colored bunting. It was mass production, politically applied, and it stunned watchers. . . . On the night of November 3rd the clubs in Chicago and New York were filled with men who never drank and were not drinking, but gabbled drunkenly among men who spilled champagne on the floors as they waltzed with each other, for it was over; McKinley was elected. Trains were creaking from the cities of Ohio toward Canton, loaded with Republicans who howled. . . . It was all over, but it did not seem true. A funny disbelief ran through the streets. Workmen who had been told that their jobs were lost if Bryan was elected were afraid

163

to go home, as if he might win yet should they leave the telegraph boards or the saloons. And some emotions cracked in the darkness, since the new Lincoln had been madly followed, insanely trusted with a violence which would not be believed today. . . . A little girl watched the bonfires from her father's steps in southern Ohio, sleepily pleased that he had been returned to a petty office in the town, and a German stumbled up to her, mumbling, " Cross — golden cross — cross. . . ." It was the Populist who had been defeated today by her father. She was not afraid. He was a simple, big, dull creature. But when he carried her into a toolshed behind the house, she was scared and began to scream, wailing so that some of the man's friends heard her as they looked for him, worried by his daze at supper. When they broke in the door of the shed, he had driven one nail through her left hand into the door itself: she was to be hung there, an expiation for her father's sins. This golden cross burned his poor mind. He was taken to an asylum. She grew up, and one day watched Mr. Bryan's eyes as he stared at the long scar trailing its purple down her hand on a balustrade in Florida. . . . There were suicides. Embittered men moved from towns to escape chaffing. Reactions showed. Democrats bragged of pleasure in the Silver Knight's defeat. Republicans denounced McKinley.

As for Mr. Hanna, he was now a huge grotesque, an image of mud stained with dollars in the cartoons. He swelled into national legend as a figure of gross wealth, a fantasy of money's power and coldness. Some men had grown fond of him, as men grow fond of a man who will not be beaten, who shows himself resilient in the midst of bad news, hard in a pool of cowardices. But he had been little seen; he was a dot on McKinley's porch, a shape in an office or in a smoky room of some hotel. The sensitive John Hay stopped bantering and wrote his astonishment to a friend in Paris: "He is a born general in politics, perfectly square, honest and courageous, with a *coup d'œil* for the battlefield and a knowledge of the enemy's weak points which is very remarkable . . ." and there were other compliments. But members of a prim minority in the Republican party were much offended. They had not been consulted and, you see, they had not been flattered. The proprieties had not been respected. Mark Hanna simply unveiled the springs on which men are manipulated into greatness.

"He has advertised McKinley," Theodore Roosevelt told my father, "as if he were a patent medicine!"

This was Mr. Hanna's crime. He had openly made use of the full powers of propaganda. He had dealt with politics as if the birth of a company was being arranged. He had thrown a hundred thousand tons of advertising into the nation, against Mr. Bryan's voice, bad logic, and good intentions. He had won, but he had upset these men whose fortunes he had certainly saved from a renewed panic and the domination of inexpert governors. He had made a President, and he had done it visibly. It is hard to forgive such realism. And now they wondered what he would do next.

CHAPTER IV

POWER, OF A KIND

I

Count Cassini, ambassador of the Tsar, arrived in Washington ill-informed as to the political and animal life of the United States. When a little black and white beast minced from some bushes in a garden beyond Georgetown and ladies shrieked, the Russian advanced upon the peril affably and Senator Frye had to take his arm, explaining the inexplicable in frenzied words. Mr. Hanna picked up a pebble and aimed it at the skunk's shameless composure in the pathway.

" By God, he looks like an office-seeker! "

His pebble missed and the party retreated up the gardens. M. Cassini went on talking to a girl from Louisiana. He could not understand her prejudice against Mr. Hanna. Suppose, then, that the man had bribed town councilmen in Cleveland to renew franchises of his tramways? What else was expected of town councils? This was the habit of democracies; you put common people in power and they, of course, hunted bribes and chances of blackmail. *Cela se voit!* . . . Miss Le Blanc retorted that Mr. Hanna was head of a capitalistic conspiracy seeking to control the

167

United States. The foreigner shrugged. What of it? In a democracy the mob controlled or the rich controlled. There was no aristocracy to be responsible. There was no Church to advise. There was no *esprit de corps* of the educated. It came to a question between the mob and the rich. Mr. Hanna appeared to him the best solution of the case, and how amiable a bourgeois, and what a good host, and what a quick wit! Miss Le Blanc gave it up, here, and allowed some other lady to attract the diplomat.

This was the spring of 1899 and Mark Hanna, for two years, had been a Senator. He had lately scandalized a dinner-party by observing that all questions of government in a democracy were questions of money, thus preceding Oswald Spengler in the opinion by two decades.[1] He would presently announce that communism seemed to him a method of increasing incompetence by making sure that nobody had any incentive to progress. Life, he thought, was a matter of competitions. All the men around Lyman Gage's dinner-table had got there by being better at their jobs than someone else. Miss Le Blanc sniffed, and the Senator's brown eyes settled on her.

"This sculptor in Paris you went to see, this man Rod-dinn, now. . . . Did you go to see him because

---

[1] "What is here described as Civilization, then, is the stage of a Culture at which tradition and personality have lost their immediate effectiveness, and every idea, to be actualized, has to be put in terms of money. . . . Democracy is the completed equating of money with political power. . . ." *The Decline of the West*, Volume II, page 485.

he's the top of his profession or just because you wanted to have him say how good-lookin' you are? "

They sparred, the Southern girl declaring that Auguste Rodin had not come to fame through competition and the Northern plutocrat answering that the word " fame " itself implied a competition. But competition meant a hustle for prizes to her and she resented it, as she resented this society of hard diplomats and ladies always asking, " Who *was* she? " as if they were used to meeting people who, once, had been nobodies. And she recoiled from Marcus Hanna with a profound instinct of her vanishing kind; the daughter of a landholding society recognized an enemy of her traditions. Since the Black Death in the fourteenth century these burghers, wielding massed money as a club, had come pounding down doors and climbing walls into the sanctuaries of aristocracy. Etienne Marcel leading the guilds of Paris to slaughter the well-born councilors of the scared Dauphin was the prototype of this conquering class. There were now no sanctuaries left; she had seen that in Europe. Aristocratic society was at the mercy of the financier who permitted its existence as a river permits a congeries of water hyacinth to idle in a warm bayou; the landholders were not important enough to be destroyed, at the end of the nineteenth century. Land, once the title to all privileges of earth, had fallen to be merely one form of speculation. Mr. Hanna did not own fifty acres, although he was a stockholder in the use of

thousands of square miles. But that this powerful adventurer was just a stockholder made him an ogre to
the descendant of a lady whose head was struck off in
1792 because she knew kings. All defensive fictions
of the declining landed power established Mark
Hanna in the wrong set. She looked at him with
horror, and now wonders why.

Mr. Hanna was an exception rather than a full
member of the plutocracy. He did not share the complete superstitions of his tribe. His provincial character exempted Hanna from some ideas of the metropolitan capitalist in Europe. He was, for instance,
not an imperialist in the sense of European and English plutocrats. And he still failed to believe in revolutions. Instead of being high leader of the capitalists
managing the United States, so far as they did, he was
on poor terms with many of them and died suspected
of gross treachery to capitalism by a lot of them. He
did not hold with several of their schemes for controlling peoples. His troubles commenced while he
was advertising William McKinley from his rented
house in Georgia, in the spring of 1896.

As the decadent American sects took up fads, these
were utilized by prudent financiers and industrialists
to mask their own wishes. Miss Frances Willard could
proudly indicate on the roster of contributors to her
Christian Temperance Union names of great factory-
owners. In March of 1896 Mr. Hanna had to face a
committee of Prohibitionists with letters of introduc-

tion signed by a Baptist millionaire. McKinley's backer might truthfully report that he himself had never tried wine until he was forty years old and that his candidate drank almost nothing, but his interview with the committee became a matter of tactful evasions. To get rid of them he asked if they had heard President Cleveland's answer to a like committee: "If you suppress the use of alcohol in America, you must seize Canada or build a string of forts all along the Canadian border." This gloomy challenge made the Prohibitionists argue among themselves until it was time to catch their train. Mr. Hanna shook hands with them, having promised nothing in the way of support for their cause.[2]

But another sectarian influence was not so easily steered out of Mr. Hanna's reception room at Thomasville. The question of Cuban independence brought itself to McKinley's manager half a dozen times before Grover Cleveland ironically presented a war with Spain to his inaugurated successor. Here again was a fad among the religious in small towns and a topic of orators in meetings of the American Protective Association. When some Catholic country had to be cursed, Spain often served as a butt of Protestant indignation. Mr. Hanna would make no formal promise

[2] Another version of Mr. Cleveland's remark is: "If the United States is to be cured of drinking beer, you will have to make a pie-crust of forts on the Canadian border and grab all the ships of Europe," this latter version being made in 1895 to Mrs. Stewart Warner. Mrs. Warner may well have reached Mr. Hanna with this witticism, as she visited Cleveland in 1895 and met Mrs. Hanna in society.

of doing anything for the Cubans, but he was put strongly on warning that something might have to be done, and he talked to McKinley frequently on the choice of consuls in the Caribbean countries. Three autographs dated in January of 1897 show him refusing consular posts near Cuba and one of these, addressed simply to "Dear Jones," contains a closing sentence almost rhetorical. "God forbid," he wrote, "that the United States be called on to intervene on behalf of these miserable people but if that need should arise it is to be hoped that our representatives in the region of Cuba will all be able men. . . ." Dear Jones, whoever he was, cannot have liked this eloquence, as it implied a doubt of his friend Mr. Huntley's ability. Mr. Huntley — whoever he was — would not do for a consulate in the tropics. But, as Theodore Roosevelt testifies in his memoirs, Mr. McKinley did find able men for the posts in Latin America. One of them was fairly ordered by Mark Hanna to leave a more profitable job for the consular service. He could not afford it? Very well, Mr. Hanna would take charge of his small capital and get it invested so that he need not worry, and he has not worried since 1897.

But able consuls in the tropics would not put off this question of Spain and her bullied colony. Mr. Hanna morosely grunted in Cleveland that the United States must not have any damn trouble with anybody. His language in February was heated by a social event, for it pleased a rich ninny in New York to

172

give a ball so consummately advertised that it was
talked of by positive princes abroad, while starving
workmen fed at the bread-lines a few blocks from the
hot hotel where ladies and stockbrokers sweated in
their costumes, for one brilliant night. This did not
gratify Mr. Hanna. His annoyance had, as so often,
a doubled reason. He disliked the host of this entertainment, and the whole thing struck him as cruelly
reckless. It would serve the New Yorker right if some
terrorist heaved a bomb into the ballroom and blew
dancers to spangles and red paste. "*Theory of a
Leisure Class?*" he grunted, staring at a book in the
library of Cushman Davis. "What's their theory?
More damn fancy-dress balls?" The discipline of his
mother's ancestors wrought in Mr. Hanna: men ought
to work. Hearing that an agreeable young artist who
sketched Mrs. Hanna that winter would paint perhaps only three portraits in six months, he rubbed an
ear. What did the boy do with the rest of his time?

His own time was well taken up. Office-seekers had
at him, now, in profusions of six or ten the day. The
majestic tariff bill was being manufactured beforehand. The smart men rallied and came to call on Mr.
Hanna with astonishing projects in mind, monstrous
concessions of land to be dealt out by the government
to the right people and quaintly arranged swindles of
many kinds. Some of these propositions amused him
so that he talked of them to his friends, and it can be
certainly recorded that, about February of 1897, Mr.

Hanna was offered shares in a company which proposed to secure from the government the whole western seacoast of Florida, with Mr. Hanna's assistance. Yet most of his time was taken by the office-seekers, and, before any announcement of Mr. McKinley's Cabinet had been made from Canton, cold information circulated in the East: Hanna was not doing the right thing by the metropolis.

The Eastern magnates were placidly neglected in the formation of the new President's immediate council. It is true that Cornelius Bliss, of New York, was made Secretary of the Interior after the appointment had been refused by John McCook, and that Theodore Roosevelt was to be Assistant Secretary of the Navy. But Mr. Bliss was not warmly friends with the Republican machine of New York, and Mr. Roosevelt was an amusing oddity who could be jocosely presented to strangers as " our police commissioner " or as Douglas Robinson's brother-in-law. He had no profession; his father, a secondary financier of the last generation, had left the vivid young man an income. He was erudite, as these Americans understood erudition, but that did him no good in the clubs, and he wrote books, which seemed strange. . . . These two appointments were all that New York got from Mr. Hanna's friend. The Secretary of State was old John Sherman, of Ohio, and his first assistant was William Day, also of Ohio. The Secretary of War was Russell Alger, of Michigan. The Attorney General was a Cali-

fornian and, worse, a Roman Catholic. The Postmaster General came from Baltimore. The Secretary
of Agriculture was a Scotch person out of Iowa, and
— unbelievably! — the Secretary of the Treasury was
a Democrat from Chicago, Lyman Gage. New York
had certainly expected that Hanna would take the
Treasury for his province. His own friends imagined
that he might ask for the post. But he said to William
Saunders, " Me in the Cabinet? All the newspapers
would have cartoons of me selling the White House
kitchen stove! " [3]

He had plenty of reasons for preferring to be a Senator. He must attend to the pruning of the tariff bill
at close range. He knew that the power of declaring
war lay with Congress. He liked the notion of being a
Senator. So he became a Senator, filling John Sherman's place by appointment. The appointment lagged;
Mr. Asa Bushnell, Governor of Ohio, hesitated for
some awkward days and had to be civilly advised by
Senator Joseph Foraker that Mr. Hanna must be appointed. It was done. He arrived at Washington and
was sworn in at once. IIis tall hat shimmered with all
those other hats of solemn gentlemen behind Mr. Mc-
Kinley and Mr. Cleveland on the platform as the new
President took oath of office.

[3] Mr. McKinley did offer the Postmaster General's place to Mr. Hanna
in a preserved letter, and Hanna refused it. Several memoirs and notes on the
period state that he wished to be Secretary of the Treasury, giving no
authority for the statement. Mr. Croly makes no such point in the biography,
and the testimony of Mr. Saunders, Mr. Leonard Hanna, and Mr. Joseph
Kimball contradicts the legend.

The exaltation of John Sherman into the Cabinet
was a privy scandal of Washington that spring. Dis-
tinction and experience had nothing to do with the
case, in gossip. Mr. Sherman was hauled up to make
place for Mr. Hanna in the Senate. But Mr. Sherman
was offered the State Department before the tenth of
January, and Mr. Hanna did not refuse a cabinet post
until the middle of February. There was no question
of a sudden lust for governmental powers on Hanna's
part. A deeper motive was apparent to the retiring
President. " I suspect," said Mr. Cleveland to Mr.
Victor Ward, "that Hanna knows McKinley likes
popularity too well." Mr. Hanna was placing himself
where he could correct that tendency. Acts that might
strain McKinley's will in case of a needed veto need
never pass the Senate. His affection for the President
was not blinding Mr. Hanna to some possibilities. He
might be useful; he would be powerful.

Whatever he was to be, he was not noisy. Mr.
Hanna appeared in the Senate and sat there, correctly
sedate in his chair, much gazed upon by visitors in the
gallery. He was obviously a plump man in his sixtieth
year who seemed short unless he lifted his head to
stare across the Senators at a speaker. The caricatured
Hanna, described as a braggart in the journals, turned
out to be a blunt, quietly amused personage at dinner-
parties. He might get so enthusiastic as to say that
Mr. McKinley's private secretary, George Cortelyou,
was a fine boy or that he liked the Vice President's

wife. Still, his monotonous voice did not rise in the Senate and a lady who met Mark Hanna at the end of March 1897 remembers mostly his silence.

Timidly invading Washington, Miss Edith Sims and her mother managed to find an Episcopal church on the morning after they arrived at the capital, and sat observing this society. The widow and her daughter had been to Constantinople, to Abu-Simbel down the Nile, and to Copenhagen. But they had never explored the United States. A trip to Syracuse in 1870 convinced Mrs. Sims that she was not quite safe far from New York. She came to Washington because her eldest daughter's husband had been transferred to duty at the War Department and she wanted to be in the capital when Marion and the babies got there, escaping from wild San Francisco.

Miss Sims presently was watching a lady seated three pews away who looked back at her, or at her mother, with a familiar sort of smile. She was not young, but she was handsome, erect, and pleasant in a somber dress. She had a little the look of those German great ladies one saw at Baden-Baden, surrounded by mussy, shy daughters and dogs. She smiled, though, in a special fashion and the girl knew that her mother was watching the other lady's face. Kate Richardson and Lottie Rhodes hunted each other through the masks imposed by thirty-five years of living. When the choir boys had taken themselves down the aisle, Mrs. Sims and Mrs. Marcus Alonzo

177

Hanna met with the sentimental crash expected of such reunions in the latter nineteenth century. Miss Edith was duly kissed and was told — truthfully — that she looked like Mrs. Hanna's youngest. She is still sometimes asked on trains if she is not Mrs. Medill McCormick.

Senator Hanna was waiting for his wife at the hotel, with another white waistcoat and top hat beside his Sunday clothes. It was a thrill to meet Mr. John Hay, the new ambassador to England, and to be enveloped in his bantering conversation. Mrs. Sims had met him, somewhere in Europe, and he pretended with great skill to remember all about her.

Marcus Hanna pretended nothing. He was utterly silent, with his cigar. But Mr. Hay babbled agreeably. He had been dancing in and out of Washington for two weeks, talking to Mr. McKinley " around senators and through office-seekers," and now he must go to luncheon with John Sherman. He said to Mrs. Hanna, " Smile at me, Mona Lisa, as I go to this ordeal."

" John Hay, if you call me that again I'll be sorry Mark didn't let them have Whitelaw Reid made ambassador to England instead of you."

Senator Hanna grunted. Mr. Hay's eyebrows twitched. Mrs. Hanna colored and then whispered that she didn't think anybody heard her. The diplomat said it didn't matter, and went away. When she had her newly found old playmate upstairs in her rooms,

178

Mrs. Hanna chuckled. In Washington, she said, you had to pretend not to know what everybody knew, and, thank heaven, she was going home to Cleveland tonight for some days. Then she began to talk about the Senator.

"She was charming about him," says Miss Sims. "I wrote down some of her stories a few days later in an irregular diary I kept in those days. But she was so upset about his health. She asked us how we thought he looked. I am afraid we were not of much comfort to her, as we had never seen him before. She said candidly that she was afraid he would overwork himself trying to manage the Republican party in Cleveland and do his work in the Senate. My mother knew absolutely nothing about politics, and neither did I. One of us innocently asked if Senator Foraker could not help Mr. Hanna in the Senate. Mrs. Hanna had to explain that Mr. Foraker and Mr. Hanna were hardly on speaking terms and that Ohio was divided between their two factions. But she spoke very decently of Mr. Foraker. She said that Mr. Hanna had been rather tactless toward him at the Republican National Convention" — of 1888 — "where their quarrel began. Then she quite broke out in regard to some of the politicians in Ohio. I find in my diary: 'Mrs. Hanna said that she regarded many of Mr. H.'s associates in politics as not worth his attention. They fawn on him for campaign expenses and ask for favors while they envy him. Interesting story: One of these politicians asked Mr. H. to have a street in Cleveland paved past a certain point. Mr. H. refused. The man then said, "I have helped to have you granted franchises for your street-car lines and now you will do nothing for me." Mr. H. answered that it did not cost the city a penny to grant him a franchise, but that it would cost a hundred thousand dollars to pave this street, and that the man wanted it done to increase the value of some real estate. Mrs. H. said that this man had now turned into a bitter enemy of Mr. H. She does not believe he will be really happy in Washington, away from his friends in Cleveland.' She told several other instances of these enmities that had come about through the Senator's refusal of some political favor. I cannot pretend to recollect them. My mother asked her if Mr. Hanna had not great power over Mr. McKinley. Mrs. Hanna said that he had power, of a kind. I remember the qualifying phrase so distinctly. . . ."

Next day Miss Sims was taking snapshots of the White House from its gateway when Senator Hanna bustled past her. He said, " I'm Eliza crossing the ice, and there come the bloodhounds." He fairly trotted up the drive. The girl saw some gentlemen hastening toward her and was alarmed, although they did nothing when they got to the gate. They settled into a watchful group, strolling to and fro on the sidewalk as they waited for Mr. Hanna's outcoming; she had her first chance of observing the office-seeker's prowl, that gait combining the hungry wolf's trot with the prouder pace of a righteous woman about to vindicate her claim to a new frock.

Mr. Hay, then, went to his duty in England and commenced the delicate performance of the task to which he had been appointed, while, in New York, men wondered why he had been appointed at all. Senator Hanna remained in Washington, beating off the bloodhounds and bluntly telling his private callers that the Dingley tariff was not an invitation to keep foreign goods out of the American market. "Mr. McKinley stands for protection, not exclusion," he told a furious maker of surgical instruments. The man yelled that he had contributed ten thousand dollars to McKinley's campaign fund, and this was how he was paid! Mr. Hanna's mouth became a line in his hot face. He shot a pointed finger at the loud person and shouted back, "Got your receipt? . . . You never turned in a cent!" His memory of fact was dangerous. A joke passed out around Washington. If you were claiming something from Hanna, you must have a receipt to show him.

The tariff was lifted. Mr. McKinley sent off his useless commission to Europe on behalf of bimetallism, as he had promised the Silver Republicans. There was a trivial improvement of business at large, but no boom. American confidence had been poisoned since 1890 and men of affairs did not brag of American opportunities as their fathers had bragged under

Grant. Wall Street showed its discontent all summer
long and, in the autumn, there were rumors of protests
made by big men to the President, although what they
protested to Mr. McKinley is now obscure.[4] Then, in
October, Mr. Asa Barnes, lunching in the region of
Wall Street with an importer of tobacco, heard the
voice of Mr. Edward Lauterbach proclaiming from a
table close to him that Mr. Hanna was to be dispensed
with. It had been decided between a boss in New York
and a boss in Pennsylvania that Mark Hanna was
no good. He had not got some bills passed in which
big men took an interest. He had loaded all these
Westerners into the Cabinet. It was risky, said the
agreeable Mr. Lauterbach, because Hanna was not so
foolish as he looked and might not take his removal in
peace. But he was to be spanked and returned to his
coal bins in Cleveland.

To Asa Barnes this was awful. Mark Hanna had
always been his fancy of a terrestrial god. Mark Hanna
gave him dollars when he was a little boy in Cleveland
for carrying notes to Miss Charlotte Augusta Rhodes.
Mark Hanna noticed him slaving in a bank and
planted him on better pay in the office of a coal mine.
In 1894, when his small business in New York was
nearly gone, a check had come from Hanna and Company, at the dramatic last moment, with a message

[4] I judge from a note of Mr. Abner McKinley to my father that
various steel interests had expected an enormous increase of the Navy to be
made directly and that some representation of this kind was made to the
President through Mr. Long, the Secretary of the Navy.

telling him to hang on. Mark Hanna had limped out of a group of dignitaries in the autumn of 1896 to cross the lobby of the Holland House and shake hands with Mr. Barnes, as though the partner in a mere tobacco shop was someone very grand indeed. So the voice of Mr. Lauterbach sent Asa Barnes to the nearest telephone. Mr. Hanna was not in his office at Cleveland, but on a train somewhere. The tale was told to Mr. Leonard Hanna, who answered, "So we hear!" and then spoke busily about Wall Street's politicians. Mr. Barnes felt better. Christmas passed. Then, after New Year's Day, newspapers flashed headings. There was a revolt at Columbus, Ohio, against Marcus Hanna. State senators and assemblymen pledged to return Mr. Hanna to the Senate, by election, had fused with Democrats and Silver Republicans. The Governor and the mayor of Cleveland were mixed up in the fuss. All Ohio was boiling. Mr. Barnes packed his clothes and fled on the next train to Columbus.

When practical politicians turn fantastic, they outdo poets. Mr. Robert McKisson was a practiced and affable politician who wanted to be a mayor of Cleveland and applied to Mr. Hanna for backing. Mr. Hanna declined him. He had no dislike of Mr. McKisson, but he preferred to back someone else. However, in 1895, Mr. McKisson got the Republicans of the big city to make him mayor, for the truth is that Mark Hanna's control of Cleveland was never so absolute as legend asserts, and Robert McKisson was then able to begin the contrivance of a personal machine for his own ends. This man is now such a shadow that the fact of his next performance seems sheer lunacy. He came to Columbus in the first week of January 1898, and there told a meeting of Democratic state legislators that he would have to be a Republican "before the people," but that, if they would send him to the Senate in Washington, he would act upon the principles of the Democratic party as set forth in the Chicago convention of 1896. This turned the stomachs of three Democrats and they refused to vote for the providential secret convert to Democracy. But Mr. McKisson was handsome and his voice soothed the rest of the caucus. On Monday, January 10th, it was known that he was the candidate for Senator against Marcus Hanna.

The details of this political cinema are fully given in Mr. Croly's biography of Mark Hanna except one feature of the muddle which was plain only to men who knew the Republican party in New York. Items of the party's metropolitan machine appeared in bars and hotels at Columbus, but their function was not discerned by Mr. Hanna's volunteers from the East. As Mr. Asa Barnes and Mr. Walter Held ranged the streets, they encountered these strangers, but never at Mr. Hanna's rooms in the hotel, where he smoked among his friends. For the five days ending with January 11th these spectators were visible. They were not helping Mr. Hanna's supporters to keep the wobbling assemblymen in line. They stood about. Mr. Held got in conversation with one of them and made nothing of his answers. He was just "watching the fight."

It was a fight. There are still five men living who tackled the legislators for Mr. Hanna, and none of these used money. Mr. Lee Durstine operated on an assemblyman from Union County by means of the waverer's son; Mr. Barnes cornered Silver Republicans in bars and raved at them; Mr. Walter Held and his brother were effective as men are effective who stand six feet three and have thundering throats; another survives who had a pious uncle in the opposition and found the old man reasonable when it was explained to him that Mr. Hanna did not drink whisky. As for the rest of the doubtful voters, they may have been paid to be loyal to their pledges, or they may have been cowed by another force. The voice of the people is at least the voice of the people. All that week the people sifted into Columbus, and Hanna's friends amazedly heard farmers and Silver Republicans of the small towns demanding that Mark Hanna, the Cleveland plutocrat, be returned to his seat in the Senate.

Why? It had happened in September and October. Senator Hanna came before the plain people not as a smiling image in a white waistcoat behind other speakers on a draped platform, but as a speaker. He could not make an oration. He stood barking out short sentences at the crowds, challenging anybody to prove

him an enemy of the labor unions or to deny that he
paid the best wages in Ohio for a day's work. Farmers
grinned when the Senator rubbed a fist on his red ear
or said, " Wait a minute! " as he stooped to pull up
a loose garter. He went on in this simple way: " Mr.
Bryan said just one thing in his big speech at Chicago
last year that strikes me as true. He said that farmers
and workingmen are business men just as much as
any banker or lawyer. Well, that's true. I like that. If
you men will study business methods and learn how
to look after your interests we won't have to hear any
more wishy-washy stuff about how Wall Street's
abusin' you. Now Johnny McClean went to the trouble
to bring Mr. Bryan all this long way from Nebraska
— hope he got a pass on the railroad for him — to tell
you that Mark Hanna is a labor crusher and God
knows what all. My brothers and I employ six thousand men. Some of them are here in this crowd. Let
any of them come forward and say that he hasn't had
a square deal from M. A. Hanna and Company and
I'll shut up! " It was not oratory, but the people stood
silent under it and applauded it. They had heard Mr.
Bryan's rhythmic nobility a few days before, in these
same towns. But here was this plain man's frank
attack on their pride. Were they not business men?
" Bryan's mistake," says a witness, " was a constant appeal to self-pity. Mr. Hanna sounded grumpy
and pretty bored with the whole thing. It may be
strange that this was effective, but I certainly think

186

it was. . . ." One must judge by the result. In the first week of January some of these plain people came to Columbus and cried in the streets that they wanted Mark Hanna sent back to Washington. Legislators heard, roared at them in the familiar speech of their town, that they had to vote for Hanna. This influence was unpaid, and it persisted through Monday, even after Democratic papers charged Mr. Hanna with attempting to bribe an assemblyman from Cincinnati through an agent.

Everything now had been done. A legislator had been kidnapped and drugged. There had been fights in bars and alleys. Armed guards were posted throughout the capital of Ohio. On Tuesday the legislators voted. A handkerchief waving from the steps of the State House announced to watchers in the street that Mr. Hanna was elected Senator, and the signal passed to his hotel. He said, " I'm too fat for a Juliet," staring down into the crowd. Then he sent word to Mr. McKisson that a baby in diapers would be able to beat him if he tried to be mayor of Cleveland again. Mr. John Farley, who defeated Mr. McKisson in the autumn of 1899, was no baby, of course, but the weakness with which the Republicans supported Mr. McKisson was notable, and Mr. Farley's friends had a lot of money to spend.

As to the spectators from New York, they had disappeared when Walter and Philip Held made a round of the hotels that evening, collecting some small bets.

Four or five days later Mr. Edward Lauterbach idled up to Cornelius Bliss, lunching at the Lawyers' Club in New York with certain friends, and told the Secretary of the Interior that he knew a couple of men who were worried for fear Uncle Mark had been hearing nasty stories about them.

"They might send him a bunch of violets and a pretty note," Mr. Bliss suggested.

"I told them not to do it," Mr. Lauterbach said, "but they wouldn't listen to reason."

"You might tell Tom Platt to send a hymn book and some cigars along," Bliss laughed.

Everybody grinned around the table, all these powerful men were amused, watching the machinery twinkle. Power had become their amusement, though journals talked of their mania for money. Some of them had no money at all, but they had power. They would spend a month of intrigue on finding a place in a governmental bureau for a widow out in Oregon, and the point was not that they liked the widow. They had never seen the woman. But it was something to do, a minute display of force and craft.

They had talents for other games than this. One of them sang well and collected rare ballads in all tongues; one of them had five thousand books on history, bound in old Spanish leathers or Indian brocades and spun a theory of civilizations in a lisping drawl; one of them fascinated Bryce and afterwards Lord Haldane by the gay agility of his talk. But America

188

did not summon them to show their power otherwise
than among the machines erected as emblems of success. They worked. Leisure was for fools, women, and
failures. And work, since they so believed, was their
pleasure.

Their bodies thickened. They died at ages of fifty-
two and fifty-three. They swooned on bright tables at
meetings of directors and were lugged down to slick
private cabs waiting on the slope beside Trinity
Church. Courage might shred under the shock of a
favorite daughter's death, and they were loaded on
steamships for a weary trip abroad. They took no exercise and looked disapprovingly at John Jacob Astor
sipping white wine at lunch while they tried to fire
their energies with the alcohol of sweet food. They
lurched off to Turkish baths where masseurs kneaded
life into them before an evening conference in the
yellow clubrooms beside Fifth Avenue. But this was
their pleasure, although they did not live to explain
it in memoirs. Few of them had time to make their
wills, death was so importunate at the end, introduced
by a secretary's scream or the rush of servants in some
lobby to a tottering bulk in furs and a rolling hat.
Wives shivered; doctors cursed them. They might
drag out two months in Europe and be seen busy with
American newspapers at Karlsbad or Vichy. But their
game went on, a tangling movement of letters and
messengers on the way to Washington or Cleveland
or, later, to Oyster Bay. Most of them wanted nothing

out of it save this thrill of making a point, an official
had been created, or a bill, about which they did not
care, had been killed in Congress. " See," one of them
shouted to Stuyvesant Fish, " I got my man in! " He
had put a collector of customs at a trivial port, to spite
Thomas Platt, after spending ten thousand dollars on
mighty dinners in Washington. This was pleasure, to
be able to wave a telegram at Stuyvesant Fish in a
club.

One of them saw Hanna buried and then gave up
the sport. He roamed, and came yearly to a dive in
Budapest where gypsy violins told him stories while
he sat out nights in the circle of his mistresses and
their complacent husbands. One of them had a house
in Spain and a room hung with photographs of the
men he had put in office. And one of them, in much
the finest, began to telephone one afternoon. His dry,
Western voice sped through wires into offices, scaring
old clerks as he summoned the dead to a meeting. A
friend was told and brought a doctor in a closed car
to the door on Broadway, then intruded and found
the tall man raging. Some fool in the central at Cleveland was trying to tell him that Mark Hanna had
died in 1904! But this was 1896! The machinery of
his mind had reversed, as it broke, to the autumn of
1896. He could be persuaded that Hanna was in town,
in rooms at the Holland House; the doctor and a
hidden needle filled with sleep were waiting in the car.
After three days he joined the rest of them. . . . But

they had a good time. This was their pleasure. They had power, of a kind.

II

A superstition followed Mark Hanna from Cleveland into Washington; he was " lucky." His disasters turned out well. If a client of his ship-building company could not pay for six vessels built at great cost, it would prove that the client had an iron mine which Mr. Hanna could develop for him and get back his money in no time. That the matter of finding capital for the development of the mine in a panicky year was very difficult and that it took brains to do anything with the mine at all were ignored in Uncle Mark's legend. The " Hanna luck " saw him through anything, and this luck was communicable. He lent or gave money to displaced workmen on the streets of his town in the winter of 1894. Some of them saved a silver dollar or a dime from his gift for a luck piece. As he marched back into the Senate in 1898, elected to succeed himself, a Western Senator leaned out of his seat to touch the jinni's shoulder for luck. Men smiled, but Mr. Hanna held a reception in the Marble Room at the end of the day's business. The affair at Columbus had echoed back favorably to these legislators. Senator Hanna was now Senator by election, after an awful fight for it, and they heard truly that he had shown good humor and pluck. "People are glad to have Warwick back," Thomas Reed wrote to a lady. "We need anybody divinely blessed with common sense at this time. . . ."

But Marcus Hanna needed something more than common sense, as the Congress assembled in 1898. He needed all those things possessed by Mr. William Jennings Bryan, arts of appeal and emotional display, the music of sentimental phrase, physical charm. He hadn't them. He was a business man in politics, able when it came to nursing the great tariff act along and a good persuader in conference. For once he wished to be an orator. He must try to head something back, cool a charge of the plain people, and every quality of his equipment was wrong. He had already been dramatized in the journals as Wall Street's man in Washington, and Wall Street was anxious to have no trouble with Spain, so the journalists declared. There was trouble with Spain already. Riots broke out in Havana; loyalists and a rabble of Spanish officials paraded the white streets yelling against McKinley, who dared to interfere in the island's government, and cheering General Weyler, who had established the re-concentrado camps, in which people died of starvation and stank of scurvy. Weyler had been recalled by the new premier, Sagasta, in the autumn of 1897 and hazy promises of autonomy were made to the Cubans, much too late. The insurgents would have full independence. Professor Sumner's outline of colonial history was filled: the island had been plundered and was now Spain's enemy.

Mr. Hanna read no foreign language and so was spared the exposition of European statesmanship which remains amply recorded in the journals and published correspondence of 1898. He was even able to maintain, up to the tenth of April, some belief in the good sense of Europe. His mind cut into the facts before the end of January. " I have just seen Mr. Hanna," Henry Adler wrote to his half sister, not knowing she had left Frankfort to join him, " and he seems to believe that a good deal of the sentiment against America is kicked up by financial elements in Germany and France. . . ." This was not what other Senators and members of the Cabinet believed. They believed and said that decadent, aristocratic Europe was trying to uphold monarchic Spain against American democracy. Under this babbling about chivalrous Castile they did not perceive plutocratic imperialists annoyed with America's invasion of a colonial question. The United States must not be allowed to trifle with empires; Spain's control of a colony must not be criticized. It was dangerous precedent. It was insolence. French royalists, Austrian landholders in debt to German banks, and the German highborn imperialists rallied to this whistle. The *Saturday Review* fell delirious in London and published marvels of that oddly vulgar invective which supplies the place of dialectic among English and American specialists in conservative refinement. But the continental show outglittered any British

HANNA

invention and is still quite interesting in its evasion
of the patent facts: Cuba was in a condition of anarchy, its agriculture and industry both wrecked and
its people two thirds adjudged rebels.

What European observers did not care to know was
that American morality had become emotional again.
The music of the Abolitionists pulsed up, after years,
and the infecting notion of rescuing the oppressed
flavored sermons. Religion, or rather the Protestant
sects, had gathered the suffering Cubans into a topic
of sentimental value. The plain people stirred, in the
West, as the awfulness of Catholic Spain was revealed
with pungency to ladies in black silk who wanted to
believe every word of it. Mr. Hanna could beat down
a Bryan, but he could not cope with women who
were asking the pastor to write to Mr. McKinley
about Cuba, and making children sign petitions to be
sent to Congressmen. "You have no idea," Abner
McKinley wrote on January 26th, "of the pressure on William from religious people. . . ." [5] Letters
from English Methodists reached the White House
while an American squadron gathered at the tip of
Florida, in the last week of January. Before the
first of February, Mr. Hanna was denounced in a
Baptist church of San Francisco for holding Mr. Mc-
Kinley back. "By God," he said, "Christians are remarkable!"

Statesmen in Washington were also remarkable.

[5] Abner McKinley to Walter McCabe.

194

A candid war party existed in the capital and gained allies in the Cabinet. Simple jingos herded with humanitarians. Cuba must be free. They learned how to pronounce the phrase "*Cuba libre*" from officials of the Spanish ministry and mispronounced it at dinners. Henriette Adler heard it garbled in the heat of a reception on the night of February 9th as she backed from the active elbow of a burly gentleman until she was against a wall and could not escape his flailing sleeve. His teeth flashed and his eyeglasses sparkled. He was alarming in the force of his objection to Mr. McKinley's uncertainty. When his elbow ripped a silken rose and some gauze clean from Miss Adler's shoulder, she said, "*Mon dieu!*" and this verbal velocity was now aimed at her. He spoke in French with speed, abandoning all the nouns of his apology, but making himself clear. Miss Adler liked him.

A lady called Nannie had a pin. Senator Orville Platt and Senator Cushman Davis made themselves a screen for the committee on reparations. Mr. Hanna came trundling down the room to see what was being done to his guest, and then the talk was a vortex. Miss Adler saw that these men had a point to make with the Senator. The battleship *Maine* lay in the harbor of Havana, sent there to notify Spain that American citizens in Cuba were not to be molested. Senator Davis seemed to want Mr. Hanna to agree with him on the value of this move. The burly charmer with the teeth thought it a bully idea to send the *Maine* to Havana. Mr. Hanna had no opinion, but stood with his chin sunk on his white tie, staring at the talkers.

They seemed queer to Miss Adler, chattering as though Europe did not exist for them. Surely they knew that France and Germany would resent any assault on Spain's imperial property? She said so, quoting what she had heard in Paris two weeks ago. It did not seem to impress the man with the teeth or the bald Senator from Minnesota. Let France and Germany resent it, said Senator Davis. The burly gentleman didn't think France serious in her talk. But Spain must be kicked out of Cuba.

" I hope to see the Spanish flag and the English flag gone from the map of North America before I'm sixty! "

Senator Hanna stared and drawled, " You're crazy, Roosevelt! What's wrong with Canada? "

The Assistant Secretary of the Navy had not said that anything was wrong with Canada except its English flag. But he was in a state of mind about the foreign flags on American soil just then and had written his prejudice that day to his friend Moore. Mrs. Hanna explained Mr. Roosevelt to her husband's guest as they drove across Washington. He was really amusing and his wife was one of the nicest women in Washington, but he did get violent about things. Mr. Hanna grunted behind his cigar that, thank God, they hadn't put Roosevelt in the State Department, as Cushman Davis wanted done last year.

"We'd be fighting half the world," he brooded.

He sat with Miss Adler in the restaurant of the Arlington over a pint of champagne and asked questions about the feeling in Paris. Her half brother always spoke of Marcus Hanna as a comedian, but this grave, worried man of sixty said nothing funny. He had not liked the sending of the *Maine* to Havana. It was "waving a match in an oil-well for fun." And her reports of European opinion depressed him. We never got credit for our motives, he said. And what did she think of the French army? . . . They talked a long time.

"He was very frank, it seemed to me then. He said that Mr. McKinley had realized the possibility of this situation before he was elected and would do all he could to keep the peace. His own aversion to a war was very plain. He said the economic condition of the country was just beginning to improve and that a war was undesirable from every point of view. I have an impression that he hoped for an intervention of England, which was generally friendly, and some of the other Powers. Of course I had the European attitude in the question and thought that the reports of cruelty in Cuba were gross exaggerations. But Mr. Hanna assured me that reports of the American consuls and travellers bore out the worst statements. He was strongly in favor of getting the Cubans freed. But he said five or six times, 'I hate the thought of a war. You don't know what a big war is like. Suppose the French come in with Spain against us?' . . ."

This notion of powerful allies joining Spain oppressed him. The *Maine* was destroyed on February 15th. On February 23rd Mr. Hanna's secretary telephoned to Mr. William Collins Beer, asking him to come at once to Mr. Hanna's office. The Senator abruptly ordered his caller to get back to New York and find out there what the biggest international bankers thought of the French sympathy for Spain. But Mr. Beer had come to Washington to pry, through the State Department, into the history of a bank in South America, for the New York Life Insurance Company. Very well, Mr. Hanna would wire the damn thing's pedigree to John McCall before Mr. Beer could get to New York. He did so. Three days later, Mr. Beer reported that J. P. Morgan and Company did not take the French newspapers seriously, but that something might be feared from Germany in the way of interference. . . . In this transfer of opinions it seemed strange that Mark Hanna, Wall Street's tool, had to appeal to capitalists for opinion through the attorney of an insurance company. Why had not Mr. Hanna telephoned to Mr. Morgan?

"Too many damn ears on the wire!"

Men came into the smoky room. War had started for some of these legislators. There was a terrific oration on the strength of the Spanish fleet. Mr. Hanna listened, fiddling his cigar between his lips, until he had to grin.

"Bah! We can lick Spain in six months!"

But nobody believed that. The journals said differently. Mr. Hanna was left to his delusions and his cigar. The excited men walked down to the bar of the Raleigh, where it was argued that Mr. Hanna would force a war for the sake of his friends in the steel business. He gave out an interview, in two days, implying that he wanted no war just now. But next week Mr. Beer returned to Washington and found theorists in the Raleigh bar assuring each other that Mr. Hanna was trying to force a war for the sake of his friends in the railroad business. Then, in the first week of March, Mark Hanna became an unpatriotic demon trying to prevent a war in the name of Wall Street. He was nightly stealing into the White House and turning the President against the cause of freedom. He was willing to let Spain keep Cuba. He had not said any of this to anybody, but they were all sure of it in the Raleigh's bar.

Mr. Beer's head spun. He heard in Washington that Wall Street was solidly lined up against a war with Spain. He retired to New York and men grabbed his arm as he entered his club, asking what this insane Hanna meant by trying to head off the war? He noted that the solidarity of Wall Street was imperfect. John Jacob Astor wore a buttonhole of red, white, and blue flowers. John Gates, Thomas Fortune Ryan, William

Rockefeller, and Stuyvesant Fish all were sounded, before March 24th, and were found to be feeling militant.[6] On March 28th it was announced by George Walbridge Perkins that John Pierpont Morgan was to put his yacht at the service of the government and that the financier saw nothing to be gained by more talk of arbitration. The news spread in the Lawyers' Club at noon, and men thought of their grown sons.

But McKinley waited. Mr. Hanna smoked cigars and growled in his office. Let the damn brokers go war crazy if they liked, this thing could be stopped. England was friendly. The Powers ought to interfere. Then the Pope made an error in dealing with the United States. He appealed to Spain and her antagonist in hope that Eastertime would not be defiled by an outbreak between two Christian nations. Archbishop Ireland went to Washington to plead for peace. Protestant pastors at once saw a profound danger to American independence which they must avert, and came to Washington by dozens. "Well," said Mr. Hanna, "that just about settles it!"

On April 7th the ambassadors of six nations, led

---

[6] The great life-insurance companies made this inquiry. My father interviewed Colonel Astor and Mr. Ryan. It was his opinion that the steady opponents of the war among financiers were simply the life insurance men and small bankers. A carbon copy of a letter to his friend Dudley Evans of Wells, Fargo and Company, dated March 26th, 1898, says: "Nothing but war talk. Hill seems to be the only prominent railroad man who is fighting for peace. The Pennsylvania crowd say that nothing can be done to stop it since C. K. Davis and Alger are pushing the president. It can not be stopped from this end [New York] and I do not think Hanna can stop it in the Senate."

by Sir Julian Pauncefote, presented a vacuous note
to Mr. McKinley, stating that they hoped further
negotiations would restore order in Cuba and maintain peace. The President longed for something else,
a deliberate offer of arbitration by a council of the
Powers. He replied civilly, twisting and reversing the
phrases of the ambassadorial twaddle, but presenting
a counter comment on the note's evasion. Their ex-
cellencies, he hinted, had not observed that a humane
cause was at stake in Cuba. This was rather hard on
the English diplomat, who had prevented a much
more insolent note, it is said, by informing the Con-
tinentals that England would not assent to an attempt
at coercion of the United States. The nations now
symbolically withdrew and Mr. McKinley waited for
fresh news from the civilized Old World in the morning. None came. Europe washed its hands of him and
his affairs, he must have thought. . . . About noon
a letter arrived in Mr. Hanna's office, where Joseph
Kimball watched the Senator playing solitaire on his
desk. Hanna read the line from the White House and
made a noise inside his mouth, a swallowed oath. He
was beyond discretion. God damn the lot of them!
Why wouldn't they offer to arbitrate?

Here a high statesman in the White House would
have turned on Europe and called for arbitration,
ignoring all the rant of the French and German newspapers, asserting the value of Cuba's case and forcing
the tale of Spanish stupidity on a table in full light.

201

But McKinley had never been abroad. He sensed that
Europe was trying to bully him, but he does not seem
to have known that Europe could be bullied back. And
he was an American. The will of majorities had a
special meaning for him. War cries banged in his ears.
Roosevelt had said across a dinner-table to Mark
Hanna, "We are *going* to have this war!" Cushman
Davis, Alger, Frye, a mob of Congressmen and officials, his own brother, and his friend Herman Kohlsaat were telling him to go ahead. He delayed. He
would not send his message to the Capitol unless he
heard that all Americans were out of Cuba. Then, on
April 11th, he sent what it wanted to Congress, and
so declined into an artist in popular government.

"If Congress had started this," Hanna said, "I'd
break my neck to stop it." But his own President had
let Congress have the lead. He sat glum in the Senate,
approving when Teller of Colorado insisted that the
Cubans must govern themselves when they were freed.
He voted with the majority and walked through the
Marble Room, staring at the floor, when the matter
was concluded on April 19th. Reporters got some
words out of him, but no sentiment worth print. A
rumor lasted a few days. Hanna was said to have
quarreled with Mr. McKinley. On May 2nd he was
dining at the White House and the rumor wandered
off in the herd of that month's lies.

He must have his say, though. "Now," he told some
Senators and correspondents in the Marble Room,

202

"look out for Mr. Bryan. Everything that goes wrong'll be in the Democratic platform in 1900. You can be damn sure of that!" They broke out in hoots of laughter. Bryan? What about the Silver Knight? Why, the man was a cipher! Uncle Mark was crazy. Only Senator Spooner shook his head. He thought that Bryan wasn't dead just yet.

"But," said Henry Cabot Lodge, "will not the Democrats hesitate before offering Mr. Bryan the nomination?"

"Hesitate?" Hanna growled. "Does a dog hesitate for a marriage license?"

He left the group. Senator Orville Platt asked the correspondents not to print Mr. Hanna's remark. He might not want it known that he thought such a thing. A solicitude for Mark Hanna grew among the Senators. He made no speeches, even in debates on the tariff, but they began to be fond of him. He was loyal to his President, and obliging about little jobs for a client of some friend, and his passion for arbitrating a row was useful in that nervous spring. And then he was an encyclopedia, ready in awkward moments of debate. Questions whispered along to his chair brought back a scribble of the number of negroes in Arkansas, the depth of Mobile Bay, or the size of a railroad station in Chicago. He was a good neighbor in the Senate and he gave a good dinner at his hotel. So they did not want to humiliate him by having it known that he was still afraid of Mr. Bryan.

Plutocratic imperialism now displayed itself in the Orient. In the first week of May it had to be admitted that something serious had happened between the Spanish and American fleets in the bay of Manila. On May 7th it was known that Commodore Dewey's ships had mashed up the defending flotilla and that Manila was due to be taken whenever American troops arrived. Within ten days Joseph Chamberlain and Lord Salisbury uttered speeches broadly friendly to the United States, and Americans in clever Paris heard that the Philippines were to be sold to England as soon as the subsidized Yankees had possessed the islands. The German official press twittered that Yankee insolence ought to be suppressed.⁷ On June 3rd Vice Admiral Von Diederichs arrived at Manila and commenced his grotesque abrasions of neutral etiquette, facing the English commander, Chichester, past the American fleet. The situation was plain even to an eighteen-year-old seaman in the American pay. "These Dutch," he wrote to his mother in Fort Wayne, Indiana, " are trying to see if they can get up a fight with the English boats by busting all the rules. If we have a fight with them they can start a fight with England out of it and grab all this country out here." Seaman George P. Smith was in tune to

⁷ An editorial of the *Kölnische Volkzeitung* on May 7th is partly quoted in Peck's *Twenty Years of the Republic*. The files of this particular newspaper, from the moment of Dewey's victory to the signing of the peace with Spain, are luxuriously informative as to the quality of German propaganda, in 1898.

the operations of imperialistic statecraft, which are
those of eighteen-year-old boys. The game of grab, as
glimpsed through portholes of his hot navigating home
impressed him for what it was. On August 13th, if he
was watching, he saw the British vessels steer forward
between the rear of the American fleet and the moving
German ships. Von Diederichs chose to follow the
Yankee cruisers and transports steaming toward the
city in assault, and Chichester chose to interfere. This
ended the matter, in 1898, and historians may go on
talking of the precise intentions demonstrated for a
long time yet.

But the tension at Manila was quietly known in
New York. The American plutocracy began to worry,
not at all caring to have the United States drawn into
a monstrous world war. In June, John Pierpont Morgan sent an agent to Washington to represent to
Mr. Hanna that a victory in Cuba might make Germany recoil. Mr. Hanna rudely answered that he was
not in the victory business. Still, a victory was supplied. On July 3rd Admiral Cervera led his squadron
in flight from the bay of Santiago and it was destroyed
by the blockading ships. Santiago fell. The war was
all over. Spain had been licked in less than Mr.
Hanna's six months.

He had not liked the war. "Oh, God," he said, reading the list of deaths at El Caney, "now we'll have
this sort of thing again!" On the news of Santiago's
fall the Senator swung out his cane among the ladies

in a veranda and stood for minutes slowly stamping one heel on the floor. " Remember," he told a young girl, "that my folks were Quakers. War is just a damn nuisance. . . ." But in July he saw that the joke was on him, and he recognized the forces which had made his pacifism ludicrous. The United States had won something that could be assayed. European propaganda had vehemently advertised the wealth and the resources of the loathsome Yankee. Investors from France and Germany appeared in New York with notes introducing them to Mr. J. P. Morgan before the destruction of Cervera's ships. All summer Herr Otto Heinrich was summoned from his desk in Dresden and brought to explain American securities to grave clients of his uncle's bank. He clicked his heels before a widowed countess and promised her that the city of Saint Louis was habitable and its bonds good. So the Hanna luck held. Mr. Hanna's President was now the ruler of a nation which, said a French statesman, "has entered the council of the Powers and is entitled, despite its youth, to the consideration of an equal. . . ." Its gunners could shoot and its bonds were good.

For all this, Mr. Hanna had not liked the war. Yet it did things for his President beyond the Mississippi; the West was pleased by this adventure; for twenty years every other lounger on a station's platform would tell tourists that he had been a Rough Rider in Roosevelt's regiment at San Juan Hill, and would accept a drink on the strength of that. The frontier was gone, and there was not much free land left to be parceled among sturdy men on the precedent of Mr. Lincoln's Homestead Act. Magnets which had drawn settlers to the West rusted out their attraction, but the strange thing called "earth hunger" still kept this Western population astir. A ghostly committee of Western legislators asked Mr. Hanna, in July, to find out whether Mr. McKinley would not keep the Philippine Islands.[8] The star of Empire was gone glimmering to its farthest and now beckoned from the Orient. Mr. McKinley had somehow led a war of expansion, without meaning to, and took the profits.

In the East, also, the war had done something unexpected. There was a new folk-hero born, and his rise amused Mr. Hanna, doubly. In the autumn of 1898 Senator Thomas Platt had to accept Colonel Theodore Roosevelt as the Republican machine's selection for Governor of New York State; an unlimited enthusiasm declared itself in the clubs while journalists caught up the commander of the Rough Riders into a glamour that ended by infuriating

---

[8] Mr. Joseph Kimball was with Mr. Hanna when they called on him. Mr. Warren Watson informs me, in a letter dated July 1st, 1929, that: ". . . [in] the very first letters I received in Manila after the troops took possession of the town in 1898 was a funny request for information about 'farming land' in the islands. The sender was a rolling stone whom I had occasionally helped with tiny loans when I was a clerk in Cheyenne, a typical ne'er-do-weel of the cow country. I do not care a straw what is now being said in histories of the period. The Westerners regarded the Philippines as a conquest and liked the idea of a colonial empire. . . ."

officers of regular troops which had also been employed in Cuba. Mr. Hanna was entertained so keenly that he laughed himself into an access of the cold indigestion that had troubled him ever since his typhoid fever of 1867. Why, the chilly metropolitans were like anybody else when it came to a military hero! They had made Roosevelt Governor of New York for charging a hill in Cuba. And how would Tom Platt get along with the crazy man? He wrote to Asa Barnes: "Mr. Roosevelt is really a very able man. He was a great help to Mr. Long last year in getting the navy ready for war. He took up a matter for me in a very effective way. . . .[9] I should expect to see him make a good record as governor unless he has bad times with Platt. He certainly did not ' shrink from office,' did he? "

Mr. Roosevelt unshrinkingly looked toward office and thus could not be sent to Paris with the commissioners as his friend Cushman Davis wanted when peace was discussed. Mr. Davis himself was selected and sailed with William Day, George Gray, and

[9] The case of the Gathmann torpedo, presumably. Mr. Hanna's passion for mechanics led him to interest himself in schemes offered to the Army and Navy in 1898. He rejected outright a grenade of the type afterwards used in the Great War, invented by a man named Vick Walter, of Chicago, saying that the cruelty of the device would damage American prestige! I have been shown a letter written by Secretary Long stating that Mr. Hanna had been of " inestimable help " in getting rid of " foolish inventions " tendered to the Navy Department. On the other hand, Mr. McKinley was rather given to clogging the department's work by sending along inventors and busybodies. Mr. Roosevelt complained of this in January of 1898 in a note to Jacob Riis.

William Frye to join Whitelaw Reid in France, remarking languidly that for once in his ill-spent life he would not be told by reporters how much he looked like the appalling Benjamin Butler. He was an obvious choice for this expedition, it seemed to Mr. McKinley, as he read French and Italian and, although Senator from Minnesota, suggested the heavy stateliness of an Eastern personage.

He was a personage, oddly forgotten by historians, a reformer, a jingo, an imperialist, and yet a critical patriot. It was Davis who launched an economist's demand for the control of big corporations in 1886, denouncing the theory of *laissez faire* as a profound economic fallacy spawned by Adam Smith. It was Davis who retorted in 1892 when a German imperialist invited the Reichstag to secure the decent dismemberment of the United States by planting colonies of civilized Europeans, commanded by their own ecclesiastics and speaking their own tongues, in yonder savage nation. The Senator from Minnesota thunderously told the Senate that this notion was less civilized than the political ideas of Confucius, and then was found by reporters in his office reading an unknown work named *The New Spirit,* by Havelock Ellis. He drawled that Dr. Ellis was a sort of improved Emerson and told the journalists where they could read the ideas of Confucius. The prose of *Moby Dick* moved him, but so did the rhythm of Tennyson's moral poems. He read constantly, slumped on a couch beside a box

of violent cigars, and dallied with essays on Madame
Roland and the law in the plays of Shakspere. He
thought of a volume on musical instruments, described
a history of prostitution in America that ought to be
written by somebody else, and collected Napoleonana.
But the war had done for him, he yawned. He would
never amount to a damned thing, after the excitements and maladies of soldiering in the sixties. It took
another war to rouse him. He set off for Paris ready
to laugh aloud when the Spanish commission proposed that the United States accept the debts of Cuba
along with Cuba.

John Hay's gay voice, meantime, had succeeded the
politic silence of William Day at the State Department. The new Secretary talked so frankly that he
seemed wholly indiscreet to callers. Yes, he had
worked hard in England to secure the United States
an open hearing in the newspapers. It had cost a
pile of money. Such things did. But the sinking
fund of the department had been at his disposal. He
shrugged . . . " *Ça vous étonne, monsieur?* " . . .
The superior Englishmen were on our side, but a
friendly propaganda for use among the people had
been necessary, and English dinners were expensive
things. One talked best to journalists over champagne.
. . . He was talking with Mr. Hanna, at lunch, when
a wonderful interview of Cushman Davis reached him
on December 12th, 1898. The Senator had been ex-
pansive to an English reporter, and had let his mind

arrange a configuration of England, America, and Japan in the Orient, opposing the *Dreibund* of Germany, France, and Russia. To this marvel he added some thoughts on the utility of England as an ally, saying that the English had five hundred years of vigor left. " Heavenly union! " said Mr. Hay. " Davis has run amuck! " He hurried to the White House, paused in the telegraph room to tell Colonel Montgomery, " Do let me hear if Mr. Davis has another attack of statesmanship! " and then the door of Mr. McKinley's office shut on the Davis *Dreibund*.

The peace treaty was signed on December 10th, 1898 in Paris, and its terms promised Spain twenty million dollars for the Philippines. Now Mr. Hanna faced the revolt of the East. He knew that the West did not care, or favored keeping the islands. But only one Eastern Senator, Orville Platt, had been persistent in urging Mr. McKinley to hold the Philippines. Others had wavered and, outside the government, professors, editors, and a few bankers were protesting. They were not impressed by McKinley's prayers for guidance, and they did not know that Mrs. McKinley was charmed with the thought of Christianizing the Igorrotes.[10] Carl Schurz, William Sumner, Charles

[10] " Mrs. McK. talked ten to the minute about converting the Igorrotes. I hope you know how to spell the name of this tribe because your fond father does not. Anyhow she wants you and Alice to pray for the Igorrotes or Iggorotes. Tell your mother that Mrs. McK. asked for her. She was wearing a pink kind of dress with green spots. . . ." William C. Beer to his son, October 23rd, 1898.

Francis Adams, William James, and Moorfield Storey were not infected by earth hunger. The Anti-Imperialist League was born at Boston in December of 1898. Senator Hoar and Thomas Reed headed the rebellion of Congress. Democratic legislators strayed, looking for a leader, when the treaty was sent to be ratified in January.

Leadership was bestowed. Mr. William Jennings Bryan appeared in the Marble Room and stood among the Democratic Senators, slowly gesticulating, beautiful, and still tanned a little by exposure in the camp of a volunteer regiment which he had peaceably commanded. His presence excited Mr. Hanna to telling Orville Platt that he'd like to see Mr. Bryan play Hamlet. Mr. Bryan's public performance had this purpose: the treaty must be ratified, to end the burden of war on the plain people. The people could then dispose of the Philippines by its sovereign will. He was well heard. On February 5th the treaty was ratified and an issue for the campaign of 1900 had been contrived. "This simple minded strategy seemed Machiavellian to him," says Charles Willis Thompson. "His idea was that if he could get the treaty ratified, the people would blame McKinley for it, because it was a McKinley treaty."

Mr. Hanna was not disturbed. On February 19th the New York Life Insurance Company learned, "He says that Bryan's trick can be discounted. McKinley consulted hundreds of people of all kinds on his trip"

(McKinley went to the Exposition at Omaha in October) " and finds western sentiment generally in favor of holding the islands. He implied that our good understanding with England would be damaged by letting Spain retain the Philippines, as they would be instantly sold to Germany. He said in a very forcible way, ' I wonder what these people in Boston would say if we listened to Hoar and turned the islands over to the natives. Why, Germany would take them in a month! Spain is selling all her other islands to Germany as it is. Hoar is crazy. He thinks Germany is just fooling.' He said a great deal more in the same strain. . . . I find a widespread feeling down here that Mr. Hanna is not much in favor of holding the Philippines but let himself be persuaded by Hay and [Orville] Platt. Hay is supposed to have practically pledged the country to keep the islands out of Germany's control.[11] Mr. Cortelyou had nothing to say on the matter. . . ." [12]

Now that Mr. Hanna had entered the sphere of conscienceless world-politics he dealt with it realistically. One's friends stood by one handsomely, in wars as in elections, and one paid them back. Let Hoar keep his

[11] Hay's letter to Mr. McKinley, dated August 2nd, 1898, states that " our English friends " would be disappointed if the United States relinquished the Philippines. Myron Herrick, in conversation with Mr. George Poldmann, in 1927, told him that Hay was obliged to argue Hanna into supporting the treaty. An autograph of Mr. Hay addressed to " Dear Hall," dated October 30th, contains the sentence, " I have had to talk Philippine business to Hanna for six hours."

[12] William C. Beer to George Walbridge Perkins, from Washington.

illusions. But he was moved by the old Senator's tirades, because he liked the Yankee and enjoyed hearing him make an oration. He esteemed these men who could get up on their feet and become periodically eloquent. He always sat out a speech of Joseph Foraker, listening to his rival from Ohio with every attention. Mr. Foraker was abler and abler, now that the showiness of his time as Governor of Ohio had peeled away from him. He talked simply, driving his sentences along in a pulsation of ready, sharp words, and men feared him. Even toughened journalists in the gallery would watch Foraker support a bill of the Administration on some trivial matter with an interest in his method. He was a lonely force in the Senate, an item of the machine, but a patent will, too little conciliating to be a leader and too cool to gather on himself the affection which came to Hanna or to Hoar and Orville Platt. And Mr. Hanna admired him, with detachment, since we have no other word for the mood in which the disbelieving mind observes the process of establishing belief.

Mr. Hanna believed in what Mark Hanna had done. His President was admired, and the business of the country swelled through 1899, fed by European investments, spilling manufactured products back into Europe. Industrialism's object was attained, and ever so comfortably. " The factories send up smoke; the workman's dinner-pail is full." Tariff had not brought revolution, and revolution did not come when the

Congress fixed gold as the standard of value in the United States. The country bankers called on Mc-Kinley, and said, "God bless you!" in sincerity. Wages went up. Mortgages were paid off. A flutter of social display was constant. The intake of insurance companies was so rank that their presidents awarded to themselves salaries of invincible tragedians without a protest from charmed stockholders, and express companies showered free turkey and tinned oysters on clerks at Christmas. It was grand.

But the jinni in the midst of this golden vapor had moments of speculation. Mr. Hanna's general attitude toward workmen wasn't unctuous. He never flattered his engineers, his street-car hands, and his shipbuilders. He lent them money to set up a house or to send a promising boy to college, and he was not particular about being repaid. His life was wound in a series of personal relations. This series included friendships with common mechanics and servants, for his cook adored him, and the waiters in his clubs sent roses to his funeral. People were people. He liked them, or he didn't. But what was all this bosh he began to hear at dinners where Eastern owners of coal mines and railroads prosed about "the lower classes"? "You mean working men?" he asked a Philadelphian banker. "Or do you mean criminals and that kind of people? Those are the lower classes."

This was not a pose. Mr. Hanna held and said repeatedly that a certain sort of workman would never get up in the world. God knew why, but they were born to be damn stupid folks. They stuck their fingers in machines, lost their pay envelopes and gabbled that the world owed every man a living when the foremen fired them. " I'll take back a drunk three times, but I won't have fools working for me. They get everybody in trouble." His mouth tightened when a young reformer, wiser since, protested an idea then afloat in social discussions, the castration of male morons. " It ain't pretty," said the pragmatist, " but what's the sense in increasing the supply of damn fools? We've got plenty." And what, he asked Jacob Riis, were you going to do with men who " won't save money, won't look after their kids, and won't stick to a job when they get one given to them? " So the mention of communism made him snort. What? Give all the damn fools in the world equal rights with good men? . . . By God, no!

But he detested this patter about the lower classes, so smoothly turned out by men who owned a coal mine or a railroad fed by coal mines. He viewed some of the great Pennsylvanian owners with a distinguished and rather visible contempt, not diminished by the fact that they rallied to his enemy Matthew Quay. " I hear," he said very suddenly to William Beer, " that there's going to be a revolution pretty quick, over in Pennsylvania. Heard of it? " Mr. Beer had, because a friend who happened to be president of the Pennsylvania Railroad Company was worried by the talk in the coal country. "Hoh," said Hanna, " it'd serve 'em all right!" This was in 1899. When the strike of 1902 did come, Mr. Hanna grunted his challenge to the Pennsylvanians, " Serve 'em right if Roosevelt seizes the mines. Go and tell Baer I said so!" [13] And so they had been criticizing the Civic Federation and himself for trying to avert the strike? " All right! You tell them that if I hear any more of that kind of talk I will go to New York, hire Carnegie Hall, and give them something to talk about!"

If he could not stand the workman fool, he could not stand the employing fool. In final fact he had an aversion to fools. When Jacob Riis argued with him on the topic of the Civic Federation, alleging that it was fatal for the delegates of the labor unions to come in contact with the rich, who would be sure to overawe them, Mr. Hanna said, " But the union men aren't fools, young man!" and scowled at the journalist in plain offense. He was annoyed by the superfluous fools who came calling at the White House to take up the President's time. One day in May of 1899 he stood watching a deputation of some kind filing out of the place and said, " What would happen, do you think, if some crank got in there with a revolver in his pants? "

[13] Mr. Baer was the remarkable president of the Reading Iron and Coal Company, who believed or said that God had put the operators in control of the mines, and then told Mr. Roosevelt that coal-mining was not a religious business. I happen to have heard Mr. Baer talk several times, and he remains one of the most indurated specimens of the platitudinizing mediocrity I have ever met.

III

In June he went abroad to see what Europe could do
for his rheumatism. Before leaving Cleveland he told
the men of his street railways that they would be so
good as not to join the strike planned by carmen of
other lines in Cleveland. He then sailed and drearily
took the cure at Aix-les-Bains, dodged up into Germany to consult American consuls about the law ex-
cluding American life-insurance companies from doing business in the Kaiser's territories, and then came
home, uncured, and outraged by the absence of the
American flag on the seas. " It's just a shame! " he
cried, at luncheon in New York. " Where the hell are
our ships? " Mrs. Hanna put her hands on her ears
and hurried the Senator off to Cleveland, where
Maggie, his legendary and noble cook, waited to
soothe him with baked hash, stewed corn, and hot
biscuit. His carmen, of course, had not joined the
savage strike which scared the city while Mr. Hanna
was away. He had gold coins added to the pay in a
thousand envelopes on the next Saturday and bustled
down to Washington to look at his President, wearying Charles Nolan on the train by a lecture about a
subsidized shipping for the United States. He saw the
American flag drifting on ships as they passed through
a canal cut across Nicaragua or the isthmus of
Panama. He talked half through the night, shoving
his cane back and forth on the floor of his state-

room. . . . Europe? Oh, yes! Pretty interesting, but about these ships — [14]

In October the Democrats of Ohio hopefully selected John McClean, a rich and practical politician, as their candidate for Governor. Mr. Hanna used, against this serious antagonist, some of his technic for national elections. There were many hired speakers, much propaganda, and ample checks for workers. "Hanna is buying the cities of Ohio," said Mr. Bryan. But it turned out that Mr. Hanna's candidate did best in the country or in little towns where Mr. Hanna made speeches, in the last weeks of October, while Mr. McClean's strength seemed to lie in the corrupt cities, not among the plain people.

In December some men in the lobby of the Raleigh at Washington were discussing McClean's defeat with Senator Richard Pettigrew of South Dakota. Mark Hanna was proving a good stump speaker. Mr. Warren Watson described the effect of Hanna's talks on the rural crowds in Ohio and praised the Senator's power of retorting offhand when he was heckled by Democrats in the audience. Mr. Pettigrew jeered; the Democrats were hired helpers from the Republican sty at Cleveland, he said, and Hanna drilled them

[14] He had proposed an act to subsidize a merchant marine in December of 1898. This became a mild mania with him for the rest of his life and he was admittedly tedious on the subject. A more interesting hobby was a notion of a governmental school for scientific research. He discussed this with Professor Langley and once with Henry Adams, at a dinner given by John Hay. Mr. Adams told Mrs. Charlton Paull that Hanna had quite an elaborate scheme for this school.

beforehand in what they were to say. Would a thief like Hanna risk answering a sincere question, impromptu? Here a mild stranger outside the group said, " But, Senator, you wouldn't call Tom Johnson a thief for planting people in an audience? " Mr. Pettigrew denied that the Democratic reformer would do such a thing. The mild stranger meekly said, " But, Senator, he did it all the time in New York when he was campaigning for Henry George," (in 1897) " and I know he did, because he paid me ten dollars a meeting for asking him questions." Mr. Pettigrew got up and walked away.

Mr. Pettigrew had never forgiven Mark Hanna for ruining Silver in 1896. He was a quiet man, but he quarreled easily and carried a grudge to the public extreme of loud speech. " See," he said to Mr. Watson in a theater, one night, "there goes Hanna's wife. Every diamond on her is bought with blood! " Mr. Watson chuckled at this rhetoric, and Pettigrew would not speak to him for months. He was feared in the Senate, because he specialized in personal attacks. Having deserted the Republican party in 1896, he seemed to loathe everybody in it, except Hoar and Mr. Wilson, the Secretary of Agriculture. He pushed a scene with Henry Cabot Lodge in the Marble Room, in the autumn of 1898, by sneering at Theodore Roosevelt on some forgotten ground. Nobody was safe from him. " Here comes pale malice," Cushman Davis said, when Mr. Pettigrew strolled near him. " My

God, Pettigrew," Senator Wolcott asked, "do you spit lemon juice?"

This character was perhaps a manufactured, defensive thing. Mr. Pettigrew could be kind, and his charities are remembered. He took care of poor relatives, bothered at home about sanitations and grain elevators in the small towns, and had friends who were appalled by his manner in the Senate. But his hatred of Marcus Hanna was acute, and it broke out once in December of 1899 before Oscar Underwood so flamboyantly that the gentleman from Alabama thought the Westerner mean and mad. They were standing on the steps of the Capitol, and close to them Mr. Hanna was comparing socks with Cushman Davis. A Yankee representative approached the jinni and put in a request of size, asking to have part of the Atlantic fleet sent to a port in Massachusetts for a celebration in the spring. Mr. Hanna thought and refused, rubbing an ear. The Congressman simmered and puffed steam. "You had a consul sent to Aix to doctor you! It doesn't matter what you get out of the government!" Mr. Hanna stiffened his neck and seemed tall. "It cost the government two dollars to send a cable. I paid his fare from Nuremberg to Aix an' back. Do you know what it'd cost in coal to send some battleships to this show? . . . No? Well, go and ask the Navy Department!" The Congressman was blown down the steps. But the gentleman from Alabama had to hear an oration by Richard Pettigrew on privilege and corruption. "He made it sound as though the whole consular service in Europe had been corrupted," Mr. Underwood said in 1919, "and if it had not been so foolish, it would have been pathetic to see an intelligent man so excited. But it was downright lunacy. He raved at me."

Mr. Pettigrew then moved to his doom. He sat in the Senate just ahead of Mr. Hanna, but never spoke to him. On June 5th, 1900, while Hanna was answering a charge of the Democrats for the Republican National Committee, Senator Pettigrew began fiddling a printed report, flipping its leaves so that men noticed it in his hands. It was the report of a minority in the Senate's committee on Privileges and Elections, asking an investigation of the tale that one of the assemblymen had been influenced to vote for Mr. Hanna in 1898 by unfair means. It was an inconclusive, wandering business, and the Senate had not bothered with the thing, as there was no real evidence of bribery set forth. But Mr. Pettigrew attacked Hanna with this clumsy bludgeon for ten minutes. The Senators grinned. Pettigrew was at it again. When the Senator from South Dakota ended his performance and sat down, they expected nothing.

But the Senate rippled as Hanna jumped up, yelling, "Mr. President!" and men hurried in to hear. He pinned together long sentences, comma by comma, and slung them at Pettigrew's shoulders in a continuous war song. He announced by the tone of his clattering words that he was sick of being lied about, caricatured, and called a knave, and a legend grew that he had cursed Pettigrew in the grandest manner, although he said little about the malignant orator. But he had found an eloquence. This was wrath. The indifferent god of the office-seekers had turned a new power loose. When he left the chamber, he pushed aside friends and went straight to the White House.[15]

He had not proposed to have this yarn spread in the campaign or to have it said that he was afraid to answer Pettigrew. In 1896 his friends persuaded him to keep still for McKinley's sake, when his son's lawyers had listed one hundred topics in an action for libel against Alfred Henry Lewis. But he was done with keeping still. He was going to "see about" this Pettigrew. When he had time, he would attend to the Senator from South Dakota. And there was Mr. Bryan. He would attend to Mr. Bryan. Immediately, he saw, there was a third case to be attended to.

Theodore Roosevelt, Governor of New York, went

[15] Colonel Montgomery told my father that Mr. Hanna's anger was cumulative in this case, as reports of Mr. Pettigrew's language about him had reached Mrs. Hanna, who was not well. Charles Willis Thompson in *Presidents I've Known and Two Near Presidents* points out that Mr. Hanna respected the dignity of the Senate. He disliked to hear personal attacks exchanged in the chamber. Mr. Pettigrew's speech reads unimpressively, as does Mr. Hanna's answer. The tones of the two men formed the melodrama of the episode. Mr. Pettigrew's feeling about the Silver issue was extravagant before 1896 and one of his relatives tells me that his hatred of Hanna was an obsession. He would believe anything said of Hanna, no matter how absurd.

into the West and made speeches. The plain people called him Teddy — not that Mr. Roosevelt cared for the trick — and thrust up placards lettered "Roosevelt in 1904!" from crowds at stations. A constant need of self-assertion in Roosevelt's adolescence had given him a curious, unforgettable exaggeration of facial gesture and he had picked up from Senator Cushman Davis an excellent motion of the right hand in speaking. He drove forward whatever points he was making with a kind of stabbing thrust — the hand rose almost to the level of his shoulder and slanted down a trifle as the arm stretched. It was hypnotic and useful, for his voice was not pleasant when he spoke loudly, although its quality was charming in ordinary speech. Before New Year's Day of 1900, there could be no doubt that Mr. Roosevelt at last was a national personality, and in February Senator Thomas Platt had decided to transfer Roosevelt from the governorship to the vice presidency, for the convenience of Thomas Platt. This project seemed wisest to Mr. Platt, since it would cost an ugly, open battle in the Republican party to stop a second nomination of Roosevelt for Governor. He allowed it to be known that Mr. Roosevelt's friends were anxious to see him preside over the Senate.

Indubitably some of Mr. Roosevelt's friends wanted just that, and Mr. Roosevelt, in March of 1900, surprised John McCook by asking at a dinner whether it might not be better for him to accept the vice presidency rather than to disrupt the state's Republican party by a muddle over his reforming policies in New York's financial affairs. Colonel McCook advised him against the dull job in Washington, and then had a difficult hour with Mr. Platt when his advice was reported to the easy boss. But by May Mr. Roosevelt seemed to be set against the vice presidency and he appeared as the national Republican Convention collected itself in Philadelphia in June, with his mind made up: he would stay in his own state. Mr. Platt, however, had been busy. He had friends enough in the West to promote his wishes out there, and the natural feeling for the Rough Rider among the plain people was now solidified by some machine-made tacks and rivets. Western delegates got off the train at Philadelphia assured that dirty work was being done against Mr. Roosevelt, to cheat him of his dues. This feeling had caught even some of Roosevelt's intimate journalists, and they rushed about in the heat hunting Hanna to demand that he stop kicking their friend in the face, as one of them memorably put it. And in addition it proved that Mr. Matthew Quay had arranged a feeling for Roosevelt among the Pennsylvanian delegates.

"Our babe is in the manger," said Mr. Quay; "the kings have seen his star in the East and are come to worship him."

Mr. Roosevelt's sombrero passed among the Western delegations and the man under it assured his

friends that he wanted to stay in New York for
another term as Governor. Cynics chuckled a little
about the soft and conspicuous hat. It was an acceptance hat, said one of them to Arthur Dunn, and
others wondered why Colonel Roosevelt wore this re-
membrance of the Cuban campaign. On Monday and
Tuesday the hat was everywhere, and everywhere
men pointed out to each other that Mr. Roosevelt's
Eastern backers were very busy. On Wednesday
morning Cushman Davis and Knute Nelson were
hunting the Governor of New York, and Mr. Davis
angrily bade Bruce Higginson tell Roosevelt that the
Westerners would not stand for much more of this.
The party wanted him to be vice president; the party
might stop wanting anything of him, if he flouted its
wishes. . . . Platt saw an advantage; messengers
pounced on Mr. Roosevelt in the lobby of the Hotel
Walton and drew him upstairs into Senator Platt's
rooms. He rejoined Frederick Holls an hour later and
said, nervously, that he must not disappoint his Western admirers.[16] That afternoon Charles Dawes telephoned to the President, reporting the tension in
Philadelphia, and late that night Mr. Hanna invited

[16] Mr. Kohlsaat's account of this episode differs trivially from a note
of Frederick Holls to my father, written on Wednesday. In *From McKinley
to Harding*, Mr. Kohlsaat quotes Nicholas Murray Butler as an authority
and states that Mr. Roosevelt was obdurate until Platt sent for him. Mr.
Holls wrote: " He was getting weak on Tuesday night. Platt sent [Lemuel]
Quigg to find him. We happened to be standing in the Walton, with N. M.
Butler. Roosevelt came to see me after an hour and seemed very nervous
and strange. He said he had given in to prevent trouble with the western
crowd."

the convention to nominate Mr. Roosevelt for the vice presidency unanimously. This was done.

"All right," said Mr. Hanna to a powerful man from New York; "all you gentlemen wanted Roosevelt out of New York. You've done it. Now, who's going to win your campaign for you?"

For three days there was an unreported, hot panic among the great powers. Hanna would not run the campaign, someone told someone. On June 21st Senator Thomas Platt was telephoning to most obscure men who were supposed to be on good terms with Hanna, asking the news. This one remark of the fetish had caused such a rumpus among hardened, middle-aged capitalists and politicians. Everything would be lost without Uncle Mark. But on June 23rd there was sweetness blowing. Mr. Hanna had guffawed when he was directly asked if he wasn't going to play. The machine was being polished and oiled. Uncle Mark would do the right thing.

The incident did Mr. Hanna an indirect service. Journalistic certainties weakened a bit. It was plain, absolutely known, that Hanna had objected to Roosevelt's nomination, when that nomination was wanted by the chiefs of finance. Finance and the Westerners had forced Roosevelt on the Administration. Perhaps, then, the link between Hanna and Wall Street was not absolute? For the three years left to him, Mark Hanna was allowed to be fairly independent by some of the reporters. But when he died, the necessities of dramatizing him conveniently caused journalists to forget what they had learned at Philadelphia in 1900.

Mr. Bryan duly swarmed into sight, talking against imperialism, advocating more free silver, and, of course, anxious to preserve the nation from the Trusts. He was to be curiously supported, this time, by Richard Croker and Tammany Hall, while several inland bosses worked for him with a fair enthusiasm — nothing headlong or lavish, but a pleasing warmth. Mr. Hanna's machine then functioned, and the campaign went on smoothly and economically. Mr. Roosevelt was shot into the West and minor speakers were flicked into towns just after Mr. Bryan had made an oration or just before. Many babies were named for Mr. Roosevelt, but Mr. Bryan scored over him, in one instance. Mr. William Bryan Wells was born in the crowd listening to Mr. Bryan's remarks and, he is told, in a temperature of ninety-seven degrees. Roosevelt never had the effect on women which was at Mr. Bryan's constant disposal. In this campaign a Yankee virgin of seventy spent incalculable money, buying and sending through the mails photographs of the Silver Knight to public schools and Sunday schools. On the other shore of the continent a widow of greater wealth paid the whole cost of the Democratic campaign in a city of twenty-eight thousand. Everywhere the female mind was at this orator's service; he was a religious symbol to uncounted lonely creatures.[17]

In September an unbelievable rumor crept; it was said that Senator Hanna was to go out on a tour of the Northwest, making speeches. This caused another unreported little panic at New York, where the wise men saw at once that Hanna would be murdered by some Populist if he set foot in Michigan or Wisconsin. New Yorkers could sit amused in cabs on Union Square listening to immigrant Socialists and even to Terrorists denouncing Wall Street, but, out there on the map, beyond Buffalo, there were terrible people ready to slay. Deputations addressed the President, saying that Mr. Hanna's life ought not to be risked. Mr. Henry Cabot Lodge put forth a special kind of pleading. He begged Senator Proctor of Vermont to use his large influence with Mr. McKinley to keep Mr. Hanna out of sight lest the good done by Theodore Roosevelt's speaking trip be lost to the party. The Senator from Vermont was tickled and didn't keep this plea to himself. It reached Mr. Hanna on October 3rd. He tossed Mr. Proctor's note to a caller and

[17] It was my father's task in 1900 to find out for the Republican campaign committee just what the real capabilities of applicants for funds were. Hanna was determined to waste as little money as possible. In consequence Mr. Beer heard a good deal about the private mania for Mr. Bryan. He always asserted that people who had no connection with the Democratic campaign committees lavished enough money on Bryan to bring up the expenses of the orator's campaign in 1900 to the level of the Republican expense. In 1900 Mr. Hanna remarked to Mr. Walter Stoeffel that he knew of a widow in Cleveland who had spent a hundred thousand dollars on Bryan.

asked, " Isn't it nice to be told that you're not fit for publication? "

The President sent the Postmaster General to discourage Mr. Hanna, with tactful oral messages. But the Senator sent back word that God hated cowards, and went off to attend to Richard Pettigrew and William Jennings Bryan in a private car, with assistants and a secretary, and nine reporters. He was announced by telegraph. If anybody was going to shoot him, he said, there was time to get the guns well loaded. " By heaven," said Tom Johnson, in Cleveland, " he has sand! " For all Americans are credulous about other Americans. As they had arranged a seraglio for Roscoe Conkling, delirium tremens for Grover Cleveland, originality and sincerity for William Bryan, and inhuman valor for Theodore Roosevelt, so they now built up an unqualified loathing of Marcus Hanna among the plain people. Dramatically, this should be.

The plain people was interested to look at Mr. Hanna. Wives fried breakfast at two in the morning and the buggies and spring wagons set off, filled with sneezing children, to the tracks eight miles away. Proletarians clotted at stations and piled on the roofs of freight houses, waiting for a mountainous brute in clothes splotched with dollar marks. Dollar Mark, the Red Boss of Cleveland, the fat brother of the Trusts in cartoons, was now to appear. An old man in a gray suit came limping out on the brazen balcony of the last car and told them that protected industry meant "more wages for the working man, more money in the banks, better prices for your crops." Smart lads swallowed twice and yelled questions at him, over the heads. What about the Trusts? "Well, what about 'em? All you boys have got foolish reading the papers. You'll see that big combinations of capital end up by forcing down prices. Why's one wagon company sell your dad his wagon ten dollars cheaper than the next one? That's what comes of these big combinations, in the long run. . . . Any old Grangers in the crowd, here? . . . Good morning. . . . I ask you this. Didn't the Grangers combine to run prices up, so's your families could live comfortably, and didn't you fight the railroads like — like Sam Hill, to get rates regulated? Of course you did! It was sound business and good practice. Anybody abusin' you people now? All right, combine and smash 'em! . . . Combination is the life of business, and of politics, too! . . . Huh? Yes, I believe in capitalism. Set something up against it as a better system for promoting prosperity and I'll believe in that, when it works. . . . And now listen to Mr. Dolliver a minute. He makes a lot better speech than I do."

News returned to Washington. Nobody had shot the Senator, and crowds bigger than those greeting Mr. Roosevelt came to hear him. He meandered through Iowa, Michigan, Minnesota. Then he swept into Nebraska one morning. At Lincoln the crowd was immense. Mr. Hanna pounded his little fists on the railing and shouted at Mr. Bryan's neighbors that the Silver Knight's latest statement of Republican corruption was " false as hell." He had promised himself to denounce Bryan as a demagogue in his own town, and here he was doing it. Having done it, Hanna beamed at the crowd and blew his nose before resuming his graceless remarks. He was giving himself a good time.

Out in the press William McCready's old Populist father turned on his son and said, " But he don't look like he ought to, Billy!" The human image asserted itself against the cartoon, and in South Dakota it asserted itself at close range, since a law of the state forbade orators to speak from trains. Mr. Hanna trundled two hundred feet to a platform and spoke thence, while boys crept so near that they could smell his cigars. The demon pock-marked with dollars vanished in this sunlight; it was just a man standing there, without diamonds on his thumbs. . . . So Mr. Richard Pettigrew was defeated by a Republican candidate on election day, and the state of Nebraska was disloyal to Mr. Bryan.

Cushman Davis was dying all this while. When they told him that Mr. Hanna had started for a tour in South Dakota he said, " Captain Ahab is after his White Whale!" Mr. Hanna did not understand the allusion to *Moby Dick* and it had to be explained to

him that a man named Herman Melville had written
a tale of a crazy captain who chased a whale which
once had hurt him. Oh? That reminded him. In 1896
some bookish person asked if he wasn't related to
that Herman Melville, on account of his brother's
name, and he had answered, "What the hell kind of
job does Melville want?" Melville was dead, was he?
That was why the bookish person laughed so. The
Senator laughed, then talked on about Cushman
Davis, and his eyes filled with tears. . . . Davis died.
The newspapers forgot his speech against *laissez faire*
in 1886 and twaddled about his books and a quarrel
of his second wife with another legislator's lady in
Washington. The man who had written twenty thousand letters to secure a law regulating capital's powers,
who had done all he could to give the West its war in
1898 and then all he could to give imperialism its
place among American policies, now vanished, and is
nothing but a footnote in the memoirs of Theodore
Roosevelt.

Senator Hanna rested, in his manner, at Cleveland
and played bridge in the Union Club. He seemed, for
the first time, an old man when Henry Adler made
his last call at the house beside the Lake. Some rust
now showed on the human machine. But the Senator
was gay; his chase of Pettigrew had delighted him
and he felt nothing but good humor toward Mr.
Bryan. The orator always did the wrong thing. Free
Silver was dead, and the people didn't care a damn

whether the government kept the Philippines or set them free.

"And do you?"

"Not much," said Mark Hanna.

But why had he made such a kick against mentioning a canal through Nicaragua in the Republican platform? Mr. Hanna would not answer until he was pressed. His mouth hardened. He hadn't wanted McKinley committed to a canal through Nicaragua or through the isthmus. But why not? Oh, he hated being bulldozed into a thing, whether he wanted it or not.

"Look," he said, "I've had enough things forced down my throat in this campaign!"

It was whispered about, in 1900, that a faint coldness grew between the Senator and his President. Mr. Hanna was no longer the minister without portfolio, distributor of federal jobs, but the leader of the Republican party in the Senate. This power, he told a friend, he would not exchange for the presidency. He was proud of it. He existed in the chamber and the Marble Room utterly apart from William McKinley. He had woven himself into the life of the Congress. And how? Well, he was a business man in politics. Let some Congressman run to him with the case of a shipmaster bullied down at Buenos Aires by the venal authorities of the port, and Mr. Hanna's telephone clicked. The Senator was speaking to the State Department, to Mr. Hay himself. Let some Democrat approach him in the Marble Room wailing that Hay

and the President were dragging the United States
into world-politics too far by demanding an open door
for the trade of all nations in China, and people drew
close to hear Hanna retort, for American trade.
Nothing was too small to interest the Senator from
Cleveland. He adjusted anything that was business.
An engine driver had been crippled while helping to
unload supplies at Tampa for the Army? All right!
He would look after that, for Mr. Oscar Underwood,
and he lectured the tall gentleman from Alabama on
the dignity of engine drivers. " I've talked to hundreds
of 'em. Never met one fool, either. . . ." A cargo of
mahogany, the sorrows of an insurance company shut
out of Germany, the complaint of a lady whose son
had been reprimanded at Annapolis for trying to
invent a new torpedo, the inefficiency of a laundry
machine in a government hospital — bring him anything that touched his instinct of a trader or that
had to do with a machine, and Mr. Hanna's voice
would be loud for the persons in trouble. A thousand
such obligations bound Senators and Congressmen to
Uncle Mark. He rose, in this simplicity, by his use-
fulness, and superstition clustered on him. He was
luck, he was force — and there was something else.
Dazedly and unwillingly, people came to see that the
old jinni loved his country, as he queerly loved his
city and his state. It was unaccountable, almost inde-
cent, when he had been dramatized as a mere plun-
derer. But there it was. "I won't have an American

235

abused," he growled, in the State Department, "and I don't give a damn if he has a jail record and ain't got a cent! You get those Swiss to let him loose!"

He towered. When there were rumors of descending tariffs and perhaps some regulation of business itself in the summer of 1901, men at New York were afraid to ask the jinni questions. They heard how he had yelled in a shop at Washington when an American glove split on his hand that the manufacturers were "squatting behind the tariff like a lot of God-damn rabbits" and cheating the public with bad goods. His paternalism might swell out and grow critical, unless something was done about him. Suppose he started his own war on protected industry? The alarmed millionaires began to woo him with invitations and elaborated blandishments.

Then the murder of Mr. McKinley at Buffalo tossed all calculations in a heap. Men who had wanted Roosevelt out of New York because he intruded on matters of franchise and seemed likely to regulate everything financial remembered Hanna's outcry to Arthur Dunn at Philadelphia, "Don't you understand that there is just one life between this crazy man and the presidency if you force me to take Roosevelt?" Now they had something worse than a reforming governor on their charts of possible accident. All tendencies of political criticism in America latterly drifted toward a notion of central reform; the people were to look to Washington for redress of the balance between financial weight and popular weight. Finance had lifted Mr. Roosevelt's uncomfortable quality from the small area to the grand map. It was known that he thought a President entitled to powers of this critical kind. Now, what?

Of course he would discard Hanna, at once. Hanna had opposed his nomination at Philadelphia and Hanna would pay for that. The dramatization was swift. They didn't ponder enough on the new President's singular relation to the Congress. With Cushman Davis dead, Mr. Roosevelt had no spokesman in the Senate. There was Lodge, but the Yankee scholar was not a leader. Who was to be leader of the party at the Capitol? A story wandered loose in which Mr. Roosevelt and Mark Hanna were supposed to have come to terms on the train bringing McKinley's body from Buffalo, but that was sure to be a fake. No. Hanna was all over.

Late in November an agent went down to consult the Secretary of State for an insurance company on the case of a mess in China, with suspicion of European influence. Mr. Hay read the statements and then was evasive. Perhaps the President should see this. Could he arrange an appointment with Mr. Roosevelt?

"Certainly," said John Hay; "come along. The President and I are both lunching with Mr. Hanna."

CHAPTER V

JINNI

I

When Lord Pauncefote died, in 1902, the President ordered the flag of the White House brought down to half-mast and thus presented Count Cassini with a topic. The Russian sat at luncheon and purred to his guests that Roosevelt had so honored the death of an English ambassador from a profound envy. Mr. Roosevelt would like nothing better than to be a great landholder, with horses and dogs. " *C'est son paradis laiteux.* . . ."

One of the guests laughed. Hadn't the President and the Attorney General just brought an action against the Northern Securities Company which must end in dissolving James Hill's huge combination of the northwestern railroads? Did that look as though he envied wealth? " You 've vulgar ideas," said the Count. Who had spoken of wealth? He was sipping brandy. After a little brandy the Russian ambassador did not care what he said about anybody. He smoothly chewed all Washington, the Cabinet, the insufferable Senators and their fat wives, those enraged cows the idiotic journalists, even dear friends of a handsome

238

girl who was hostess at his embassy, and spat out the
pulp. . . . Who had spoken about wealth? Bah! The
President's milky heaven was to be such a creature
as Cromwell, a false aristocrat who roused the filthy
people to follow him. Had one not heard Mr. Roosevelt make a case for Cromwell? And then all that
reverent babble about his mother's family in the South,
with the lands and the hunting dogs! . . . He saw
offended eyes, and turned the talk to himself, gayly
deploring that he soon would be promoted. He would
be minister of foreign affairs in Saint Petersburg, or
maybe prime minister. "Then will come the dirty
moujik with a bomb — and I shall go to heaven!"
He faced the calamity, with a smile. They laughed.
The Count was so amusing.

He came near to a sharp statement of Mr. Roosevelt's position in 1902. The plutocrats and their imitators had for some years busied themselves with a
decoration of country-houses, gardens, horses, ken-
nels, and bastard oak paneling. Ladies in 1902 were
trying to use the word "bitch" technically without
flushing; stockbrokers fitted on pink coats and fell
off tall hunters in great quantity. Mr. Roosevelt
seemed to be a shape in this movement. His horse on
the driveway of the White House and his pleasant,
simple estate on Long Island were possessions that
tuned in this music of fresh wind. Abject journalists
assured inland women that Mr. Roosevelt sprang
from "two of the most aristocratic families in the

United States . . . " and old ladies in New York or
Georgia took that news as they might. An exacer-
bating dandy, who had lived within a quarter mile of
Mr. Roosevelt all their two lives without meeting him,
told James Huneker in the lounge of the Metropolitan
Opera that the President was quite decently English.
He shot and rode and all that, he'd taken a regiment
to Cuba just as the best Englishmen took regiments
to South Africa, and so he was quite all right.

This suggestion of the country squire rose whole-
somely among moneyed men whose photographs be-
tray hepatic insufficiency and social leaders in whose
portraits faces seem masks of rosy dough stretched
on wire. His other attributes soon made Mr. Roosevelt a sun god to many differing groups of Americans.
He was antiplutocratic to weary theorists. His ortho-
doxy soothed clergymen worried by the swell of free
thought. He was a model of sportsmanship useful to
schoolmasters busily prodding introspective lads away
from the amusements of intellect toward the baseball
field. To the fathers of such lads he was the holy gos-
pel of action, since nothing in the President's advice to
the young could be construed as an encouragement of
dreaming. He was food and light to sentimentalists;
his qualities could be identified with almost any wish.
The cult increased. He was advertised as a patent
medicine, a panacea, until in his last phase youngsters went to call on Mr. Roosevelt well prepared to
hate him.

They met a personage, charmingly alert, whose egotism floated in a tidal sweep of conversation which billowed twenty gayeties in an hour. If they were tactful they found that one must not argue when the Colonel happened to call Goya, Flaubert, or El Greco morbid rubbish, pronounced the renovated psychologies of Jung and Adler nonsense " and such dirty nonsense," or approved paste nymphs and useless flowers of his friend Saint Gaudens as " bully," in the nicest tone. They discovered, if they had a sense of likeness, that they were hearing merits of Dickens, Thackeray, and Mr. Dooley extolled by their own father. He was genially adverse to enigmatic discords of high art as was your uncle George. But they must not make a mistake in speaking of history. The man in riding boots could snap out the date of Louis the Fat, recollect after one blink the name of a peerage conferred on Nell Gwynn's brat or the number of men at arms seasick in the fleet of Medina Sidonia. He could extensively report the language of Oliver Cromwell to the silly Parliament. You found that history, to Mr. Roosevelt, consisted somewhat largely of facts in the lives of great popular leaders, and that most great leaders were popular leaders. Civilization was an eventual absolute and not a recurrent state in races. Morals were not customs of some period, but eternal verities, just as they were to your father. . . . And you could not hate him, especially when he told you, one fist pelting into the other palm, that what the nation needed was action. Action!

Action was assertion. He was not impulsive, sane men saw, while fond journalists represented the President as a prancing kitten. But from resolve to effect, with Roosevelt, was a streak of exerted emphasis, and that this emphasis was right must not be questioned. " Why did you call Mr. Hill a fat spider, sir? " he was asked in 1902, when that epithet sent a friend of the railroad builder furious out of the White House. " But that's *my* way of putting it, Montgomery! " And this way of putting it was to annoy sensitive men who keenly wanted to admire Mr. Roosevelt, until January 6th, 1919, because it recalled too much of Roscoe Conkling and was too like those homely moments of Mr. Bryan's roadside invectivation when the orator forgot elegance and merely yelled names at his oppressors. Lenient psychiatrists tell us that this necessity of assertion was a survival, in the strong man, of the myopic, sickly child who had to feed his thin self-confidence by doing everything violently, so as to be sure of his heroic existence. Less friendly observers took it for a condescension to tricks of the ordinary political moralist who puts his enemy in the wrong by exploding him. Anyhow, it was a bully effect.

The trouble was that these effects began to influence Mr. Roosevelt's minor prophets when he was Governor of New York. " Forgive this short note," William

James wrote, in 1900; " I have just escaped from an insufferable admirer of Mr. Roosevelt after a terrible trouncing. My offence was that I made a small objection to something in his last book. I am now in the condition of the feline caught too near the cream-jug. . . ." [1] As the cult expanded, an ugly swagger grew among the faithful. What T. R. did was right, what he said was bully, and what he was said to have said was sacred truth, even when he said in print that he had not said it, and so God damn you if you doubted anything. " Just two classes of Americans are not Roosevelt enthusiasts, fools and crooks ! " The cheapness of that, its mendacity and its inferior bravado, sickened the scrupulous, as they were driven to note that Mr. Roosevelt, who had deprecated Hanna's advertisement of McKinley, did not seem to mind this sort of thing. No doubt it bored him, but he was engaged as virtue's impresario and perhaps he felt that his prima donna excused these flowers. The fine English art of bragging by indirections is not transplanted in America. Americans brag of themselves and their heroes with the simplicity of children and French patriotic statesmen. The damaging factor, in Mr. Roosevelt's case, was that a man of genuine sensibilities appeared to swallow this coarse diet and to thrive on it. " Remember Disraeli's advice about using a

---

[1] Unprinted, to a lady on her private affairs, October 11, 1900. I am permitted to quote a striking sentence at the close of the letter: " And so I have given you no real advice, as advice is never a realistic thing but a form of friendly hallucination which rises from the ego of the giver. . . ."

trowel," said the Attorney General, in 1903, taking a friend into the White House.

But, against all these semblances, Mr. Roosevelt was not immodest. He asked advice; he gallantly pointed out where he had accepted advice from his ministers; he would permit, up to a point, any amount of argument. Yet in these arguments his own sense of a conflict's violence led him to strain statements. Early in 1903 he strolled with several guests from his office into the dining-room of the White House and sank in his chair at the table, announcing, " I have just had the most *ter — rible* scene with Aldrich over the new act." Men who had been listening to a chat between the President and the Senator from Rhode Island over the draft of the Expedition Act stared at him. " But it was clearly evident," says one of them, " that Mr. Roosevelt really thought there had been a scene. Mr. Aldrich was in the best form possible. I cannot recall that he even put up a strong argument. Mr. Hanna winked at me across the table, without closing his eye. . . . Can it not be that Mr. Roosevelt imagined a kind of malevolence in his opponents and that it affected his thought during such scenes? . . ." [2]

[2] On the other hand, a real scene displayed Mr. Roosevelt at his best. Just after the settlement of the coal strike in 1902, Colonel Montgomery wrote to my father: " He came through it like a bird. We are all proud of him. He was justified in throwing chairs at them " — the operators — " but he even made excuses for Baer after it was over. They bullyragged him as badly as the war crowd bullied McKinley before the declaration in '98. I had to be in the room three times. It truly made me sick to listen to those men. . . ."

Something affected the thought of Mr. Roosevelt's friends. McKinley hadn't been buried two months before a situation was arranged in melodrama between the White House and the Arlington Hotel. A hero confronted a purple demon; the President met the leader of his party almost daily and horrid battles took place. Details were known in the bars. Chairs had been upset; oaths hurtled. George Cortelyou was forced to drag the raving Hanna out of Mr. Roosevelt's office. "I have not heard such silly talk," said old Senator Vest, "since the boys had it that Mr. Cleveland was horsewhipping his wife every night." When Mr. Taft had become President a lady standing with Philander Knox at a reception asked if he, as Attorney General, had witnessed any of Hanna's rows with Mr. Roosevelt. "Yes," said Mr. Knox, "I did. Hanna got into an argument about the old Granger movement with Roosevelt. Roosevelt thought the Grangers were a lot of maniacs and Hanna thought they were useful citizens. They both got pretty hot. . . . And now," he concluded, glancing into the Blue Room, where Mr. Taft loomed amiably, "let us go in and eddy around the President. . . ."

But the boys had it that Roosevelt was fighting Hanna for permission to bring an action against James Hill's Northern Securities Company, the trust which would have placed all the railroads of the Northwest in the control of Hill and Morgan. Mr. Roosevelt had not to ask any permission for this action, and asked none. The Senator grunted, very coldly, in his parlor at the Arlington, " I warned Hill that McKinley might have to act against his damn company last year. Mr. Roosevelt's done it. I'm sorry for Hill, but just what do you gentlemen think I can do? "

Still, Mr. Hill's friends were aggrieved. The jinni ought to raise some smoke or waft away the papers of the action brought at Saint Paul. It began to be said in New York that he was selling out his friends to the President in exchange for federal jobs; he was trading loyalties for a postmastership or a clerical place in the Treasury. He ought to do something, something final to stop all this. The exaggeration of what Mr. Roosevelt was doing leveled to the fantasy of what Mr. Hanna could do. For a superstition of the nineteenth century held all these talkers. They were like the credulous critics who established painters and novelists as unlimited, permanent qualities. Against the pullulating mediocrities created in literature and public life by the force of journalized sentiment, a man of any real power rose, in that century, to a tremendousness. Since Mr. Hanna made Presidents and governors, and led the Senate, he could do this other something. He somehow could abolish the presidential will.

Mr. Hanna laughed, turning the talk. A fortune teller had told him he would lose the rest of his hair and another tooth in 1903, he said. Or had his callers seen Maude Adams in her new piece? And what did they think of Clara Morris's yarn about McKinley in this magazine? And if they would excuse him, he had to drive over to see the President. But what was he going to do? . . . The Senator drew himself up and was tall in the smoke. "The Senate passed the Sherman Anti-Trust Law," he said; "how can I take it off the books?"

Meantime he had found a new plaything, although it was not advertised. Having sported with money, with a city and a state, with extraordinary powers and dangers, he came to one of his last amusements. A few people noticed it, but not his own wife. A sentence would be shed with ash from his cigar, between two rambling jokes. Quentin Roosevelt had said a good thing for a baby, the other day, or Mrs. Roosevelt didn't like the baby to have too many toys, or the small boy was in a gloom because a pony had a sore foot. He walked up the driveway of the White House with men whispering at his other side and listened to the garrulous child that hung to his cane. "This is important, gentlemen. . . . I'll talk to you in a minute. Go on, bub."

Otherwise he did not cultivate elderly sentiment. He boasted that he would not build a dog kennel to his own memory. He yawned when a lady tendered him plans of a new orphan asylum, with a pavilion to be named for Marcus Alonzo Hanna. "Mr. Bryan would say I was corrupting the orphans, ma'am. . . . How would a check for five hundred do you?" This living body of Mark Hanna was all that he cared for as Mark Hanna. No monuments were to report his power. Wouldn't he look grand in a pair of wings sitting on the roof of an asylum named for him? Wow! And there was his check.

He had always given without any system, to a pair of begging nuns, or to a wretched old reporter, to a waiter at his hotel who had an ailing daughter, to anybody needing some money. In the autumn of 1902 while Hanna was helping Roosevelt to secure the committee of arbitration in the coal strike, he rolled up yellow bills, sitting in a cab on Pennsylvania Avenue, and tossed them into the hat of a man begging for the strikers. Let 'em have it. Some time or other there would be no more strikes. Business would be too finely adjusted to permit such waste. And coal would one day lose its value. There was enough water power in the one state of Pennsylvania to drive plants by electricity along the whole Atlantic seaboard. The government ought to take that up, some time. Enough would come back from even the lowest rates charged for this power to pay half the federal salaries — why the hell shouldn't the government run power plants? [3]

[3] While revising this passage I have been privileged to listen to a redoubtable lawyer employed by a great coal-mining company as he expounded the horrors of " socialism " in an argument against the use of American water power as Hanna and a dozen others have prophesied it will be used. The gentleman talked through three cocktails about the nefariousness of governmental power plants. He is also in favor of Prohibition as a benefit to the laboring man, he has written strongly against the possible decrease of protective tariffs, and he hopes to be elected to Congress soon.

He was closely noticed, in these years. People who had not to talk to the Senator about a job or an act of Congress pondered him. One of them found that this pragmatist did not know of William James, save as one of those anti-imperialists up in Boston, but that he had studied out a difference in human natures for himself, much as James saw it. " See," he told a girl, " make your father find your brother something to do that's not real business. *The boy's all inside himself*. He can't run folks. He'll be a failure in business." Advice was wasted on a good, hard-headed man enamored of strenuous living for everybody in trousers. His eldest son must get out in the world and " do a man's work." There is a horripilent diary left to record the effect of a man's work on the young fellow at whom Mr. Hanna looked twice or so. The machinery of the strenuous life shook him for fifty months, and then all his notes on Kant and the diary's cover in the open drawer of his desk were stained by the discharged blood and the exploded brain.

But the extravert intelligence was happiest when he could deal with men who went in for achievements of fact. John Rockefeller, he said, was a kind of economic super-clerk, the personification of ledger-keeping. Coal Oil Johnny would never have been any good in Jim Hill's shoes, for instance. Charles Francis Adams was no business man at all, but a man who ought to have gone in for politics. John Hay, now, had found the real job of his life. The Lord had always

meant Hay to be a Secretary of State. He was openly
proud of having sent Hay to England in 1898. . . .
As for the Lord, it seemed that this remote character
had the function of an assembling engineer, who fitted
the machine of destiny together and set it going. But
what men did was of their own will or their peculiar
folly. If they were idiots enough to excuse their failures
by blaming God, it showed they were bigger fools than
Mr. Bryan and Tom Johnson. Predestination? Swill!
. . . Roosevelt was President by accident, wasn't he?
" If you don't believe things happen accidentally,
you're crazy as an Anarchist, by God! "

He admired Roosevelt's drive. The little cuss could
work like a nigger, persuading and hinting until he
got his way. He knew how to handle people. So did
Mr. Hanna, and in 1902 the team of powerful men
took all those malleable things at the Capitol and
arranged them to their own wishes. They had come by
power and used it. Both materialists, they made a
double point in that high materialism which delights
poets five hundred years after its force has thrown up
that vastness of a wall against a flood, that roof, that
pyramid. They chose to build.

II

Otto Paul Heinrich left his young wife in a milliner's
shop at Aix-les-Bains and ran out to stare at a pro-
file, a cigar, and a white waistcoat in a victoria passing
him. He had stopped being a journalist in 1896, when

he permanently left America, but a craving roused again in August of 1899. He set off after the carriage and tracked it to a big hotel. Monsieur 'Anna would see no callers. Mr. Heinrich wrenched the neck of his conscience and threw the corpse away. He wrote on his card, " A friend of Hermann Kohlsaat " and sent it in to Senator Hanna. Doors flew open. Trying to remember the appearance of the editor whose name he had used, Mr. Heinrich came before Mark Hanna and demanded an interview.

Mr. Hanna would not be interviewed for any newspaper. Mr. Heinrich assured him that this was just a case of taking notes for a book on the United States. He had lived three years in America and meant to tell his experiences. Mr. Hanna hoped it would be a better book than Paul Bourget's *Outre-Mer*. He thought that about the wishy-washiest slop he had ever read. Mr. Heinrich agreed. He would have agreed to anything just then, with the Senator defenseless before him.

Mr. Heinrich: You do not care a great deal for books?

Mr. Hanna: Not as a rule. I like some of Mr. Howells's, and I used to read Thackeray. But most of these popular books seem pretty thin to me. I don't like *Ben Hur* or Mrs. Grand's book [*The Heavenly Twins*], or things like that.

Mr. Heinrich: I suppose you prefer the newspapers?

MR. HANNA: I don't think much of most newspapers. They waste a lot of time. The editorials are too long. Editorials only ought to be printed about twice a week. I guess I am spiteful about newspapers because I made a fool of myself trying to run one.

[He then interviews his interviewer on German newspapers, down to the details of printing and the pay of typesetters. Mr. Heinrich struggles and changes the topic.]

MR. HEINRICH: I suppose you consider Mr. W. J. Bryan a very dangerous person.

MR. HANNA: Why should you think that? My friend Mr. Dawes has known Mr. Bryan for a long time. Dawes says that Mr. Bryan is a good fellow. I do not go around saying that people are bad because they oppose my friends in politics.

MR. HEINRICH: Still, you would have been afraid to see Bryan elected in 1896.

MR. HANNA: Of course. You know how bad the financial condition was in 1893, and from then on to the war. We are just getting back into shape now. Mr. Bryan's election would have brought on a panic.

MR. HEINRICH: I believe that is so. You believe that it is the business of your government to protect industries?

MR. HANNA: Yes. So does your Emperor.

[More conversation which was not written down. Mr. Hanna interviews Mr. Heinrich on the limitations of the Emperor's powers, or something of the kind.]

Mr. Heinrich: But I do not understand why Americans find the government ownership of railways so objectionable.

Mr. Hanna: I will tell you. [His reserve, as usual, is breaking down under an agreeable presence.] I have been in the Senate for two years. You cannot understand how hard it is to get legislation pushed through Congress. Suppose that the government took over the railroads. We have just about one half of the mileage in the United States that is needed. If the government owned the lines it would be an awful job to get systems extended. Any fat-head [rendered as " sheep's head " in Mr. Heinrich's German] from Maine would be unwilling to see a new line put out in Minnesota. Senator Davis would have to fight for years to get such an act. Our nation is too big for one part to know what another part needs. Then, in case of strikes, what a terrible situation you would have! You know what Mr. Pullman's foolish friends made him do in 1894. Now, everybody blamed Mr. Pullman for refusing to arbitrate that strike. I blamed him myself. But it was one of his big stockholders who caused the trouble. Let us suppose the government owns the railroads. The unions ask for more pay. The case comes to Congress, and some silly Congressmen refuse to listen to reason. What have you got? Revolution!

Mr. Heinrich: But the people should not be allowed to strike.

[Mr. Hanna roars. He is then lectured on the rights of the State and the profound indecency of opposing the State, for quite a time.]

Mr. Hanna: That may be true in Germany. But it would not do in the United States. Our working people are not so weak as that. I have been dealing with labor for thirty-five years. I should not be surprised to see the government take over the railroads in forty or fifty years. At this time it would be a bad thing. You forget how big our country is. The people in the East know nothing about it. That is why Mr. Reed would have made such a bad President. But he is a very clever [he probably said " smart "] man.

Mr. Heinrich: You mean that the provincial feeling of the various states makes legislation difficult? Enterprises are not nationally felt?

Mr. Hanna: Yes. Now, as an instance, there are two good propositions in which Mr. McKinley takes a great interest. One is to do something for the irrigation of the dry states in the Southwest and the other is to have a serious discussion of a canal from the Caribbean to the Pacific. Senator Davis is opposed to a canal through Nicaragua. He may be right. He has studied the matter a great deal. But you cannot get a serious discussion of these matters from most of the members of Congress. [He then draws back into his reserve.] I am not criticizing Congress. The trouble is what I just said. It is the size of the country.

MR. HEINRICH [diplomatically]: I understand. Would you be opposed to legislation determining the hours of daily labor?

MR. HANNA: Yes, if it was a case of national legislation. That is a matter to be fixed by the states. A great deal of the legislation proposed for the good of the working man is a case for the state and not for Congress. Conditions differ according to locality.

MR. HEINRICH: Did you ever read Henry George's book *Progress and Poverty*?

MR. HANNA: Yes, of course. Everybody was reading it when it came out. There is some good writing in that book. But I do not believe in Mr. George's principles. I do not think the single tax would do what he says it would. The final value of property is not in the land, but in the uses of the land. I have talked this over with many people. Mr. George's proposition is bad.

MR. HEINRICH: I agree. But you do not believe in most of the social reforms that are proposed?

MR. HANNA [very slowly]: No. They seem to end up in producing some kind of condition just as bad as anything we have on our hands now. Take the proposition of making all incomes equal, with the government owning all property. Now — [Mr. Heinrich interrupts to ask what party among the Socialists believes this.] But that has been talked of. You must have heard that. I heard John Ellsler talking about that many years ago.

MR. HEINRICH: Did Herr Ellsler write this in a book?

MR. HANNA [bored]: No, no. I mean the actor John Ellsler. [He is suddenly bitter.] He is one of the men I am supposed to have ruined. It was when he was producing a play of Mr. Howells's [October 25, 1878]. He was a very smart man, a great theorist.

MR. HEINRICH: A Socialist?

MR. HANNA: No! But he liked to talk theoretically. . . . But do you see where this proposition would end?

MR. HEINRICH: It appears to be like some of the English propositions. [They discuss the idea. Mr. Heinrich forgets to take notes for a while.]

MR. HANNA: That seems to me the defect. I know people who will do good work for nothing. But most people are not like that.

MR. HEINRICH: You think that special talent ought to be rewarded specially?

MR. HANNA: Of course I do! Suppose they had said to Henry George that he would not be paid more than a boy on a newspaper gets for writing his book! [He discovers that Mr. Heinrich is translating his words into German.] I wish I could speak some foreign languages —

But that was all. Mrs. Hanna came into the room, telling the Senator he was supposed to be taking a nap. Mr. Heinrich fled. His holiday was over. He and his pretty wife went back to their pretty apartment in Dresden, and Herr Heinrich attended to the English correspondence at the bank while Frau Heinrich worked on prophetic little shirts or practiced the piano. Only, a restless nibbling affected Herr Heinrich. He spun the commercial globe in his office, and the United States seemed a patch of raw, bright, alluring bulbs. He read over and over a copy of Rudyard Kipling's American notes picked up in a café. . . . In September his wife shed tears on the pier at Bremen. Otto had gone mad, her parents thought. He, so well placed at the office of his rich uncle, to return to that desolate and uncivilized Chicago! It was lunacy. The young man could not explain just why he wanted to go back. Something had taken him, while the Senator talked in the smoke of the cigar at Aix. In this way Mr. Hanna, without knowing anything about it, contributed a tall young machine gunner to the armies of his nation, in the year 1917.

This scant, unfinished interview raises two points. Mark Hanna's interest in the irrigation of the Southwest does not appear in Mr. Croly's narration of his life. But he had shown an intelligent willingness to raise this topic during McKinley's presidency. In the spring of 1897 he brought his follower Joseph Kimball to the White House and made the President listen to the shy little man for an hour while the Westerner explained, stammering, the possible location of high dams and reservoirs. In the autumn of 1898 he had the visit repeated. Mr. Kimball stayed to luncheon, but the meal was interrupted by one of Mrs. McKinley's epileptic seizures. In 1899, before he had learned to use his voice in the Senate, he suggested an irrigation scheme to be introduced by Senator Spooner and turned Mr. Kimball loose on the clever man from Wisconsin. Other people were now attracted. Articles in magazines and newspapers were frequent.

"The thing is coming along," Mr. Hanna wrote to Mr. Kimball, in September of 1901. "I should not be surprised if it was seriously discussed in the short session. I would advise you to have a talk with Mr. Roosevelt when you come to Washington. He can do a good deal with some of the New York men if he wants." Mr. McKinley's death disheartened Mr. Kimball; he fancied that the power of Mark Hanna ended here, and was startled in the spring of 1902 when Mr. Elmer Dover wrote to him from Senator Hanna's office, saying that things were shaping for the passage of an act and that Mr. Roosevelt was working vehemently in its behalf.

The great proposal enchanted the new President, and all his dazing resources of conversation were behind the movement that took form in the Newlands Act. He summoned legislators; he dazzled callers; he wrote to powerful editors. But toward the end of May

258

there was a hitch, a flare of provincialism. Some Senators and Representatives saw no sense in irrigating the deserts; the Southwest was too far from their embarnacled, Yankee perception. Mr. Roosevelt came, flushed and sweating, down the hallway, arguing with a pair of these parochial statesmen and, twenty minutes later, tired callers in the outer office watched Mr. Hanna pass through. Mr. Roosevelt had opened the brazen bottle, evoking the jinni of the Arlington. His agitated falsetto broke out as the Senator approached.

"Uncle Mark, do you think you could explain to some of these *complete* idiots that there is such a place as Arizona?"

Uncle Mark thought it possible, and did it in his own manner. He roamed into the New Willard Hotel and summoned the bloodhounds of the lobby from their chairs with a motion of his cane. He could command these men because they liked him, feared him, or might need something from him. They had their orders promptly. They were to go to work on Senator This and Mr. That. "Bring in some scalps," said the Senator, "and make it fast." The bloodhounds wagged their frock coats and did what they were told. On June 17th the Newlands Act, creating a huge reservoir of money from the sale of public lands, became a law.

Mr. Hanna took no part in the debates, and journalists wondered if he was not secretly in opposition to the measure, until Mr. Roosevelt set them right by a word to Arthur Dunn. He had fulfilled his function in the unspoken treaty between the White House and the Arlington Hotel, and the credit could fall where it might. "People have not paid much attention to this business," he said, "but I tell the lot of you that it's a damned big thing."

So it was. It came on one man as a final release from a course of action to which he had bound himself when he was a boy. Mr. Joseph Kimball packed his modest trunk and vanished forever from the city of Washington, where he had spent months of each year since 1886, lurking in grand offices with his black hat and his roll of plans spread on his knees. Too shy, too gentle for the task he had set himself, he had been obscure or ridiculous in this pale city. He was pointlessly insulted by Thomas Reed and laughed at by reporters who knew, from some profundity of their trade, that it was impossible to irrigate the deserts of the West. Until Mark Hanna took him up, he had been without a powerful friend, a gray, slim figure in antechambers, a person known to secretaries and clerks as the fellow with the irrigation scheme. But he had hung around, timidly badgering Congressmen and Senators, and now other men triumphed for him. Mr. Hanna took him to the White House to thank the President. Mr. Newlands sent him a cordial line. He went back to his deserts and soon died. His name means nothing, save to his children, written here, but it is written to remind a few that a nation has — sometimes — unselfish servants who are not paid. . . .

260

Mark Hanna's interest in a canal connecting the Atlantic Ocean with its neighbor by way of Central America is a more definite set of facts. He had periodically talked of this since the Civil War. He bored his guest Henry Adler by a long discussion of the matter in October of 1890, at the Union Club in Cleveland. The affair presented itself to him then merely as a technical topic. His mechanical intelligence was entertained by the possibility of cutting such a canal. In the spring of 1896 he was talking of the canal again, this time to Mr. Theodore Hamill, a youngster of twenty who had lived in South America. In the autumn of 1897 Mr. Hamill appeared before him more seriously, full of an agreeably piratical scheme of seizing the isthmus at Panama for the United States, confiscating the property of the French canal company, and building a canal. Mr. Hanna must have enjoyed this project in patriotism, because he gave Mr. Hamill a note to Cushman Davis and sent him across Washington to call on the Senator from Minnesota, who laughed outright, but kept the boy talking about the geological structure of the isthmus for some hours. Yet, however lightly Mr. Hanna took this chatter, he thought enough about Panama to address a letter in his own script to Senator Allison, asking what his real opinion of an interoceanic canal was. "I have recently," he wrote, " heard a lot about the Panama route which impresses me favorably. Mr. Henry Villard and some other solid business men in New York have been

interested in the French concession. You know that
Davis has no use for the Nicaragua route. He has been
into the business very thoroughly and is dead against
that project. I should like to hear from you on this
point." [4]

Then, in 1900, he showed the frankest reluctance
when Mr. McKinley was eager to include an interoceanic canal among the show pieces of the Republican
platform. His objection was double. Mr. Bryan, he
told one friend, was likely to grab at the plan as another gesture of imperialism. And he said to Myron
Herrick, " It is bad business playing poker with other
people's chips." The phrase echoed a long way, as did
many of Mr. Hanna's rough figures. You must remember that his babyhood and young boyhood had
been passed beside the ruinous canal at New Lisbon,
the ditch into which so much money had been thrown.
Age was not making Mr. Hanna cautious, but his
President would be blamed if the canal through
Nicaragua or the one through Panama, favored by
Mr. Herrick, proved a failure.

He begged and ordered speakers to go easy on the
topic. Neither the lordly contribution of the Panama
company's American attorney to the campaign fund
nor the pleasure of stealing a Democratic plank for
his own party's platform made the canal dear to Mr.
Hanna in 1900. He thought it bad politics, and said

---

[4] Mr. Oswald Villard tells me that his father had no interest in the
French company, but that his name was used to promote sales of stock.

so, and his subsequent performance has thus been described by professorial historians as flagrant opportunism. But, in the technic of politics, he was fully right in 1900. The canal was dangerous, although not much attacked by the anti-imperialists, and the hazy condition of the whole scheme made it more ticklish still. It haunted him, though — this gashing of mountains and blending of seas. McKinley was not six weeks dead when an engineer chatting with some friends about the route through Nicaragua, in the Holland House, found a page offering him a card; Senator Hanna wanted to know if he might join a conversation that had drifted across the hallway to him where he sat with his cigar. It is not unlikely, after all, that Daniel James Mason's denunciation of the Nicaraguan scheme, fifteen minutes long, did as much as anything to harden the Senator in favor of Panama. " You are," he said, " a damned sight more enlightening about this business than anybody I've listened to on it."

But he had heard a great deal about the business. In the flux of easy satire since 1920 it has become strangely necessary to regard an American man of business as a jackass. To assert the contrary for a number of dead men of business, some of whom had no favor among the sanctimonious, is an exploit, here undertaken with a certain nervousness. Quite independent of Myron Herrick, Nelson Cromwell, and Colonel Bunau-Varilla, a quantity of political business men in New York and Chicago moved in favor of the Panama Canal. They were not only independent of the French Panama company, but they were independent of each other. A few of them, such as John McCall, George Perkins, and Thomas Fortune Ryan, directly approached Mr. Hanna. Others approached Mr. Roosevelt. The feasibility of this canal and its advantages over a canal through Nicaragua were discussed at luncheon and dinner by men whose pockets would not swell by a dime's width if the canal was built. It interested them; they liked to talk about it. John McCook drew Edward Harriman into a chat, in 1901, and found that the dark collector of Western railroads was not at all averse to a Panama canal. Far from damaging his California properties, he said, a canal would help them. "People would get so sick of looking at water on the way out," he explained, "that they'd come home by rail." To this selected audience, then, it was exciting to hear privately, in March of 1902, that Mr. Hanna might oppose the measure languidly debated in Congress, empowering the President to arrange the construction of a canal by way of Nicaragua. But when Mr. Hanna appeared in the Senate on the fifth of June and spoke for Panama, his act bewildered half of the journalists and most of his friends.

He came into the Senate, followed by his secretary, whose hands were full of pamphlets, and commenced his conversational support of Senator Spooner's

amendment to the Hepburn Bill before a scant gallery.
Ten minutes passed; telephones had jingled and
people hurried to the Capitol. Soon rules were broken.
Ladies and diplomats, reporters, agents of the powers,
all jammed the gallery's aisles. This plain old person
in a dull gray suit was doing something and a drama
heaped itself in the warm chamber while he drawled
along, explaining this investment to the Senate without an eloquent phrase. He talked, glancing at two
shreds of note paper scrawled with figures, as if some
client had asked his advice about a sale of bonds. It
seems the driest speech, and yet it thrilled. Up among
the witnesses the Russian envoy began to murmur,
" *Mais il est formidable!* " and this, they say, is true.
Mark Hanna was formidable: he stood talking of
costs and labor and convenience, the foreman of an
age. Machinery spoke; the blue prints of engineers
and the coal in bunkers found a voice here. A monstrous, docile power made itself heard. This was a job
that the nation could take on, if it wanted to do it.
This was work. He stood drawling, and another mood
overcame people hearing him. He had spoken for an
hour. It was seen that his ailing legs were stiffened
under him as his face grew yellow, damp with effort.
A woman gulped, so that Senators heard her, " Oh, do
make him sit down! " and Senator Frye twitched in
his chair. But he talked on. His report was not yielded;
he would be heard out. His knees sagged at the last,
and when he dropped into his chair a gasp of true

relief whirled through the Senate before the applause began.

Gossip and rancor exploded in the hotels that night. This had to be explained away by Mark Hanna's enemies. They must find a dirty trick in it somewhere and, literally, by midnight men were assuring one another that Mr. Hanna was wrecking any hope of a canal by causing a deadlock between the Senate and the House. He was doing this, of course, on behalf of the railroads. If that story was not suitable, another served: he had been bribed by the attorney of the French Panama company to cause the United States to buy its worthless properties. In fact, everybody had been bribed. The Secretary of State, the Cabinet, Mr. Hanna, Mr. Spooner, the President's elder daughter, and Leonard Wood were sharing sums of thirty and forty million among them. "It is the most expensive lying since the Civil War," said Mr. Hay. "But where is the money supposed to be coming from?"

Meanwhile, at the Arlington, Mr. Hanna was tirelessly receiving callers. His control of his project was not complete. He could count certainly on the strong and utter opposition of Thomas Platt and Matthew Quay in his own party, and the perpetual protector of the Nicaraguan scheme was the agreeable Senator Morgan of Alabama, one of the most popular Democrats. As Hanna startled the public on June 5th, he now stunned experts by his private management of the affair. Congressmen and their friends were summoned to his rooms. The lobby took its orders. He promised nothing. No favors were to be doled out in exchange for obedience. "He has his campaign face on," said Senator Frye. On June 13th a Western journalist canvassed the House of Representatives and knew in advance that Nicaragua was done for. Mr. Hanna had won; it would be a Panama canal.

But he was paying for his conquest. Mrs. Hanna fretted and one of her friends found her quietly weeping on the afternoon of June 14th. He was killing himself, she said. He just would not realize that he was an old man now, and nobody could make him behave, not even Ruth. And the strain was extraordinary. He himself tried to slacken it, dashing along the Potomac in a fast launch one night, and stamping into John Hay's library one Sunday morning, saying that he was two thirds crazy, he was so tired. Mr. Hay was entertaining Daniel Hoyt Marvin with some literary gossip and Mr. Hanna listened to the talk a while. It recalled something he had meant to investigate.

"What about this poet Walt Whitman?"

"He's still dead," said Mr. Hay.

Mr. Hanna knew that. But someone had told him that a Postmaster General discharged Walt Whitman for writing a book. Mr. Hay handed him *Leaves of Grass* and the Senator examined it for half an hour silently, as if it were a report of bankruptcy proceedings. He put it aside with a snort.

"The Postmaster General must have been a fool."

267

He rode back with Mr. Marvin to the Arlington and took this stranger into his confidence on the subject of automobiles. His wife was the only person in the family who believed that automobiles would ever amount to a thing. His brothers and his son were skeptical. But he saw the automobile revolutionizing commerce. " It was just like reading," says Mr. Marvin, " one of those articles you see twenty times a year about what the automobile has done, but with everything put in the future tense. His only error was that he counted on a long war between the steam motor and the gasoline motor. He said that someone would put a motor on the market at prices suitable to small farmers and change the whole nature of life in the country. I did not believe a word of it, of course. This was my only encounter with Mr. Hanna, and I thought he was going into softening of the brain. . . ."

On June 19th he had his triumph. The Senate voted. Mr. Hanna stood in the Marble Room with Senator Spooner receiving compliments. Reporters and diplomats pressed on him. He grinned with a particular sweetness when Thomas Platt came up to make a chilly speech, for he knew that Mr. Platt and Mr. Quay had been deviling the President behind his back. They wearied Mr. Roosevelt until he arranged one of his amiable duplicities: Colonel Montgomery was summoned and stayed beside the desk while the President importantly scribbled nonsense on a dozen telegraph blanks, the names of his children or sentences from headlines of a newspaper. The bosses tired of his polite inattention and left. Mr. Roosevelt lay back in his chair and asked with violence, "Montgomery, does the spectacle of human imbecility ever alarm you?"

This was known to Mr. Hanna, and his grin must have burned Thomas Platt. But he triumphed affably. He said to some Democratic Senator, "I'm sorry you wouldn't vote with us. You'll find that we've sold the boys the best horse." It was a business man's victory; he had sold the nation the better of two propositions. It was victory on his own terms, a solid argument of costs and convenience against oratory and scandalous hints. "We've saved the Treasury about seventy millions," he said, limping down the room on Mr. Spooner's arm; "so let the dogs howl!"

The dogs howled and are howling yet, in cheap biography and histories. This act so admired by men who hated Hanna's power is slobbered with conjectures as to his motive. He did what he chose. But in America we have reversed Goethe's saying, "The doer is conscienceless; no one has a conscience except the spectator. . . ." Through all that June of 1902 spectators played the conscientious, linking the President and the Senator in a flurry of conscienceless accusations. Large things had been done, and they must be diminished by many little breaths; the quality, the fine heat of performance, must be cooled down. Gentlemen of the press and the bars knew all about it. The President had enormous holdings of dry land in the Southwest, or he had friends who had dry acres. Hence the Newlands Act. And Mr. Hanna was putting millions in his banks by this trick of Panama. So the dogs howled. But the hills were cleft and the oceans joined, where Hanna willed. Ships sail through this ditch of Panama, guarded by young Americans in badly fitting uniforms. High dams spill down their harvested flood for a harvest's good upon those plains where, when I was born, a horned skull might glimmer on unending dust, challenging man, and the train jarred past a ruinous house swept out by heat, past orchards murdered by the sun. These are facts, these achievements that once were dreams or trickeries of politicians. There could be no canal, it was innumerably proved in bars and drawing-rooms, and watering the desert was a child's notion. But the great ditch and the rills among trees all panoplied with fruit are facts. Let the dogs howl.

III

Hanna had fulfilled himself. It was felt. Anecdotes thickened on the Senator, envious or flattering. He was a national possession while reforming journalists raked him with the rest of the muck; he was a national disgrace while ambassadors and touring celebrities wanted interviews. He was more than ever the fetish of luck and force. His chuckling secretary showed privileged callers letters written in obscure houses and towns of the West, wheedling the Red Boss of 1896 to

270

get a pension granted or to find an office. Mothers asked advice on proper books for growing boys, and to one such matron the old man wrote: " I have never been a great reader. When I do read it is generally something pretty practical. If your boy is a serious fellow, would suggest that you try to get him a very good book of Baron Humboldt. Either the book is named Cosmos or that is the first essay in it. You probably know this was a favorite essay with Mr. Lincoln. I admired it a great deal when I was a young fellow. I do not mean," he admitted, " that Mr. Lincoln and I grew up just the same way. . . ." But legend will have it that Mr. Hanna did not know the meaning of the word " cosmos," and legend prevails, in these cases. He will remain, then, a coarsely ignorant person, without intellect, yet, somehow, a consummate manager of men, a comic *arriviste* at whose table members of the Cabinet, authors, scientists, actors, and painters cheerfully mingled. Oh, come!

Hanna talked plainly, but he talked honestly, and this honesty somehow accorded with a revolt of the sensitized against an insipid society. The old Senator spoke his mind. To people who did not confuse intellect with an appreciation of paper roses his mind was an interesting thing enough. He recognized the absurd in the creation of all these great fortunes; he did not gape at money, as money. One Western millionaire, he would say, had a bank slide on his head and sat up in the clay to see lumps of ore twinkling at him, and the anecdote is true. Another had a mother who gleaned a third of her boy's pay from his pockets by night, and returned him five thousand dollars of it when she heard of a good investment in stock of a steamship company, on the Lakes. He divided these goats from the sheep; the millionaires by chance did not rank with those banking or industrial plutocrats who knew what they were doing and deliberately did it. Also he disliked fussy shams. There was a giggle at Senator Spooner's house one night when Mr. Hanna glanced at an ideal restoration of the Roman Forum and said it looked a " second-rate World's Fair." Proper æsthetes shuddered when he called the rococo Library of Congress a German wedding cake, or they stared as politely as they could when he said his brother's new motor launch was a damned sight more beautiful than a lot of these foolish statues you had to look at. Everything hard, limbered, and strong pleased the Senator's mechanic eye; the prow of a motor boat, his slim daughter on a lean horse among the pines at Thomasville, the high line of a mast bearing a flag. Finally, he defended the interior economy of money-making itself, for one night in John Hay's library talk turned to intellectual achievements. Elihu Root and a lady survive from the group that laughed when the Senator claimed the invention of double entry book-keeping as a grand feat of intellect. Hanna growled, " Well, it is ! " and went away with the Secretary of War. But

Henry Adams roused in his corner and murmured to a woman, " Goethe thought it was, too . . . " and the murmur stays with her.

The Senator was not afraid of women. He dared even to scold one, if he liked her. The daughter of a friend came gleaming into Washington with ten trunks filled at Paris in the spring of 1903. Hanna took the girl, encased in a wonderful frock, to a dance given by naval officers. The Roosevelts appeared. Many partners said pretty things, and ladies purred over the French gown. Her exhilaration lasted until Mr. Hanna wanted to leave and led her down the room. She asked him confidently which was the best-dressed woman in the place. His head jerked sideways to a simple black robe in a knot of blue and gold uniforms. The girl saw nothing stunning about Mrs. Roosevelt's costume. It was just a nice frock.

" That's all that a lady has to have, sis."

A lady was a lady to the political pragmatist; the minister without portfolio was sedulous for the dignity of the lady in the White House. The harmless son of a military official was bouncing a tennis ball in the gutter of Dupont Circle one day of April in 1903 and the plaything hopped into a passing victoria. Quentin Roosevelt tossed the ball back, and its owner stood alarmed, wondering if this would cost his father a promotion, although Mrs. Roosevelt had smiled. Then a cane smote the end of his spine, and Mr. Hanna furiously grunted, " You! You ought to take your hat off when any woman speaks to you. When Mrs. Roosevelt speaks to you, keep it off a week!"

He was old. People saw it or would not see it, because his vivacity continued and his pace down to his chair in the Senate was stiffly competent. Seen from the gallery, Mr. Hanna was not unlike a finely adjusted toy in motion. His world amused him still, and he would dodge off on trips to look at things. Workmen in the plant of the Otis Elevator Company at Yonkers did not know the stout man in gray quietly poking among them, asking sensible questions about weights and slides, as if he was a graduated workman himself. But he was old. He talked, sometimes, a little wonderingly about other people's memories. His own was unimpaired. It puzzled him that Mel and Leonard should forget their father's swooning fit on election day of 1860. The whole family had been in the house, and how frightened they all were! But his brothers forgot that. . . . It distracted him, at breakfast in the Arlington, with men watching his lips. They had come down to head him against Mr. Roosevelt, but he would only talk to them of memory through the meal. . . . Take the nomination from Roosevelt in 1904? Rubbish! He was leaving for Saint Louis with the President in a day or two, to open this Fair. . . . He wanted to talk of his past.

Exasperation rose in New York. What did the old devil mean by speaking for the commercial treaties with Cuba, instead of against them, and why didn't

he fight Roosevelt openly from the floor of the Senate
on all these damned reforms? He had not stopped the
act giving precedence to governmental actions in Federal courts, or the act punishing receivers of rebates,
or the creation of the Department of Commerce and
Labor.[5]

A simple explanation was, of course, that the leader
of the Republican party thought Cuba entitled to
reciprocal aid from the United States and believed
some reform to be inevitable. But that was too simple.
Perhaps — John Hay's ill health was known — Hanna
wanted to be Secretary of State in a second Roosevelt
administration. Edward Lauterbach had another theory: Hanna was turning State Socialist. That was
what his Western irrigation scheme, his prophecy of
power plants owned by the government, and his chat
about the vanished Grangers with their ideas of co-
operative grain elevators, co-operative banks, and
sternly regulated freight rates, summed up to.

" To think," said a sporting banker, " that we sent
this man to Washington to look out for us! "

"We did nothing of the kind," John Pierpont

---

[5] In fact he pushed the creation of the new department. It had been discussed with McKinley in 1899 and 1900. It was favored in New York by
John McCall, Darwin Kingsley, George Perkins, and several other less-
known financiers. Howard Melville Hanna claimed in 1904 that his brother
invented the department. Senator Hanna, in a letter to Mr. Jacob Bennett,
dated October 1, 1900, says: " There should be a department capable of
handling such situations as this [the threatened coal strike averted by
J. P. Morgan and himself], and the matter is being put up to the President
in a very strong way. . . ."

Morgan answered; "he sent himself. We did not know how to spell his name in '96." [6]

It had taken much persuasion to make financiers know that Hanna was not McKinley's ruler, but an adoring, diffident friend. They were human financiers and doubted all sentiments except their own sentiments. Three of them had tried to have Whitelaw Reid made ambassador in 1897 to the court of Saint James, because they were fond of him. Mr. Morgan himself, striding on toes of clients in his waiting-room in a hurry to embrace a son just landed at New York, was a human and rather moving sight. But they could not credit that Mark Hanna had become fond of Theodore Roosevelt. . . . There must be something else he wanted. Meanwhile, why didn't he stop the President's uncomfortable activity?

"Can't you realize," a dry, Western voice asked, "that hundreds of men you all know and eat lunch with have been urging Roosevelt to enforce the Anti-Trust Law and the Interstate Commerce Law?"

They knew it, but did not want to know it. They were major capitalists. They sulked away from believing that hundreds of little rich men rejoiced quietly when the President moved to dissolve the Northern Securities Company. One of them certainly knew that the clumsy laws regulating commerce and the formation of trusts had been passed with the backing of minor capital at the end of the 'eighties. Little

[6] *Ipsissima verba*, in latter March 1903.

money had long fought big money, with the engines of democracy.

A phase of law ended in the United States. Capital was not at war with law, on the plan of Sumner and Spengler, but trying to maintain the elder code taken over from England in the eighteenth century, because old laws were too narrow to control capital, this floating, detached mass of power which illusively seemed free of the earth. Those old laws were written by learned clerks and abbots to whom money was just rent due proper landlords or tokens of gold exchanged by traders and merchants. This wealth in the hands of men without traditions and bound to no caste was not anticipated. The dead judges of the King's Bench could not bind a casteless nation large as all Europe. Democracy created American capitalists, as American capital once had created democracy.

Money had stirred with every movement of the colonists westward, always gaining strength. As the expansionist policy it had caused democracy to build its railroads, and as democracy it had urged the Homestead and all like acts granting free land in the West. As democratic morality it destroyed the slaveholders of the South. As producing industry it had granted itself subsidies, acts for the purchase of silver, tariffs and protections. As international finance it had beaten down Free Silver in 1896. As "manifest destiny" it had, a little haltingly, approved imperialism. Its private wars were clouded in moral issues and equivocations; its will speaks through shapes as various as William Bryan, John Rockefeller, or the dreary Henry Ford. It would make war soon on pleasure, learning, and criticism. For what does demos care about aloof gayeties of the mind, scholarship, frail dreams? Demos poor is wronged, and demos rich is demos powerful to wrong demos. Money does not rule democracy. Money is democracy.

Mr. Roosevelt, then, put the refreshed laws in force against democracy, and democracy applauded. For eighteen months the financiers were highly disturbed, but, by the autumn of 1904, they had sensed Roosevelt's limitation. He wasn't imaginative, after all. They spent money on his campaign for the next presidency in such bulk that his feeble opponent accused Roosevelt of blackmailing the great corporations, which was untrue and superfluous. Still, in the spring of 1903, rich men worried, and some of them gave out solemn interviews. It was at once discovered that a conspiracy against Mr. Roosevelt existed in Wall Street. The word "conspiracy" was a bully effect.

For theatrical reasons Mr. Hanna had to be part of this conspiracy. He was towering. He had smashed a heavy attack of the Democratic party in Ohio, in the autumn of 1902. His popularity puffed. A lady strolling with Matthew Quay along Pennsylvania Avenue noted a huge truck filled with envelopes and wondered what the load was.

"It's just Hanna's mail going up to the Capitol," said Mr. Quay.

Mr. Quay knew precisely the situation between the White House and the Arlington Hotel. There need be no trouble if the President's satellites and Hanna's gang would let the two men alone. But the dear boys, he told Mrs. Warner, wanted to make a fight of it. He had warned the President that the regional bigwigs and little politicians who lunched with him one day would be hunting an invitation to breakfast next morning at the Senator's hotel. But there was going to be trouble, and soon.

"We have two Executive Mansions, and the President's friends don't like that."

Here, for six weeks, everything becomes misty, conjectural. It was heard in New York by the third week of April that a new leader of the Republican party had been found, in the person of Senator Joseph Benson Foraker. Prudent magnates sent messengers to conciliate and inquire what that meant. Mr. Hanna grinned. Mr. Foraker seemed "cold, and not in the least interested" to examining agents. Roosevelt was touring the country, explaining himself to the plain people. On May 3rd an obscure, clever man, secretary to a dull, rich Senator was beckoned by the Attorney General to enter his carriage on S Street. Mr. Knox observed gently that they were both indebted to Mark Hanna for great kindnesses. He wondered, staring away from his acquaintance, if Hanna knew that some "irresponsible people" were trying to bring about a breach between Mr. Roosevelt and himself. It would certainly be disastrous and it ought to be prevented. . . . Good morning.

Foraker's perplexity, on May 14th, shook some words out of him. He was "expected" to get the Ohio State Republican convention to approve Mr. Roosevelt's presidency and to pledge itself to support his candidacy in 1904. He was "in a tight box." He pried off the lid, on May 23rd, by giving an interview in which he adroitly stated that Mr. Hanna's own retinue had raised the question of endorsing Mr. Roosevelt's candidacy in 1904 and, now that it was raised, the convention must endorse the President or refuse to endorse him.

Next morning the obscure secretary breakfasted with his Senator and the paragraph in the newspaper took the old Western adventurer's eye. Oh, so it had started! Well, Foraker would be appointed Chairman of the Republican Campaign Committee, if he could swing this trick for the Roosevelt faction. The President's friends were to repeat Hanna's performance of 1896. They would appear at the convention of 1904 with so many states pledged to the President that there could be no other candidate. Foraker would nominate Roosevelt and would mechanically be made Chairman. . . . This was being said everywhere. Washington was alert by noon. The President had struck at Mark Hanna. The jinni was to be cased in the brass bottle and chucked into the sea.

Hanna did not believe that. He assumed the trick to be Senator Foraker's invention and said so, in Cleveland. He had been joking with Roosevelt in March about the efforts of his own friends to get him to declare himself a candidate in 1904 and the President had asked to be a guest at the wedding of Ruth Hanna to Medill McCormick in June. Roosevelt would not do this to him. The men about him saw that his power of campaigns, its excitement and tension, was dear to Hanna. "By God, he can't mean to have Foraker run a campaign for him! . . . By God, I don't think he's in this!" He gave out an interview denying, for the fourth published time, that he wanted the presidency, and opposing Foraker's suggestion. Now he telegraphed to Roosevelt, in Seattle.

"The issue that has been forced upon me in the matter of our state convention this year endorsing you for the Republican nomination next year has come in a way which makes it necessary for me to oppose such a resolution. When you know all the facts, I am sure that you will approve my course. . . ."

Mr. Roosevelt was not interested in the facts at all. Strategically remote from this incident in practical politics, he handled it with ideal cleverness. He proposed to be endorsed by the Ohio Republicans. He answered:

"Your telegram received. I have not asked any

281

man for his vote.[7] I have nothing whatever to do with raising this issue. Inasmuch as it has been raised, of course, those who favor my administration and my nomination will favor endorsing both, and those who do not will oppose."

The telegram was published instantly by the Associated Press. Experts differed as to its merits. Mr. Roosevelt's backers were thrusting him forward a year ahead of the convention which should endorse his candidacy. If Hanna now let him be endorsed it would impress the public as a deliberate plan to shut off any other choice in advance, and it would be taken as an act to strengthen Hanna's own candidacy for the senatorship in this year of 1903. Hanna refused fight. He telegraphed to the President, withdrawing his objection, on May 26th, and delicately added: "I have given the substance of this to the Associated Press."

His duller admirers saw that Mr. Roosevelt had planted one straight on the jaw of the Wall Street gang and had forced Hanna himself to approve his candidacy in 1904. That he had not published Hanna's telegram to him was another sound stroke in the game. They cared no more for the facts than the President

[7] "'I have not asked any man for his vote!' Hurrah for George Washington!" Henry Watterson to Davison Weeks, May 26, 1903.

"I was terribly sorry to see Theodore descend to such an amazing quibble as his telegram to Hanna. You know I have no reason to love M. A. H. But he has been very dignified in his attitude since this happened. He knows perfectly that Theodore has been asking us all for our support next year. If Hanna had chosen to answer, his only course open would have been to say that he (Roosevelt) meant individual delegates in the Ohio Convention." John J. McCook to William C. Beer, undated.

cared at Seattle. His friends in Washington rejoiced. Senator Foraker, Henry Cabot Lodge wrote to the President, admired the telegram tremendously. Senator Foraker's way of showing this was odd.

"The whole business has been intensely disagreeable to me, for a number of reasons," he said in the first week of June.

His reasons he kept to himself. He stood on the stairs of his fine house in Washington and stared at a mosaic of Guido Reni's Aurora on the wall of the upper hallway, as he slapped the handrail. He rasped out that Mr. Roosevelt hadn't asked him to do anything. His callers watched him scowling until his small son decided to slide down the rail and gracelessly ended the serious conversation by bumping into the Senator. So ambassadors merely found that Mr. Foraker did not like the results of all this. As usual, they had seen Foraker in the yellow hallway of his house; one never got upstairs in this man's life. He received embassies on his doormat, and this embassy had been a failure. Foraker would not be reconciled with Marcus Hanna, and that was all. He led his child up the stairs. Agents of the most powerful banker and the biggest insurance company in America walked out of the house and reported that nothing could be done.

But much had been done. His brother Howard furiously circulated Mark Hanna's telegram to Mr. Roosevelt, advertising that Roosevelt had replied as to another kind of message. An impression grew among men who admired the President that he had been unscrupulous, and some said so, vigorously, in New York and Washington. They would not see Foraker or Lodge succeed Hanna as executive head of the party in the campaign of 1904. "And you can tell the President that," said Senator Orville Platt to Philander Knox, "as loudly as I am saying it to you in this room!"

On May 29th the President wrote an emollient letter to Mr. Hanna, a cadenza of soothing and smooth suggestions. "I thank you for your letter which gave me the first gleam of light on the situation. I do not think you appreciated the exact effect that your interview and announced position had on the country at large. It was everywhere accepted as the first open attack on me, and it gave heart, curiously enough, not only to my opponents but to all the men who lump you and me together as improperly friendly to organized labor and to the working men generally. . . . No one but a really big man — a man above all petty considerations — could have treated me as you have done during the year and a half since President McKinley's death. I have consulted you and relied on your judgment more than I have done with any other man. . . ."

This note bored the Senator's son. Two years later he wrote to Henry Adler: "Mr. Roosevelt soon sent father a conciliating letter, of which you will find a

copy enclosed for your private file. But he does not
explain why he did not give out the substance of Mr.
Hanna's telegram correctly to the Associated Press
when he published his own answer to it. The truth is
that he had no explanation ready. He knew perfectly
what Mr. Hanna's situation in regard to Mr. Foraker
was. But he wanted to make a Rough Rider speech
about his enemies in Wall Street to the crowd out in
Spokane and he took this occasion to do it at Mr.
Hanna's expense. Of course he had no time to learn
the effect of Mr. Hanna's interview on the public.
He answered father's telegram within a day of receiving it. He was consulting with two men who hated
Mr. Hanna at the time, and admitted it in a letter he
wrote to H. C. Lodge three or four days later. . . ." [8]

Mr. Lodge was rather indiscreet in the first week of
June. Information passed from a brokerage in Boston
to New York that the President's scholarly intimate
claimed this whole arrangement of telegrams and
challenges as his idea. The information was untrue,
but Mr. Lodge did talk a good deal. An alarmed
Attorney General began to send out rings of oil on

[8] " . . . I thought the matter over a full 24 hours, consulting with
Mellen, Byrnes and Moody. . . . I accordingly sent him my answer, and
as you doubtless saw, made a similar statement for the public press, of
course not alluding to the fact that Hanna had sent me the telegram — my
statement simply going as one made necessary by Hanna's long interview in
which he announced that he would oppose my endorsement by the Ohio
Convention. . . . I made it " — the speech at Spokane — " particularly
with reference to having a knockdown and dragout fight with Hanna and
the whole Wall Street crowd. . . ." Theodore Roosevelt to Henry Cabot
Lodge, May 27, 1903.

the torn water. " Mr. Knox says the whole affair is a
pure misunderstanding. He is doing his damnedest
to patch it up. Lodge has been talking too much in
Boston and some kind of letter he had from the President is being passed around. I am very sorry about the
whole thing. . . ." [9]

Meanwhile in Cleveland it was raining daily. There
were bets. The Hanna luck was to break: rain would
fall on Ruth Hanna's wedding day, and the President
would not appear. Magnates swarmed into the city
under umbrellas on the ninth of June. Ladies prepared
to wear a second-best gown. Then the sun rose dec-
orously next morning and the rain ceased. The President's teeth shimmered on the veranda of the big
mansion by the Lake and he said " Damn! " audibly,
catching his cuff in a twisted ornamentation of the
newel post in the hall. Out under a tent on the lawn
old Charles Foster lifted champagne to his lips, whispering, " To the next President — whichever one it
is! " The conspiracy of business men to defeat Roosevelt in 1904 had learned of its own existence in March,
but it was growing real. Senator Hanna bowed his
most distinguished guest out of Cleveland, and the
game continued.

[9] Benjamin Montgomery to William Collins Beer, June 7, 1903.
A quotation from an official on duty in the White House should not be
made without explanation. Colonel Montgomery wrote frequently to my
father, but he scrupulously refrained from saying anything of business current unless the matter had become public property, such as the meal taken
by Booker Washington with Mr. Roosevelt. He was warmly attached to
Mr. Roosevelt, but viewed some of the President's maneuvers with regret.

" A case of Wall Street versus Theodore Roosevelt," said the Attorney General, in July, "has been made out. I think it can be settled out of court. But . . . it might be wished that the defendant would . . . exercise a little reticence."

The conspiracy took the form of daylit conversations openly carried on in clubs and restaurants by all kinds of men. But conspiracy was still the word at the White House. "I thought," mused a shrewd journalist from Kansas City, Harvey Fleming, "that conspiracies happened in dark rooms and nobody knew who was in them." Still, conspiracy was the appointed word. The President was having a knockdown and dragout fight with Hanna and the Wall Street conspirators.

" I'm the person who's going to be dragged out," said the Senator. "Don't these fools in New York know I'm sixty-six years old?"

These fools who wanted Hanna to take the nomination from Mr. Roosevelt in 1904 were mostly stockholders, not the major financiers. They were men more angered by some attitudes of the President than by anything he had done, against finance. "I have known Theodore for twenty-five years," one of them wrote to a son in Oxford, "without knowing that he hated corporations and wanted to see Wall Street smashed wide open.[10] But I should like to know what

[10] This wish was reported into New York from Cheyenne, Wyoming, in June. It was widely quoted in private.

excuse he has for hating corporations. His father made money out of them and he lives on it. . . . But what disgusts me, in this exhibition he has made of himself, is that he cries before he is hit. He has taken a leaf out of Bryan's book. It may please the Populists and the cowboys to see a President of the United States make a fool of himself talking cant. Could he name one real threat made against him by any responsible person? . . . Mr. Hayes was abominably libelled through his whole administration. But he behaved himself as a gentleman should. I cannot say as much for Theodore. Every decision and every piece of legislation is announced as if he had been obliged to enter the Senate and plead to have it passed. . . ."

Here the injustice is plain. Mr. Roosevelt's satellites were supplying their hero with airs of martyrdom. Horrible things were being done to the President by his enemies. Hill, Morgan, the Rockefellers, the steelmakers, and the grand butchers were " saying things." When the Republic of Panama appeared so suddenly in November, and Mr. Roosevelt caused it to be recognized, a plaintive journalist assured the world in the bar of the Raleigh that Hanna had forced this action on the President, a sentimental invention which annoyed Mr. Roosevelt into many words on November 22nd.[11] But what Mr. Roosevelt really said, about

[11] During the composition of this book I have been told at least ten times that Mr. Hanna forced the President to recognize the Republic of Panama. Mr. Roosevelt specifically denied, on November 22, 1903, that Hanna had even advised him to recognize the Republic. He said in 1911 to

Wall Street and about his hypothetical enemies, was constantly whelmed and distorted in grotesque lies. " This wordy city," John Hay wrote to Mrs. Charlton Paull in the first of October, " poisons men, who might be friends, against each other. . . ."

The conspiracy of finance was formless enough until December, but the Senator had no peace from his proponents all through the autumn. They were at him in a hundred ways. Myron Herrick was asked to plead, and would not. John McCall, who was truly liked by the Senator, declined to bother him, saying that Hanna was too old to be made President. But loud conspirators would not be silent. They must have a yes.

" Conspiracy," Mr. Hanna said, in his rooms at the Arlington, " is the right word for it! They want to kill me!"

He growled that he was selling securities " to save Dan and the girls the bother." The whole business amused him. As soon as he told his bank to sell one famous stock, his very lawyers wanted to know if he was getting rid of this corporation's shares so as to be able to face the plain people with clean hands. That was pretty funny, wasn't it? . . . Well, he was off for Cleveland tonight. His campaign was booming. He was electing himself Senator and taking the

Mr. Charles Deshler at San Francisco, " Hanna did absolutely nothing to hinder me or to force our hand in that business." His denial in 1903 was made to a lady who sympathized with him on Mr. Hanna's reported brutality.

governorship of Ohio for Myron Herrick. Tom Johnson was out on the stump already, shouting for municipal street railways and revised taxations. Johnson, he yawned, would stay mayor of Cleveland. That couldn't be helped. But the Democratic reformer's candidate for Governor would be wiped out. Herrick would sweep the state. . . . He limped downstairs and stood in the doors of the hotel. The funeral of a notable nothing was passing the Arlington.

"Drive him fast to his tomb," said my father.

"That from Shakspere, Beer?"

No, it was from *A Tale of Two Cities*. The old man nodded, repeating the words. Yes. He had not thought of the book in a thousand years. He stared after the funeral.

"Drive him fast to his tomb? That's where a lot of 'em want to see me!"

His maintained power had grown irksome to many people. Weak men and strong men both resent this amusement called success, and he had plangently succeeded for so long, and was succeeding still. His victory in November was sharp. Letters and telegrams from thousands demanded that he make himself President. Petitions came, signed by all these people in the South and West. It tickled him, and it seemed to puzzle him. He could understand those bully boys up in New York thinking they wanted him for President, but the Westerners? "I don't see that so well," he said, and lit his next cigar.

Be President? No! The answer went back to New York, perhaps twice a week in December. A committee up there was gathering pledges and money. Pity to waste their time so. No! . . . Meanwhile it all amused him, the messengers, the lickspittle orators, the embassies of Mr. Roosevelt's worried friends. He got tired, he told George Cortelyou, of going to the White House and being sworn in. His tonsils were calloused with telling damn fools he was too old, too fat to be President. Say, though, some of these gentlemen had corns on their tongues from lying to Roosevelt about him! . . . His eyes snapped. He marched into the Senate and grinned at the funny world. He was committing his last offense against the propriety of romantic politics: he disdained solemnity.

At the White House there was something going on for Hanna's diversion. Practical politicians called and lunched with Theodore Roosevelt. Rural editors were bobbing in and out. A boss from Cincinnati showed his gay eyes. Herman Kohlsaat grew exasperated, hearing the gossip in Chicago. Roosevelt must stop hunting delegates for 1904. He came to Washington and boldly lectured the President, declaring that Hanna was too old and too ill to be a candidate and that Mr. Roosevelt was making himself ridiculous by his nervousness. The President gave out word that he would not see men who had been brought to confer with him. Kohlsaat returned to Chicago. But, on December 20th, Senator Foraker exploded to a friend,

"Root and Knox and Wayne McVeagh and I have all told him that Hanna does not mean to fight him. But he is writing too damned many letters!"

For power begets superstitions. Something about this old man, with his stiffened legs and his sagging throat, worked on the President. He would not be satisfied. A terrible legend of force hung around Hanna. This same day the President thrashed up and down his office, talking trivial stuff to Mr. Beer. The question flashed after half an hour.

"Have you seen Senator Hanna since you came down?"

"Yes. On the street, for a minute."

"Did he say anything about the next convention?"

"No, sir."

"Oh. . . ."

But Mark Hanna's wife could not laugh. Her long training made her tactfully mute when questioners came at her. No, she would say, the Senator was not thinking of the presidency. He had said so. It was absurd for people to talk in this way, and so humiliating for the President! After Christmas she made one outcry, on the cold veranda beside the Lake. Wind hurled flakes upon her furs, and her friend shivered. But if she could only stay here! She would rather freeze in Cleveland than be at Washington. And those awful people were trying to kill him. And he would have to lead the campaign next summer! . . . But she came back to Washington and appeared at receptions, placidly correct, kindly, and so tired. She was not well and the Senator was ill. They went out together, to long dinners and the play. Talk swelled as the old man passed through murmurous alleys of hotels. . . . There he was. That was Mark Hanna!

Mr. Lytton Strachey, cleverest of biographers, patented a device at the end of his story about Queen Victoria, fancying thoughts that wheeled in the mind of the dying Empress, her life reversing until she came to the trees and grass of her babyhood at Kensington. Mr. Strachey did this much too well. Since his old Queen died so, a dozen famous men have died in print to the same music, or have passed a final, measured paragraph reviewing their own times. Henry James, Nathaniel Hawthorne, the great Swift, and François Villon have been displayed on Mr. Strachey's patent, and perhaps someone will set the needle on the plate of Marcus Hanna's memories. But it is true, not fancied, that his youth came back to him on the last night of January as he lurched into his rooms at the Arlington.

There was a dinner of newspaper men. He must dress. He left his train downstairs. It was not known yet that typhoid colored his face. The white-haired woman seated with his wife stared at him entering and saw by the flush and the blaze of his eyes that he was sick.

"Mrs. Balch is afraid you won't remember her, Mark."

He did not remember, yet. He stood looking at her, and his eyes, as in 1865, seemed to go through her. She stammered that he had known her when she was a child and walked toward this being in his yellow, splotched mask of sickness, with his slim fingers thickened at the joints by rheumatism. As she came, he altered. His memory caught at her gait, or her voice, and he shouted, " Sawdust! "

He grew tall and glowed. He was her Mr. Mark again who killed the rat on the wharf with his walking-stick and gave her hearts of maple sugar from the tin box on his desk. He babbled at her, question upon question. How was — What was her brother's name? — Orion? And did she live in California? Oh, and she should see the rat the Roosevelt kids had at the White House! It would scare her stiff. . . . She was crying. He held her hands, and his fingers burned her. A sense of death on his hands made Juliet Araminta choke. But she tried to talk.

" And you've got your canal now."

" Was I gassin' about canals back then? Honest? You remember that? . . . How long ago it is! " he panted.

Men poured in, gentlemen dressed to dine. The child who had loved him, and loved him now again, looked at them with hate and heard suave voices urging Uncle Mark to dress at once. He was swept away, and in half an hour the Senator tottered into his chair at the gay dinner of the journalists. She must leave for

New York at midnight, hurrying to a nephew sick at West Point. But she had promised to come back.

On the ninth of February she read that Senator Hanna's illness had proved serious. The great Dr. Osler was in consultation, and the family had been summoned. Next morning she was back in Washington, one of the people drifting incessantly to stare at the unresponding face of the Arlington.

Hotels jammed suddenly, and on Friday night the yellow hall of Foraker's house was pungent with cigars. Furs were sumptuous huddles on a bench and the Senator sometimes stroked a black collar's softness with his light fingers as he stood coldly listening to the cool flatteries of the powerful men, and coldly answering. The pastime must go on. These lofty children played with power because they were used to the game, and it was dear. Some of them came afterwards to think that Hanna had been more conscionable than were they. He had played in a dream of advancing industry, of men and wealth in one blend, a smooth pulsation of a grand machine. He had adored, and had been loyal, when they played for the barren sake of egoism, to be known as strong. So they spoke of him, afterwards, and perhaps were not wrong.

Just then they must find a fresh alliance, and they had come to make peace with Hanna's enemy, for the news was bad at the Arlington. A courtly chatter ran in the group, an insolent palaver about nothings. They had been brought to call on Mr. Foraker, and that

was all. And that was to be all. They were told so, as
they stood there.

A fair little boy strolled down the stairs and considered these men with a child's impeccable contempt.
It was time for dinner, and the phonograph was
broken, and an older boy set to amuse him on the
landing was a weary bore. He was tired of this gathering. He yawned at them and leaned his blue clothes
on the rail, waiting for them to have the sense to go.

"Well, Arthur, we're going to make your dad leader
of the party."

"Mr. Roosevelt says there aren't going to be any
more leaders when Mr. Hanna dies," said the child.

But outside in the city people stopped one another
to ask what the news was at the Arlington. He had
grown familiar to the simple, and it was known that
he had open hands, that he was a kind father and the
best of friends. A blankness hung in Washington as
Sunday passed. He was fighting; there might be a
chance. Pages from hotels and messengers on bicycles
threshed before the Arlington that night, waiting. Reporters stamped cold feet and whispered that the big
marine over there was an outpost of the White House,
stolidly attending the death of Marcus Hanna. He
stayed until midnight and then tramped out of their
sight.

Monday was gray. The Senate idled. Lads ran in
to mutter in some ear that it had not come yet. Senators walked out in the midst of speeches and found

a telephone. Many dinners were canceled and a ball postponed before dusk, and at six o'clock watchers spread below the Arlington. The big young marine stood with his hands in his pockets close to Juliet Balch and may have seen that she was pale and weeping.

"Know him?"

"Yes. Are you a messenger from the White House?"

"No," he said. "Mamma wired me to be here. He was good to my folks out home."

Minutes marched. A new lad would come on his clicking bicycle, and a new cigar would glow among the reporters. Everything waited for the news. Carriages stopped and drivers bent down to ask if it was done. To his last he commanded a world's attention. People must wait and wait. It was half past six. It was twenty minutes to seven. A figure came through the brilliant doors and raised a hand. The young marine took off his cap and turned away. These living bodies separated and disappeared into the night.

APPENDIX

APPENDIX

No terminal essay in condemnation or defense of Marcus Hanna was designed for this book. I must admit that the morals of leaders in a democracy do not interest me. If one man chooses to get in a dubious margin of votes for his candidate by handing a check of five thousand dollars to some discreet assistant and another rouses the same voters by yowling from the end of a train that his opponents are victims of a " seared moral sense " and yet a third assures dwellers in small towns that his heart is wrung when he hears the people of small towns criticized, I find no difference in morality among the methods displayed. Morality is an exaltation of personal taste, and taste is something usually sacrificed by leaders of mankind in the mass. The materials in condemnation of Mr. Hanna hugely exist in any large public library, written by men of unquestioned and also unexplored veracity. " Let the virtuous people stick to describing vice — which they can do well enough."

A current theory of history advises us that beyond democracy lies Cæsarism, the control of the ineffectual mass by the strong individual. My dissent from the theory has been twice implied in this sketch of Hanna's

times. Democracy and Cæsarism seem to me coexist-
ent. Democracy yearns for leadership and accepts
many clever dictators before a Julius Cæsar declares
the ideational ruin of the republic and sits on the
wreckage to await his assassins. The characteristic of
Hanna's bloodless adventure in government is this
Cæsarism, and his charm lies in the candor of his approach to the mass. He appealed to materialists as a
materialist; his pragmatism was not draped in virtuous pretenses. He grinned.

NOTES

Chapter 1

The episode of Hugh Jones is taken from a statement of his
grandson, Mr. H. J. Tessman.

Leonard Hanna's cruise on the Lakes does not appear in
Mr. Croly's study of Marcus Hanna, but is authenticated by a
conversation of Mr. Hanna with Mr. Henry Adler in 1899.

There are several versions of Schuyler Colfax's conversation
with Mr. Lincoln on the day of the assassination. Mr. Ernest
Harvier, who had his information directly from Mr. Colfax,
told me that Mr. Lincoln mentioned the immigrants particularly. Mr. Colfax saw the President before the Cabinet met
in the morning, and again a little after seven at night.

Chapter 2

The intrigue which disposed of George Pendleton in 1868, at
the Democratic convention in New York, is said to have been
managed by Tammany Democrats under advice from Jay
Gould and his associates. Mr. Peter Daly and Mr. George
Grannis, who witnessed the convention, both told me that the

swing to Seymour was contrived by the constant work of a man named Ledbetter, operating from the Saint Nicholas Hotel.

Hanna's performance at Warsaw was reported in New York by Mr. Conkling's friends as a deliberate trick of Garfield to cause Mr. Conkling to recognize him, Mr. Hanna acting as Garfield's agent, and in Charles Foster's version of the episode Mr. Hanna is said to have promised Garfield that he would ask General Grant to call at Mentor. I have adhered to Mr. Croly's narration of the matter.

Chapter 3

Mrs. McKinley's interest in the Orient peculiarly impressed my father and Mr. Charles Deshler, as well as Mrs. Saxton. Colonel Montgomery boldly declared that her incessant talk on the conversion of the islanders influenced the President to retain the Philippines. On the other hand a person as closely associated with the presidential family as William Day did not notice the obsession.

The accusation of having ruined John Ellsler always gored Mr. Hanna. Mr. Ellsler's daughter is not aware that her father ever borrowed money from Hanna. The Euclid Avenue Opera House was bought by Mr. Hanna at public auction, its sale being forced by Mr. Ellsler's creditors. Ellsler remained in charge of the theater to the end of the season, accepted a benefit at the last performance, and appeared as Mark Hanna's guest at a supper afterwards. Myron Herrick and James Dempsey, two men who knew Hanna intimately, both characterized this yarn as a complete invention.

The messenger who informed Monsignor Ireland's friends in Saint Paul that the American Protective Association was trying to procure promises from the Republican party is Mr. Walter Stoeffel. Monsignor Ireland was not aware that the information came from Hanna. Mr. Stoeffel was sent with a note signed by Myron Herrick to the house of an eminent Catholic lawyer in Saint Paul, received an answer, and returned to Saint Louis.

303

APPENDIX

Chapters 5 and 6

From 1896 to 1904 my father was constantly employed by the New York Life Insurance Company and by George Perkins, of J. P. Morgan and Company, as a political observer. Copies of his long reports on events in which Mr. Hanna was concerned are filed among his papers. He was by no means intimate with Mr. Hanna and only grew to like him in the last years of their acquaintance. He often told me that Mr. Hanna's curious honesty about the shabbiness of some of his assistants was the first thing that gave him an affection for the Senator. Mr. Hanna would point out that a common politician was wholly scrupulous in his private life and wholly reliable when he was given money to spend. In the very intense campaign of 1899 in Ohio, for instance, Mr. Hanna gave several thousand dollars to a man of no character whatever to be spent on hire of carriages in rural districts on election day. The man afterwards presented all the livery bills, receipted, to the Senator, with five dollars in change. His accounts were precise to the penny. Mr. Hanna paid him two hundred dollars. The hanger-on immediately got drunk, and died of pneumonia in a public hospital.

Mr. Beer was incessantly in Washington, after 1896, and it would have been possible to fill this book's latter chapters with wild gossip and perhaps some odd facts written to him by men of consequence or journalists. He aided in the lobbying for the Newlands Act, at Mr. Roosevelt's request, and was borrowed by Mr. Hanna for the battle over the Panama Canal. In the autumn of 1902 he was sent by Mr. J. P. Morgan to attempt the settlement of the coal strike through one of the more reasonable operators. He reported his failure to Mr. Roosevelt in person on the night of the old soldier's call described in the third chapter of this sketch. In the spring of 1903 he was used as an agent in the forlorn movement to reconcile Hanna and Foraker, and for the rest of the year seems to have spent most of his time informing various gentlemen in New York that

Senator Hanna did not want to be President of the United States. It happens that he took me to Washington with him on the 9th of February 1904, and I am now the only person alive who heard Mr. Arthur Foraker's comment when George Perkins told him that his father was to be made leader of the Republican party.

In order to exhibit Marcus Hanna at close range I have added one of Mr. Beer's reports to this appendix. The campaign of 1899 in Ohio was bitter and costly. The Democrats and the independent Republicans spent enormous sums. A clerk in the office of Wells, Fargo and Company was offered one hundred dollars to vote the Democratic ticket. Unsigned private letters were circulated against McKinley and Hanna and sent particularly to clergymen. Mr. Hanna afterwards told my father that he regarded this as the most open use of money by the Democrats he had ever seen in Ohio, and that he suspected several eminent Republicans of assisting the opposition.

My indebtedness to Mrs. Henriette Adler Meyer for the use of her brother's papers, to Miss Alice Jayson for research, to Mr. David Saville Muzzey for some heartening advice, and to Mr. Charles Deshler and Mr. William McCready for most valuable information is here specially mentioned. Mrs. Henry Villard, Mrs. Juliet Balch, Colonel Benjamin Montgomery, and Mr. Oscar Underwood have now no use for my thanks.

REPORT OF WILLIAM C. BEER TO JOHN MCCALL

NEW YORK, November 11, 1899.

MY DEAR MR. MCCALL: —

In obedience to your orders, I left New York on Tuesday evening, October 31st, for Ohio.

On Wednesday, in accordance with a suggestion from the White House, I stopped off at Pittsburg and called on President McCrea, of the Pennsylvania Lines West of Pittsburg. He, unfortunately, was out of town, but his representatives supplied me with transportation on all the Pennsylvania lines in Ohio, and also gave me a good idea of the situation, politically, from the railroad standpoint. Leaving Pittsburg Wednesday afternoon, I saw friends along the line and arranged for information and help in Columbiana, Mahoning and Stark, Trumbull, Wayne, Richland, Crawford, Ashland, Defiance, Williams and Lucas and several other counties. I stopped off at my father's home in Bucyrus, Crawford County, between trains, and ascertained from him the attitude of the Gold Democrats of the State, — he being in close touch with all of the leaders of that wing.

I went on the same day to Lima, Allen County, where I had arranged to meet Senator Hanna in the afternoon (Thursday). I found him at the supper table, at the Lima House, in company with Congressman Dalzell, of Pennsylvania, and several distinguished Ohioans. As soon as Mr. Hanna finished his meal, he sent his party out and came over to where I sat. I said, " President McKinley is anxious about Ohio." He answered, vigorously, " He has — good reason to be ! " I then informed him that, by your orders and at the request of President McKinley, I had come to Ohio, being directed to report to him, Hanna, and do whatever I could in any direction, but principally among my friends in the various transportation companies. He emphatically assented to this suggestion, and having given me a general idea of the situation, he went off to the reception which had been arranged for him prior to the evening meeting, and told me to occupy his room in his absence, and start to work in any way I thought best. I thereupon wrote, by hand, twenty-two letters to railroad presidents, general managers, superintendents &c., and to Senator Platt and other prominent express officials. The letters were supposedly from Senator Hanna, and urged upon those gentlemen the extreme necessity of doing everything in their power to get every vote out among their employes and shop-men on election day.

On the Senator's return from his meeting, about 10:30, he read over the letters and signed all, except one to J. P. Morgan and a couple of railroad men whom he had seen personally, and with whom he had arranged that very matter, viz., the Lake Shore and the Nickel Plate Presidents. As soon as he signed the letters, I sealed them with sealing-wax and directed them, under private cover, to each man. After that was finished, the Senator leaned back and sketched to me, rapidly, the situation in the State. He said: "Please tell President McCall that I have had a very hard fight. I feel almost certain that we shall carry the State by a safe plurality. It has been hard work, and has nearly worn me out. We are having trouble in Cincinnati and some in Cleveland. Tell him that wherever I have been in the smaller towns and cities, I have called together the leaders, and have personally given out the necessary funds, one hundred dollars here, one hundred dollars there, and so on. I have seen to this matter myself in as judicious a manner as I could, and it has been placed as wisely as I could judge. You have noticed that I am to speak in Sandusky City to-morrow night. Well, I am going to leave here to-morrow morning at 8 o'clock and go to Toledo first. I have quietly summoned all our leaders there, — you know them, — George Waldorf and the rest, — and am going to follow the same tactics which I used to beat Jones in the Convention, — to get the delegation, — you remember? They sent word to me a few days ago that if they had five thousand, they could buy up all of Jones' lieutenants, — his head men. Those fellows understand perfectly well that Jones can't be elected Governor, and that there will be no offices, and they are not in this for their health. They convinced me as to the scheme, and I sent them a thousand dollars yesterday, and will give them the rest to-morrow."

After some further chat on the subject of my duties, the attitude of various railroad men, &c., I asked the Senator point-blank what he thought the result would be. He looked at me for several seconds before replying, and looked rather queer, but, finally, said he thought the State would go about 25,000 or 30,000 for Nash. This did not agree with his first remark to me when I met him at the supper-table, and I knew he was giving me "taffy." I did not press him, however, and bidding him good-night, left his room with the letters, and, in company with the Senator's body-guard, Post Office Inspector Gaitree, went to the Lima Post Office and mailed the letters about midnight. I then took the C., H. & D. train for Toledo about two hours afterwards, and arrived at Toledo at 7:30 Friday morning, procured a little information there, and left for Cleveland at 8:30 A.M.

You will remember I met you as I left my train, at 11:25 A.M. and immediately went uptown to the railroad and express headquarters' buildings. I had a letter from the Vice-President of Wells Fargo & Co., Col. Dudley Evans, to his Ohio Superintendent, Mr. T. M. DeWitt, and we spent part of the afternoon together, going around from place to place. We learned that the feeling in Cleveland among business men was very cheerful and sanguine for Republican success. They felt there was no particular doubt as to Ohio. Thought Cuyahoga County would give a safe Republican plurality, thought Jones would not have many votes in Cleveland, and the feeling was, in general, that the state was safe, and that Mr. McKisson and his friends would not poll a very heavy vote in Cleveland, as they would probably stay away from the polls.

Friday night, Superintendent DeWitt and I started

for Cincinnati, as your orders were to take in the big cities first.

Mr. DeWitt told me that he felt confident most of his employes were safely for the Republican ticket, and went on to relate how they *could not* be otherwise, because Wells Fargo & Co. used them so well, and the men were fully conscious of the prosperity of the country and, consequently, of their Company; how the custom of the Company is to give each man a big turkey and a can of oysters and a bunch of celery on Christmas day, and this little custom made them all seem like one big family, &c., &c.

When we arrived in Cincinnati the next morning, we went immediately after breakfast to the General Agency of the Express Company, and taking the General Agent aside, inquired as to the attitude of the men. (There are over a hundred employes of Wells Fargo & Co. in Cincinnati.) Mr. Earle replied in rather an embarrassed manner, "Well, Mr. DeWitt, I think there are a very few for the Republican ticket, but most of them are for McLean, and a good many are for Jones." DeWitt was astounded, but after a hasty consultation, he arranged to have the men gotten together by Earle, so that he could address them in bunches and individually. While Earle was getting them together, Mr. DeWitt and I went over to call on our friend, the General Manager of the Cincinnati, Hamilton & Dayton System, Mr. C. G. Waldo. We found that Mr. Waldo had already heard from the letter which I wrote to President Woodford at Lima, (signed by Senator Hanna). He was very cheerful, however, and said that his men were all right, but that in deference to President Woodford's wishes, he had communicated with their route agents, superintendents, &c., but thought there was no cause for alarm. I convinced him to the contrary, and he set to work immediately. After he had finished dictating his telegrams, Superintendent DeWitt having left us, Mr. Waldo and I went over to call on President M. E. Ingalls, of the C., C., C. & St. L. R'y Co. (Big Four). Of course, you are well aware of President Ingalls' high standing in Sound Money circles. Like yourself, he has been a life-long Democrat. In Ohio, however, Mr. Ingalls has, among the best citizens, a reputation for " shiftiness."

As we had a most remarkable experience with him, I take the liberty of setting it out in full as nearly as I can recall his exact words. He said: " No, I am not taking any part in politics this year. I did in 1896, as everybody did. I have been rather sorry for it ever since. I spent over one hundred thousand of my own money, and devoted nearly all of my time to speaking and working for McKinley, and what was the good of it all? Why, afterwards when I recommended to them not to take sides with this old fellow Deboe over here in Kentucky, they wouldn't listen to me, and although I went to Washington and told the Pre — the Administration what I thought of it, my protest was unheeded, and they did as they pleased. No, I am not going to take any part, and they can get along the best they know how. Yes, there are a good many Republicans voting for McLean now, in fact nearly all my friends are for him, and I think he will carry the State. It is true there are a good many working-men for Jones — why, my private secretary, Davie, who has been with me for many years, and has been a Republican always, is off this year. I said to him the other day, 'Davie, who are you going to vote for?' He answered, 'Well, Mr. Ingalls, I am a Republican, but I can't vote for Nash, and I won't vote the Democratic ticket; I guess I will vote for old man Jones.' You see how it goes? Yes, a good many of our men are for Jones and McLean; I guess nearly all of them. My son, up in Cleveland, who is a good deal brighter fellow than his father, keeps me posted every day, and he says Hanna is going to lose the State sure this time, that everybody is for McLean up there. And, by-the-way, speaking of Hanna, now I like Hanna personally. He is a good fellow and all that, but I will say to you, — and this must not be told either to McKinley or Hanna, not at least until after election day, — the people are sick and tired of Hanna. They are sick and tired of Cox down here in Cincinnati, but the people of Ohio have revolted against Hanna, and I guess he is done for. They do not like his methods. McKinley is a nice, pleasant fellow, and I guess the people like him, but they want to show him this time, inasmuch as Hanna is running the campaign personally, that they wont have any more Hanna, and I guess they will do it. Yes, the State is going for McLean," and here he turned and shook his finger at me significantly, " and that means the jig is up with McKinley. He won't be nominated next year. You'll vote for Dewey next year, young man! "

Mr. Ingalls did not, of course, know that I came in any way from President McKinley. I had merely repeated verbatim your message to him as one Sound Democrat to another, and General Manager Waldo had been careful to introduce me as a New York Life man — a messenger from President McCall. At the conclusion of his address, Mr. Ingalls, after a moment's thought — apparently remembering whom I represented — said, " I am sorry I can't see my way clear to comply with President McCall's wishes. I haven't said to anybody how *I* will vote. Perhaps I shan't vote at all, but you can tell him I am not working this year."

Mr. Waldo, remembering President Ingalls' great influence in Cincinnati, left very much discouraged, but got his second wind, shortly afterwards, and started in with renewed vigor to get his men in line. He promised me to see, individually, every general manager in Cincinnati within twenty-four hours.

After leaving Mr. Waldo, I went to the Hotel and telephoned to an old-time friend, Mr. H. P. Boyden, formerly editorial writer for the " Cincinnati

Commercial Gazette," now Comptroller of the City of Cincinnati, elected to that office by the Mugwump Republican-Democratic Fusion of two years ago. Mr. Boyden is perhaps the most intimate personal friend of President Ingalls. He had no idea of my errand in the city. To him I was merely a New York Life agent in the city on business. I invited him to dinner at the Grand Hotel, and after discussing other subjects of mutual interest, alluded to the political questions in Ohio, and asked him for some light on the subject, as I being a New Yorker, was rather out of touch with the situation. Upon this theme Mr. Boyden spoke about an hour, and gave me the Mugwump Democratic side of the question in full. He said, in part, " It means that the people of Ohio are through with Mark Hanna. They have had all they want of Hannaism and Coxism. No, I have nothing against President McKinley. He is my personal friend. I like him. We all like him, but he has got to learn he must cut loose from Hanna, and, of course, we long-suffering Cincinnatians have decided that George Cox must understand that *he* has reached the end of *his* string. We have stood him as long as we are going to, and this alliance between the better class of the Republican party in Cincinnati and the Democratic party, has come to stay until Cox retires from politics. No, I do not feel that there will be disastrous consequences to the party in a national way. This is our own little fight in Ohio, and it had to come sooner or later. We may as well settle it right now, so as not to interfere with the success of the National ticket next year. Well, if it means disaster to McKinley, although I do not think so, let it mean so. It is a case of self-preservation. The party in Ohio must be purified. We have deliberately shut our eyes to the consequences. We shall carry Hamilton County against Hanna and Cox by 10,000 plurality, perhaps more, but certainly 10,000."

After leaving Boyden, I went to the headquarters of the U. S. Post Office Inspectors, to see how our case against the crank (Ireland) who is writing letters to Mr. Edward W. Scott, of the Provident Savings, was getting along. I found they had had some difficulty in finding the man, but finally learned that he is a " curbstone " broker. He has no fixed abiding place, so the Inspector says, and they have had hard work to run him down. It so happened that on the very day I was there, the Chief Inspector had located him, and had sent a man out to find him and give him a scare. He expected that within twenty-four hours at least, he would be able to prepare a final report on the case to be sent to the 4th Assistant Postmaster-General, who will, in turn, send it to us.

Afterwards I hunted up George Cox.

Cox said: " We shall carry Hamilton County certainly by 6,000, and if we can only get some money from Headquarters, we will carry it by more. The trouble has been here that we are fighting the

Democrats, the Jones men and the Fusion Republicans in our own party, but we will win sure. We have been greatly hampered by lack of funds. There are 10,000 ex-city employes, all good, loyal Republicans, who have been walking the streets since the Fusion victory two years ago, and they are dead sore. You can't blame them. They have families dependent on them, and they haven't been able to find work. I guess a good many of them will work for McLean and Jones, if they can get something for doing so. Well, I cannot blame them, but if I had the money, I should at least induce them to stay away from the polls and not vote at all, if they did not vote with us. I have sent to Chairman Dick three times asking for money, but I haven't had a cent. They sent a man down here last week to help us collect money from our own citizens, and how much do you think he collected? Three hundred dollars. Our Committee was only able to collect seven hundred and fifty, and the Post Office employes here all hid themselves behind Civil Service, and how much do you suppose we got from that building? One hundred and fifty-two dollars and fifty cents. We have had some more in driblets, but nothing like what we ought to have, and I am fighting McLean's bar'l that way! If I had ten thousand, I would contract with Mr. Hanna to give him 10,000 majority from Hamilton County. If he will send me seventy-five hundred, I will give him 7,500 or 8,000 plurality. I will take whatever they send me, and be glad to get it. The more they send me, the better work I can do. Why, here we haven't got a daily morning paper in the city. McLean has bought the Republican paper, — The " Commercial Gazette." The only papers we have are evening papers. I sent to Dick and asked him to let me have twenty-seven hundred dollars to get out a morning paper for one day only, to-morrow, Sunday morning, the Sunday before election, and I would get out at least 5,000 copies and have them handed to the passers-by on the corners by boys. They would have been read by everybody, and would have done lots of good. But do you suppose he would give me a cent? No sir! How much do I think the State will go Republican? Well, it is a hard matter to say. Ninety per cent. of the railroad employes here are for Jones and Mc-Lean. The C., H. & D.? *Why*, I ought to know what they'll do. I am the largest individual stockholder in that railroad. I told you that ninety per cent. of those men are for Jones, and it is nearly the same with all the other railroads. What about the Big Four? Why, those men would follow Ingalls any where he would lead them. How is Ingalls this year? Why, for Mc-Lean sure. He is working day and night for John R. McLean. All his men are doing the same, too. As to the State? Well, of course I am paying more attention to Hamilton County than to the State, but I hear a good deal from up there. Of course, everybody comes to Cincinnati, and they tell me that we will pull through. How much do I think? Well," after a moment's hesitation, "I should say perhaps 10,000, or may be 12,000, along there, perhaps 15,000."

As this was Saturday night preceding election day, I deemed it my duty to acquaint Senator Hanna with the state of affairs in Cincinnati at once. Cox intimated very plainly that he thought Dick was deceiving Hanna, and that the State was in such bad condition, that he wanted to keep the knowledge of it from Hanna, if possible. He said he thought Dick had not transmitted to Hanna one single message from him, Cox, and that as he, Cox, had not seen Hanna for several months, Hanna could not, of course, know how bad Cincinnati really was. Therefore, I left for Cleveland Saturday night within two hours after seeing Cox.

The next morning, Sunday, I drove out to the Lake Front, where the Senator lives, and was with him from 10:30 A.M. to nearly 1:30 P.M. I reported to him the situation in Cincinnati fully, and related the conversations I had had with Ingalls and Cox and Boyden as nearly verbatim as I could. He seemed greatly disturbed, and said that a week before that time, he had made out a check for five thousand, had mailed it to Chairman Dick with explicit instructions to send it to George Cox, and he supposed it had been done long ago. He said that he could not spare any more money. That he had used up all he had had from various sources, and now was drawing on his own funds. He said that his brothers had contributed six thousand, and that other public-spirited Republicans in Cleveland had done nearly as well. He denounced Cincinnati as a stingy city, and said what a shame it was, with the vast wealth of that place, they had the cheek to ask outside help, but that it had always been so. Said he would telephone to Cox immediately and to Chairman Dick. As to Ingalls, Hanna used some very forcible language in refuting that gentleman's statements. He said: " If Ingalls said he contributed one hundred thousand of his own money, or anybody else's, he is a liar. The fact of the matter is that in '96, Ingalls came to me with a cock-and-bull story about being able to carry Virginia, if we would help him. You remember what I did for him. How we poured the money into that State, and you know what good it did! Nothing!!! *He* contributed one hundred thousand? I'll bet he didn't contribute one hundred cents. Well, you can't expect anything more from Ingalls. His action is consistent with his character. Time and again he has come to me asking for favors, and I have done them always, and this is the reward. Why, not long ago, he came to me asking for a great, big favor from the Attorney General's Office — a very delicate matter, too — you know how peculiar our Attorney General is sometimes, and I went there in person and saw Griggs. I accomplished what Ingalls wanted, and now — !!! How much does George say he will give us from Cincinnati? Is that all? How

319

much does George think we will carry the State by? 10,000?!"

The Senator went off into a brown study when I told him Cox's figures. He was silent for some time, but finally said, "I do not believe it. I think we will do better than that. We have a fine organization through the State in the rural districts, and will get out every vote. Wherever I have gone in places like Youngstown, and towns of that size, I have helped out the Committees with five hundred here and a thousand there, and I have neglected no place. Of course, all our money is gone now, and I wont ask Mr. McCall for any more. Of course, if you could get, say, twenty-five hundred more from some other sources in New York, it would be a great help, and I would send it right down to George Cox. He would use every cent of it right, and I believe it would be a good thing to do. I can't let him have it myself. I have told Dick that in cases where it is absolutely necessary, he should give the proper parties a reasonable amount, and keep account of it and let me know. I will take care of it here, and we will settle it up somehow when I come to New York. I do not want to strain my friends in New York too much, because I am going to ask them to help once more next year. I can't ask John McCall for another cent. It wouldn't be fair. He is too good a fellow. There is nobody else like him in this country. There is only one John McCall. But if you could telephone there and have your folks see somebody that

320

would help us out to the extent of twenty-five hundred it would do a great deal of good. The Catholic vote is with us. All the head men in the Catholic clergy are working with us, and John Farley, whom I helped in that mayoralty fight, although he is a Democrat, has great influence with the Catholic clergy, and they are all with us, and so is he. John is a good fellow. He is all right."

The Senator instructed me to try to communicate with Vice-President Kingsley by telephone, and to let him know, without fail, what answer I received, but to be very sure to let Mr. Kingsley understand that if any money was forthcoming, he did not wish it to be from the New York Life, but only to be *collected* by Mr. Kingsley from such other sources as he might see fit.

As you are probably aware, I followed the Senator's instructions, and received a reply next morning from Mr. Kingsley to the effect that, being unable to communicate with you, he did not see his way clear to comply with the Senator's request. I met Mr. Hanna at the door of his office, as he was going down to what he called the Ore Dump to speak to a meeting of workingmen, mainly composed of iron moulders, ore shovellers &c. He was in the centre of a group of brawny foremen and bosses, with all of whom he appeared on intimate terms. They were acting as a sort of body-guard to him, as he anticipated a little trouble, perhaps, at the meeting. On receiving Mr. Kingsley's message, he replied quite cheerfully that it was all right, that he thought Cox could get along with the five thousand he sent him, and which had left Columbus by a special messenger Sunday night, in compliance with his telephonic instructions. He said: "Give my kindest regards to President McCall, and tell him I will see him when I come to New York."

I left Cleveland Monday afternoon, and went through Lorain and Huron and Seneca counties. I was glad to find that in the smaller places the voters were true blue, and the prosperity of the country was a greater argument for the Republican ticket, than anything which could be said against it by the traitors among the Republicans, or the followers of Jones or McLean. The farmers thought that the high prices of wool and wheat were better arguments than any cry of anti-Hannaism or anti-Imperialism. There were no voters for Jones in the smaller towns, except a very few of the riffraff, and perhaps one or two Anarchists that are to be found in every community.

During Sunday and Monday, the Republican farmers took a great brace. Election day was bright and clear, and almost to a man, the Republican and Sound Money Democratic farmers hitched up their buggies and started for town. The Republican organization, and for that matter the Democratic organization, had apparently ample means for livery hire, and the full vote was gotten out. Nobody was missed. The results were:

FIRST — Republican gains through all the country districts. Thus proving that our strength lies outside of the big cities, and that the farmers of Ohio, if the present conditions continue, can be safely relied upon to carry that State for us next year, with an equally large plurality.

SECOND — That Ingalls and Boyden, and their friends, made good their threats against Hanna and Cox in Hamilton County, but they were able to do so only because of the large vote for Jones in Cincinnati. If Cox had been able to swing his customary vote with the laboring classes, he would have made good his promise. It is also my opinion that if he could have had five thousand dollars more than he had, he would have gotten a small plurality in spite of Jones and McLean.

THIRD — The disaster in Cuyahoga County is accounted for by the Republican leaders in the State, whom I saw after election, in just one word, "Mc-Kisson." This gentleman worked his game very cleverly and quietly, but it is evident now that his whole force voted for Jones by a pre-arranged plan. McLean ought to be more disappointed than Hanna about Cuyahoga County, for on Monday there were two headquarters opened in Cleveland for disbursing McLean's money. It was free as water. All in bright, new one dollar bills, fresh from the U. S. Treasury, and the word was given out that any respectable Democratic worker could have a reasonable amount of it. One of

323

these headquarters was at the Weddell House, where I stopped, and all day long there was a ceaseless procession of " workers " up the stairs to that room and down again with smiling faces. The bar did a big business afterwards, and yet McLean came out third in the race.

FOURTHLY — It is evident to the Republican leaders that the campaign next summer must be in the country, in the district school-houses, or wherever a cluster of farmers can be gotten together to listen to bright, energetic, young Republican orators. There is in the big cities a deep-rooted conviction in the minds of most of the voters, that Hanna has certain methods which are wrong. No such feeling as this exists among the farmers, and to them George Cox is only a name. None of them have ever seen him, and they neither know or care anything about him.

I will say, in conclusion, that I reported daily, by letter, to President McKinley, addressing my letters to Col. B. F. Montgomery, at the White House. At the conclusion of my visit with M. E. Ingalls, I called up Col. Montgomery on the telephone (having been requested to do so, if anything startling should happen), and informed him fully as to that conversation.

After election day, I spent a day with my parents, part of another day in Canton with the President's friends, part of another day reporting to President

McCrea, of the Pennsylvania Railroad, in Pittsburg, and then came directly to New York.

If I were to estimate the value of the results accomplished directly and indirectly by your assistance and agencies in the Ohio election, I should say, in all candor, that you supplied the margin of plurality.

Chairman Dick is not popular. Mr. Hanna is decidedly unpopular in the cities and county seats; but the effective aid given directly by you, and furnished by reason of your influence with corporations, is beyond estimate. Wells Fargo and Co.'s men all came over, and there are a thousand of them in the State. There are many more C., H. & D. employes. The express and railroad employes run into the thousands. The results of those letters were immediate. President T. C. Platt, of the United States Express, sent telegraphic orders to his superintendents, and it is quite easy to see where 25,000 votes were changed from Jones and McLean to Nash, within the week before election day.

I attach an informal note received to-day from General Manager Waldo, of the C., H. & D.

Very respectfully,

The Honorable
  John A. McCall,
    New York City.

INDEX

Adams, Charles Francis, 39–40, 211–12, 249

Adams, Henry, 157, 219, 273

Adams, Maude, 246

Adler, Alfred, 241

Adler, Henriette, 193, 195, 196, 197–8, 305

Adler, Henry, 77, 124–5, 127, 128, 129–30, 132, 163, 193, 197, 233–4, 261, 284, 302, 305

Alcott, Louisa May, 52

Aldrich, Nelson W., 244

Alger, Russell, 161, 174, 200, 202

Allison, William, 73, 113, 146, 147, 149, 261

Altgeld, John Peter, 134, 153, 156, 159

Ames, Oakes, 70–1, 72–3

Andrews, Benjamin, 72

Arthur, Chester, 34, 95, 96

Astor, John Jacob, 189, 199, 200

Austen, Jane, 88

Baer, 217, 244

Balch, Mrs. Juliet, *see* Smith, Juliet Araminta

Baldwin, John, 143, 146, 147

Barnes, Asa, 26–7, 28, 182–3, 184, 185, 209

Barrett, Lawrence, 129

Beecher, Henry Ward, 27, 38, 83, 90

Beecher, Mrs. Henry Ward, 75

Beer, Thomas, 6, 7–8, 31, 75, 109, 136, 137

Beer, William Collins, 41, 110, 121–3, 135–40, 142, 143, 144, 145–6, 147, 152, 156, 157, 158, 159–62, 165, 182, 198–9, 200, 211, 213, 216, 223, 229, 244, 282, 286, 290, 292, 303, 304–25

Beer, Mrs. William C., 89

Belknap, —, 36

Belknap, William Worth, 83

Bennett, Jacob, 275

i

iv

At a very early age Thomas Beer found a lavishly illustrated edition of *Salambo* among his grand-father's books of which he says, "By an accident, the illustration in the novel which showed the Carthaginian General Hanno taking a bath in the blood of slaughtered slaves, had a real likeness to Mark Hanna. I was considerably worried about this in the campaign of 1896 while my father under Mr. Hanna's direction was steering a carload of dilapidated Civil War generals through the middle west making speeches on behalf of McKinley." Thus, Mr. Beer's interest in his subject is of long standing and picturesque inception. Throughout his boyhood came other and more material contacts with the politicians of the day and considering the period, Mr. Hanna, and Mr. Beer, it can be seen that this book was long ago destined to take its inevitable and brilliant place among the latter's literary achievements.

This book was set on the linotype in Caslon, electrotyped, printed and bound by The Plimpton Press, Norwood, Mass. The paper was made by Curtis & Brother, Newark, Delaware.